Temple Houston

Temple Houston

LAWYER WITH A GUN

By
Glenn Shirley

UNIVERSITY OF OKLAHOMA PRESS : Norman

Also by Glenn Shirley

Toughest of Them All (Albuquerque, 1953)
Six-Gun and Silver Star (Albuquerque, 1955)
Law West of Fort Smith: A History of Frontier Justice in the Indian Territory, 1834–1896 (New York, 1957, 1961; Lincoln, 1968)
Pawnee Bill: A Biography of Gordon W. Lillie (Albuquerque, 1958; Lincoln, 1965)
Buckskin and Spurs: A Gallery of Frontier Rogues and Heroes (New York, 1958)
Outlaw Queen: The Fantastic True Story of Belle Starr (Derby, Conn., 1960)
Heck Thomas, Frontier Marshal (New York & Philadelphia, 1962)
Born to Kill (Derby, Conn., 1963)
Henry Starr, Last of the Real Badmen (New York, 1965)
Buckskin Joe: The Unique and Vivid Memoirs of Edward Jonathan Hoyt, Hunter-Trapper, Scout, Soldier, Showman, Frontiersman, and Friend of the Indians 1840–1918 (Lincoln, 1966)
Shotgun for Hire: The Story of "Deacon" Jim Miller, Killer of Pat Garrett (Norman, 1970)
The Life of Texas Jack: Eight Years a Criminal—41 Years Trusting in God (Quanah, 1973)
Red Yesterdays (Wichita Falls, 1977)
West of Hell's Fringe: Crime, Criminals, and the Federal Peace Officer in Oklahoma Territory, 1889–1907 (Norman, 1978)
Temple Houston: Lawyer with a Gun (Norman, 1980)

Library of Congress Cataloging in Publication Data

Shirley, Glenn.
 Temple Houston: lawyer with a gun.

 Bibliography: p. 305
 Includes index.
 1. Houston, Temple Lea, 1860–1905. 2. Lawyers—Texas—Biography. 3. Lawyers—Oklahoma—Biography.
 I. Title.
 KF368.H65S54   345'.766'00924 [B]   79-24049
 ISBN 978-0-8061-4131-2 (paper)

Copyright © 1980 by the University of Oklahoma Press, Norman, Publishing Division of the University. Manufactured in the U.S.A. Paperback published in 2010.

All rights reserved. No part of this publication may be reproduced, stored in a retrieval system, or transmitted, in any form or by any means, electronic, mechanical, photocopying, recording, or otherwise—except as permitted under Section 107 or 108 of the United States Copyright Act—without the prior written permission of the University of Oklahoma Press.

Contents

Preface		ix
Chapter		
1	Six-Gun Defense	3
2	Son of "The Raven"	8
3	Canadian River Empire	29
4	"A Baldheaded Whiskey Town"	43
5	"The Bloodiest Place in Texas"	61
6	District Attorney, Texas Style	74
7	War on Cattle Thieves	91
8	Texas State Senator	99
9	The "Grass-Lease" Fight	127
10	"Texas Stands Peerless amid the Mighty"	143
11	Temple Doffs his White Stetson	162
12	"Mercy, Eh! Where Was Mercy Then?"	168
13	Silver-Tongued Orator	192
14	Guns and Death	210
15	Chicago "Alkali"	227
16	Astronomy and Antiquities	240
17	Go Thy Way, Sin No More	255
18	Old Fight Over Again	272
19	Fire-Eaters Cross Swords	289
20	The Tub Stands on its Own Bottom	300
	Bibliography	311
	Index	325

Illustrations

In Texas...

General Sam Houston	10
Temple Lea Houston as a page in the United States Senate	18
Temple as a cadet in Texas A&M College	18
James Nathan ("Honest Jim") Browning	27
Charles Goodnight	32
Texas Panhandle, 1880s (map)	37
Diorama of Fort Elliott, Texas Panhandle	40
Mobeetie, Texas, mid-1880s	44
Mobeetie, late 1880s	44
Dickerson Brothers store, Mobeetie	46
J. J. ("Uncle Johnny") Long's store, Mobeetie	47
Mark Huselby	49
Frank Willis	52
Lucius Dills	52
George W. Arrington	59
James McMasters's store, Old Tascosa	63
Old Tascosa (map)	65
Equity Bar, Old Tascosa	66
Houston, district attorney, Mobeetie	75
Houston, Texas senator	100
Texas State Capitol, Austin	151

In Oklahoma...

J. D. F. Jennings	169

John E. ("Jack") Love	171
Rail Road Eating House, Woodward	175
Martinson General Merchandise and Woodward Saddle Shop	176
Blacksmith shop, Woodward, 1890s	177
Woodward County Courthouse	178
Woodward, early 1890s	179
Robert J. ("Bob") Ray	180
Oklahoma Senate members, 1895	182
Jerry Rowland Dean	184
Oklahoma Supreme Court	195
Houston at McFadden Saloon, Taloga	201
W. E. ("Billy") Bolton	203
David P. Marum	204
Alphonso J. ("Al") Jennings	214
Cabinet Saloon, Woodward	219
Henry E. Asp	221
Oklahoma Senate members, 1897	238
Houston as lawyer at Woodward	243
Houston residence at Woodward	249
Houston's collection of memorabilia	250
Houston on Republican River	251
Houston defending "fallen woman," 1899	269
Scenes from Territorial Democratic Convention, El Reno, 1900	277
Woodward, ca. 1900	302
Richard Dix as Yancy Cravat in *Cimarron*	308
Cravat defending the "fallen woman"	309

Preface

Temple Lea Houston was the first child born in the governor's mansion in Austin, Texas, the youngest son of Margaret Moffette (Lea) and General Sam Houston. He died early, at age forty-five, in Woodward, Oklahoma Territory. Yet he lived far beyond his years, realized the ambitions of his profession before reaching his majority, and drained the cup of life. For more than two decades, from 1881 to 1905, he was one of the Southwest's most brilliant, eccentric, and widely known criminal lawyers.

He has been referred to by latter-day historians as "a chip off the old block," "a true son of the Raven," "plains statesman," a "spellbinder," "defender of the underdog," and the "Texas flamboyan," who tossed a political future overboard to get away from being his father's son. One journalist has capsulized him as "a gun-toting, tough hombre and silver tongued darling of the frontier courtroom, who spouted French and Spanish fluently, spoke seven Indian tongues, quoted Greek scholars, the Bible and Shakespeare, and died with his boots on."

Temple Lea Houston was all of these—and more.

His contemporaries thought him "the most artful and capable jury lawyer ever seen in a courtroom—a very dangerous man to oppose in a lawsuit"; "he could beat any man making a speech I ever heard talk"; "as an orator he was the peer of the Southwest during his day and time."

A prominent southwestern rancher, interviewed at a Kansas City cattlemen's convention in 1897, said:

In my opinion few men are as little comprehended and understood.... He has been presented to the public as a rowdy, a roisterer, and a genuine remnant of the frontier desperado. He has been embroiled in several quarrels, but these were never of his making. He simply protected himself after the manner of the man of the border, who knew and could maintain his rights.

In fact, he is a kindly mannered, thoroughly educated man.... My company employed him at a salary as general counsel, and I do not believe a better, more painstaking or reliable lawyer ever gave advice....

What kind of lawyer is he? There are some twenty murder cases now pending in the courts of Oklahoma Territory, and Houston is defending counsel in most of them!

Here, then, is the drama of Temple Lea Houston's existence, vivid experience, and precocious accomplishments in a pioneer period when life was often reduced to its stark fundamentals.

GLENN SHIRLEY

On the Cimarron
Payne County, Oklahoma

Temple Houston

1
Six-Gun Defense

Tension and a sweltering summer heat hung over the courtroom at Enid, Oklahoma Territory. All doors and windows were open to admit the breeze that never came. Outside, locusts hummed lazily. Nature seemed at a standstill as men wiped perspiration and waited.

Everyone in the room knew that he was witnessing a drama that would be long remembered in state history.

Judge John L. McAtee of the Fifth Judicial District presided. Actually, McAtee's district embraced Woodward County, created from the extreme western part of the recently opened Cherokee Outlet; Beaver County (No Man's Land); and four counties created from the 1892 opening of the Cheyenne-Arapaho reservation—Dewey, Custer, Day, and Roger Mills counties. Enid was the seat of Garfield County, in the Second Judicial District, presided over by Judge John H. Burford. The Second District also embraced Blaine and Washita counties, in the Cheyenne-Arapaho reservation, and Canadian and Kingfisher counties, created from Old Oklahoma in the opening of 1889. Burford was holding court in Canadian County; his dockets were loaded—as they often were in the more heavily populated areas—and McAtee had been called in to help try cases.

Blacked-robed despite the heat, Judge McAtee fanned himself and tried to look as dignified as possible on his high rostrum. In front of the bench was a table covered with law books and papers.

At the table sat a friendless cowboy being tried in a case that had originated at Grand, a frontier village on the north bank of the South Canadian River and seat of Day County.

The horse-stealing charge was augmented by one of killing the animal's owner, a Day County rancher, and feeling in the neighborhood ran high.

Day County was situated in the northwest corner of the Cheyenne-Arapaho country, on the border of the Texas Panhandle, where settlers were few and cattle-range customs still prevailed. In the fear that these people "might hurry up justice which they considered a little too slow to suit the popular demand," a change of venue had been ordered to a "more civilized" locality.

The dead man had had the reputation of being a quick-triggered gunman, and the cowboy's plea was self-defense. But witnesses testified that the cowboy had shot and killed his victim without giving him an opportunity to draw. It made no difference that he feared the rancher's swift and deadly guns. It did not matter that he would have had no chance in a fair fight. The prosecution was demanding the hang rope. But many in the crowd were betting that the defendant would go free, for his attorney was Temple Houston, one of the Southwest's most widely-known criminal lawyers.

Temple Houston was thirty-three, an age when most men enter maturity, yet he had lived far beyond his years. He had realized his ambitions in his profession early, mingled with the rougher element as well as the talented, and each day drained the cup of life. He stood six feet two, lean-hipped, never erect but slightly stooped and head down like a buffalo. His face held a sinister fascination for everybody who looked at him. Swarthy and somewhat gross in its largeness, it suggested the Indian and gave color to a false story that he was part Cherokee. His mouth, straight-lined and down-curved at the corners, suggesting cruelty, was a fit companion of his small gray eyes, furtive in their glances except when strongly arrested. When he smiled, his lips were tightly drawn across white, even teeth. When abstracted, he had a peculiar habit of toying with the auburn hair that flowed in curling locks about his shoulders.

It was his eccentric dress that first attracted a stranger's attention and added glamour to his legends. He wore an extra-long black frock coat under which was slung "Old Betsy"—a white-handled Colt's revolver that he never failed to secure at a single grasp—a yellow-beaded vest, and Spanish-style, satin-striped trousers cut with a bell flare over unusually small, box-toed riding boots of the finest leather. Temple Houston never passed down a street without sparking inquiries about who he was; he was a sight not to be forgotten.

In addition he possessed qualities most frontier lawyers lacked. He was well educated, spoke French and Spanish fluently and seven Indian tongues, and quoted Greek scholars, the Bible, and Shakespeare. His every work and act were dramatic to the extreme, but behind his dramatics lay the reasoning of a brilliant mind—and fearlessness. His unique methods of impressing a jury had won him many a seemingly hopeless case on the Texas frontier. The crowd waited now to see how he would handle this one.

Soon after the trail began, Houston discovered that the prosecuting attorney had managed to select jurors who, although "good men and true," were not particularly friendly toward the defendant. After the prosecutor had presented his witnesses and Houston produced none to refute them, the prosecutor summarized his case in an impassioned speech. Horse stealing, he explained, was not a crime to be countenanced. And when coupled with murder....

On this point Houston felt certain that the cowboy had acted in self-defense. Switching his coat tails, he took a stance as far from the jury box as the courtoom would permit. In low but quick, cutting tones he related the cowboy's version of the events leading up to the slaying.

"Gentlemen, you have heard my client charged with a crime which was completely outside his realm to commit. He could no more have stood up to his malefactor than the spark from a lowly firefly could outshine the noonday sun—could no more have outshot him than the stubborn, plodding jackass could outrun the fleetest race horse. Such things, gentlemen, are utter impossibilities."

As he spoke, he moved forward with short, catlike steps.

"Gentlemen, this malefactor had a gunman's reputation, while my client here is an ordinary, hard-working citizen like yourselves, little experienced in the use of firearms."

He took another step toward the jury.

"My client was grievously wronged!" he suddenly cried. "He approached his malefactor in a spirit of charity and forgiveness, but this hard-hearted gunman spurned his friendly overtures and flew into a rage. When he saw this gunman coming at him, he knew that his life was at stake."

Houston took one more menacing step, which brought him almost under the noses of the men in the box. There he bent over the pine railing, asking in his most confidential tone:

"What would any of you worthy gentlemen have done in the face of such a character? Do you have any idea how you would have fared against the lightning draw of a gun-artist—unless you had drawn first!"

The jurors leaned toward him, their nerves taut. Then, Houston tossed his long hair and roared:

"This malefactor was so adept with a six-shooter that he could place a gun in the hands of an inexperienced man, then draw and fire his own weapon before his victim could pull the trigger. Like this!"

And, before the men could blink their eyes, he whipped the white-handled Colt's from under his frock coat, pointed the revolver directly at them, and emptied it rapidly.

Judge McAtee, judicial dignity forgotten, "made a hurried jump beneath the bench," the defendant dived under the table, and the jurors "scattered like winter's withered leaves." Some of them leaped over the railing and joined the spectators in a stampede for the doors and windows.

With equally rapid movement Houston holstered his weapon and looked around, acting surprised and innocent. Judge McAtee peered cautiously from beneath the rostrum.

"Your Honor," Houston chuckled, "you need not have been afraid. My cartridges were all blanks."

Judge McAtee returned to the bench. He ordered the bailiff

to reassemble the jury. Then, glowing with wrath, he informed the distinguished Houston that he was of a notion to plaster him with a heavy fine notwithstanding his fame and prowess.

Houston bowed low and apologized for "any seeming disrespect for the person of this court—I only wanted to show what speed this dead man possessed." In his most eloquent and convincing tones he talked the judge out of citing him for contempt, and the trial proceeded.

He made his point. But the jury obviously felt that he had made fools of them. They found the cowboy guilty.

However, the skillful attorney was not licked. He immediately filed a motion for a new trial on grounds that the jury had "separated during the hearing and mingled with the crowd."

Judge McAtee, while unhappy over the affair, admitted that a strict rule of procedure had been violated. The new trial was granted.

In the same setting a few months later, with an impartial jury and Judge Burford presiding, the cowboy was acquitted.

2

Son of "The Raven"

Supposedly Temple Houston was born under a star of destiny. Actually it was the one in the Lone Star flag fluttering above the capitol building at Austin, Texas. The first child born in the governor's mansion and the youngest son of Margaret Moffette Lea and General Sam Houston, he came kicking and squalling into the world on August 12, 1860.

Seven other children graced the Houston household: Sam, Jr., born in 1843 at Washington-on-the-Brazos, the town where Texas's declaration of independence had been signed seven years before; Nancy Elizabeth ("Nannie"), born in 1846 at Raven Hill and named for her grandmothers, Nancy Lea and Elizabeth Paxton Houston; Margaret, born in 1848 at Huntsville, named for her mother and called "Maggie," which was also General Houston's nickname for his wife; Mary Willie, born in 1850 at Huntsville and named for the general's beloved sister; Antoinette ("Nettie"), born in 1852 at Huntsville; Andrew Jackson, born in 1854 at Huntsville and named for the famed "Old Hickory"; and William ("Willie") Rogers, born at Huntsville in 1858. Mrs. Houston named her eighth child for her Baptist minister father, Temple Lea.

Temple came at a time when his father, then sixty-five years old, was serving his second term as chief executive of the Lone Star State, which he had led to victory in 1836 at the historic Battle of San Jacinto, and feeling that he had earned and could well enjoy a period of tranquillity.

General Houston had played an important role in molding the nation's destiny. He was born in Rockbridge County, Virginia, on March 2, 1793, of Scotch-Irish descent. His father, a veteran of the American Revolution, died in 1807, and his mother moved the family of six sons and three daughters to Maryville, Tennessee. Sam's formal education consisted of a few terms in neighborhood schools. At sixteen he worked in the village store. But he spent most of his time among the neighboring Western Cherokees, learning their language and customs, and developed a deep sympathy for Indian character. Oo-loo-te-ka, their principal chief, adopted him as a son and christened him Co-lo-neh, the Raven, a revered name with associations in Cherokee mythology and the appellation by which he is best remembered.

In March, 1813, he enlisted as a private in the Thirty-ninth Infantry for service in the war with England; he was promoted to ensign in July and commissioned a third lieutenant in December. In March, 1814, he was commended by General Andrew Jackson for his coolness and bravery, though severely wounded, in an engagement with the Creek Indians on the Tallapoosa River at Horseshoe Bend, Alabama. He was promoted to second lieutenant in May, and from that time General Jackson had a deciding influence on his life.

In 1817, Houston was promoted to first lieutenant and assigned to the adjutant's office at Nashville. In October he was appointed subagent to the Cherokees to fulfill government promises to the tribe and help equip them for moving west, but following a dispute with President James Monroe over the smuggling of Negroes from Florida, he resigned his subagency and military commission and began the study of law at Nashville. In 1823 and 1825, under Jackson's sponsorship, he was elected to Congress, and in 1827, he was elected governor of Tennessee.

On January 1, 1829, Houston married Eliza Allen, daughter of a wealthy and politically powerful citizen of Gallatin. In April, Eliza returned to her parents' home, and Houston, tacitly assuming the blame, resigned the governorship and went to live among his old Cherokee friends in Indian Territory.

For the next few years he served as the Cherokees' interpreter and ambassador to Washington and as good-will emissary among the neighboring Osages, Creeks, Choctaws, and Chick-

General Sam Houston ("The Raven"), father of Temple Lea Houston. Unless otherwise noted, the illustrations reproduced in this book are from the author's collection.

asaws and the warring tribes on the west, the Comanches and Pawnees. He established a trading post, called Wigwam Neosho, on the Verdigris River near Cantonment Gibson and, like many other frontier traders, took an Indian wife.

During this idyllic period a dream of empire formed in his active mind—a dream of the great Mexican province of Texas, beyond the Sabine. Making a trip to Texas in 1832, partly to report on Indian affairs there for President Jackson, he was caught up in the rising storm of Anglo-American opposition to Mexico. He was made general of the Texas forces and in 1836 defeated the Mexican armies of General Antonio López de Santa Anna at San Jacinto, which resulted in Texas independence and General Houston's election as president of the new republic.

When Houston left Indian Territory, his Cherokee wife refused to leave her people to accompany him. He considered the raven his bird of destiny, and its croaking cries seemed a forewarning that he would not return. Finally she "split the blanket"—divorced him, in Indian parlance—and married again, three weeks before the San Jacinto battle. In the summer of 1839, on a trip to Alabama to buy blooded stock for his farm, Houston met the loving, charming, artistic Margaret Lea. He married her on May 9, 1840 and, despite the new struggles he faced, began the happiest period of his personal life.

When Texas entered the Union in 1845, Houston was elected United States senator. He was prominently mentioned for the presidency of the United States in 1852. His popularity was attested to by another presidential boom in 1856. Neither drive was successful.

The nation was rushing toward civil war. Houston cried for peace. He made himself unpopular by opposing the pro-slavery Kansas-Nebraska Bill. Completing his senatorial term, he returned to Texas. He owned four homes in Texas—a cottage at Huntsville, a plantation at Raven Hill, near his residence at Independence, and a summer place at Cedar Point, on Galveston Bay. He moved from one retreat to another, seeking old haunts and old friends. Accustomed as he was to the stir of public affairs, private life soon palled; he ran for governor in 1859 as an independent and was elected. He expressed his opposition to the secession movement in his inaugural address from the portico of the capitol at Austin. An enormous crowd stood on the lawn as the grizzled war horse raised his powerful arms in a fatherly gesture and boomed, "When Texas united her destiny with that of the United States, she entered into not the North nor the South—her connection was national."

Houston's life had been a long, hard-fought battle. He had been away from home when most of his children were born. As they slipped through the interesting stages of childhood toward maturity, he had been much too busy to enjoy the changes. This last one, Temple Lea, he hoped to follow closely, to weave into his life the hopes and plans the others had missed.

Already, however, the heroes and patriots who gathered at San Jacinto battlefield in April, 1860, to commemorate the twenty-fourth anniversary of the victory, had adopted a resolution recommending their distinguished fellow citizen, General Sam Houston, a true and safe man who would arrest the growth of the spirit of disunion, as the people's candidate for the presidency of the United States.

The loyal gesture struck fire throughout the country, and Houston barely missed being nominated by the National Union party at its convention in Baltimore several days later. To stem the rising tide of civil war, Houston did his utmost to prevent the Democrats from nominating an extreme secessionist. Rabid states' rights southerners declared that the election of Abraham Lincoln, the "Black Republican" candidate, would mean secession and war. Houston denounced them as traitors, insisting that secession would not be justified unless and until the federal government attempted force against the slave states. As for Jefferson Davis, he was cold as a lizard and ambitious as Lucifer.

Houston fought earnestly to keep Texas in the Union. He

succeeded only in delaying the action until February, 1861; a called convention took matters in hand and defeated his administration by a vote of 167 to 7. Thereupon all Texas officials were required to take the oath of allegiance to the Confederacy, which Houston refused to do. Thus for the second time in his life he gave up the governorship of a state for a principle.

The old warrior was not through, however. His sonorous voice went on warning the people prophetically of the disaster to result: "Your fathers and husbands, your sons and brothers will be herded at the point of bayonets. You may, after the sacrifice of countless millions of treasure and hundreds of thousands of lives, win Southern independence,... but I doubt it."

Events came to pass as Houston had foretold. But bitterly as he was opposed to this war, he sent his adored son Sam, Jr., to fight for the South. Nor did he live to see the fulfillment of his dark prophecy. In the spring of 1863 he again was solicited to become candidate for governor but declined for health reasons. "I'm now seventy—an old man," he said.

He was suffering from a severe cold and contracted pneumonia. On July 25 he sank into a coma with his devoted wife and children gathered about him. Houston had disposed of his Huntsville home and Raven Hill plantation, and the family lived in a picturesque structure called Steamboat House.

The next morning Margaret Lea, who had sat at his bedside throughout the night, read to her husband in a low voice from the Bible. He stirred restlessly, and she put aside the book and took his big hand in hers. He murmured, "Texas—Texas—Margaret—."

General Sam breathed his last.

Temple was little more than a babe in arms, and none of the other children had reached majority. A great sorrow fell upon Mrs. Houston and crushed her spirit. In a letter to Sam, Jr., captured at the battle of Shiloh, Tennessee, and now a prisoner at Camp Douglas, she wondered if she could ever guide her little flock through the wilderness.

She sought peace through the remaining summer months and into autumn, squinting through her spectacles at the pages of her Bible and meditating in the privacy of her home. Her attitude improved as she realized that her lot was better than that of some. Starvation gripped her home state of Alabama, and a close friend had lost five sons in the war.

Late in 1864 she moved her family back to Independence, where she acquired another and different house in the center of the old town, to be near her mother and to educate her children at Baylor University. She also leaned heavily on her old Negro slave, Eliza, whom she had owned since girlhood.

Eliza had moved with the Lea family to Texas in 1839. When Margaret became Mrs. Houston, Eliza went with her mistress, sharing her joys and sorrows. "Aunt Liza," as the children called her, had cared for, loved, and taken pride in each new baby. Each one she declared to be the best and brightest. But none received in such full measure the heritage of mind and temperament of their father as did the youngest, Temple.

From his mother Temple inherited an artistic tendency that found expression in drawing. His life was shadowed, as much as a small child's life can be, by the horrors of the war. His childish sympathies were with the South, and he spent hours lying flat on the floor sketching scenes of battles the fields strewn with Union dead, the Confederates always victorious.

When he was five years old, Temple submitted one picture for his mother's approval that depicted an unusually large number of dead Yankees. The gentle Margaret, more than disturbed about his seeming love of carnage, gravely remonstrated with him: "All those poor men had souls."

"Yes," he replied as though to pacify her, "they all died Christians."

Shortly word came of the surrender at Appomattox. The Confederate soldiers began returning to their homes. One group in nondescript uniforms passed through Independence. Temple, seeing them coming, rushed into the street, waving in both hands a cavalry saber given to him by a grown admirer, and shouted to the head of the column, "If Rebels, you can pass—if Yankees, you cannot!"

The men cheered until they were hoarse.

Sam, Jr., came home, and the Houston household seemed normal again. After studying briefly at Baylor, Sam entered medical school at the University of Pennsylvania. In the spring of 1866, Nannie married Joseph Clay Stiles Morrow, who owned a mercantile business in Georgetown. The following October, Maggie married Weston Lafayette ("West") Williams, who leased a farm at Labadie Prairie, in Washington County. In the summer and autumn of 1867 an epidemic of yellow fever swept the state, and Mrs. Houston became one of its last victims. She died on December 3, and Aunt Liza remained to help the older children care for the younger ones.

Cares rest lightly on youthful shoulders, and Temple felt little of the depression that again enveloped the family. At age seven he went to live with his oldest sister at Georgetown. He seemed a happy child, assuming on occasion an attitude of self-importance and lording it over his playmates in a most regal manner, yet the next moment shrinking within an armor of taciturnity that none could penetrate.

At age ten he was elected president of his school's debating society. Rules of order and decorum were strictly enforced. One night when Temple was presiding, a corpulent character well known about town strolled in to listen to the debates and to make himself more comfortable stretched full length on a bench. Calling his name, Temple thundered from the chair, "You will please assume a proper attitude!" The man promptly complied, and the room rocked with applause and laughter.

By the time he was twelve, Temple resembled his father in physical appearance—big, rawboned and man-sized—and the wanderlust nature of the Raven for wild ways and daring deeds and the gentle, trustful spirit of the tenderly reared mother battled inside him. The mysterious longing to go forth and conquer the world finally possessed his soul. He mounted his pony and rode away from his sister's home, west to the vast cattle ranges on the Colorado and the Concho river. There he learned to rope and shoot and do other things a boy his age perhaps never should have known. His uncanny aptitude for imitating the manners and habits of grownups he met was a continual source of interest and amusement. Always a favorite of the men he worked for, he drew top wages.

He accompanied one longhorn herd to Bismarck, Dakota Territory. Bismarck was an end-of-track town founded in 1873 at the Missouri River crossing along the roadbed and right of way being surveyed for the Northern Pacific Railroad—a route that had been recommended to Congress before the Civil War as an Oregon tributary along the popular Asa Whitney Trail from Saint Paul by way of the Upper Missouri to Vancouver. Bismark was filled with squatters and land speculators. Half of the log buildings housed saloons, ladies of easy virtue, and drifting gamblers. The only "law" was the Seventh Infantry, which was stationed at Fort McKean, on a hill south of the river, to protect the surveyors and laborers. Killings and street fights were common, and there was always the dread of an attack on the town by hostile Sioux, who made forays to the north against the friendly Mandans and Aricaras.

Finally a new fort to house a cavalry unit was built under the Fort McKean hill. Called Fort Abraham Lincoln, it was more readily accessible to the town. It was soon occupied by the Seventh Cavalry under Lieutenant Colonel George A. Custer, and Bismarck became a safer place to live.

In November, 1873, the railroad work was abandoned by the construction corporation for lack of funds. But the town continued to boom as a trade center for the rapidly developing agricultural section and as a base of supplies for the United States military posts and Indian agencies. Reports flew thick and fast of fortunes in gold that lay hidden in the Black Hills, and a major war with the increasingly hostile Sioux confederation was in the offing. The following spring Lieutenant Colonel Custer, with more than a thousand men, including ten companies of his beloved Seventh Cavalry, would depart on the now-famed Black Hills Expedition.

Young Houston did not linger for these events, nor for the snow that bore down from Canada and smothered the northern prairies during the winter of 1873-74, spreading blanket upon blanket across Bismarck, until the top halves of the buildings in the town and at the fort were checkerboarded on white, flanked by the ice-locked river. Temple made his way to Fargo and took a train down to Saint Paul.

Seeking further new experiences, he got a job as clerk on a steamboat and traveled down the Mississippi to New Orleans. There he met a political friend of his father's, still serving in Congress. For the sake of the father, as well as the personal attraction of the boy himself, the friend used his influence in securing for him an appointment as page in the United States Senate.

Temple's older sisters were relieved by the news. Deeply concerned for his welfare, they were convinced that some good, stern discipline from the nation's lawmakers was just what he needed.

Temple worked in Washington, D.C., until he was sixteen. Three years in this forum ringing with oratory caused him to return to Georgetown, where he told Nannie and Joe Morrow of his hopes and ambitions and that he was now ready for an education. The Morrows placed him in the Agricultural and Mechanical College at Bryan.

The new college, opened on October 4, 1876, was a result of the policy of the federal government under the Morrill Act of 1862 (amended in 1865) of making a grant of public lands to states agreeing to establish institutions for instruction in agriculture and the mechanical arts. Temple's aspirations did not include "high-toned" farming or mechanics, but he became a serious participant in the "classical studies connected therewith," including military tactics.

He studied incessantly, remarkably retaining most of what he read. He could trace on a world map the march of the armies of the world's captains, from Alexander to Napoleon. Next to his father, Napoleon Bonaparte held his greatest admiration. His favorite pose was to pin back the skirt of his coat

Temple Lea Houston as page in the United States Senate.

Temple as cadet in Texas A&M College, Bryan.

and the brim of his hat and, with hands clasped behind his back, stand motionless in the attitude of *Napoleon at Saint Helena.* He decorated his room with pictures of the "Little Corporal" in battle and retreat—Napoleon at Austerlitz, at the Kremlin, crossing the Alps, at Lodi, at the Pyramids, as first consul. Years later two marble busts of the general would grace his desk, and his cases would hold reams of clippings and volumes of history referring to him. While Temple's spirit of revelry was not dead, he had it under sufficient control to graduate with honors and the rank of second lieutenant when he was seventeen.

The following year the first president of the college and his faculty, who had pioneered in a field without precedent, were dismissed, having failed to carry out the objectives of teaching either agriculture or mechanical arts on a practical basis. John Garland James was employed and told to close his Texas Military Institute at Austin and move his entire staff to A and M, where four-year programs were initiated.

Temple did not return to Bryan. Maggie and West Williams now occupied the old house in Independence where his mother had died. In an upstairs room was kept the silver-mounted saddle of Santa Anna and other souvenirs of General Houston's activities in Texas. Making his home with the Williamses, surrounded by his father's artifacts and papers, Temple entered Baylor University to study law and philosophy.

In 1863, Texas Baptists had called the Reverend William Carey Crane, an educator of national experience, to take over the presidency of Baylor. The curriculum was broadened and the women's department made a separate institution, Baylor Female College. From 1866, Baylor University was a male establishment. Crane, a cofounder of the State Historical Association of Mississippi and a passionate devotee of history, was an intimate friend of the Houston and Lea families. Two years before her death Mrs. Houston had asked Crane to undertake to write the life of her husband and edit and publish his literary remains. Crane's two-volume opus would not appear until 1884. Meanwhile, the trunks of letters, drafts of speeches, and mementos in the Houston attic became his particular target, and Temple his protégé.

The youth had proved that he possessed the capacity for hard work. He devoured everything he could lay hands on— law, history, the Bible, Shakespeare, astronomy, foreign languages. He even sought out Catholic priests in various towns to converse with them in Latin. The course of study embraced four years; Temple completed it in nine months, graduating at age nineteen in a class of ten with the degree bachelor of philosophy.

He applied to the Texas bar. The age requirement was twenty-one. Two other young men who had graduated in law with him were several years beyond their majority. It was agreed to strike an average age of the three applicants and admit young Houston to practice.

It is not clear why he chose Brazoria in which to open his law office, except that it was the seat of one of the leading coastal counties where, to use one of Temple's colorful phrases, "the Gulf of Mexico, in vexed magnificence, breaks against the Texas island chains." Perhaps it was the area's antebellum quality and historic significance. Here were the old homes of many prominent Texans, among them Colonel James W. Fannin and William Harris Wharton. Famous old Peach Point, the home of Stephen F. Austin's sister, stood on the Brazos not far from the mouth of the Gulf.

Brazoria was established in 1828 as a port and trading center for Austin's original colony. The Brazos was the chief artery of commerce and communication between the colonists and New Orleans; small boats navigated as far as Old Columbia. Customhouses were situated at Brazoria and Velasco, at the mouth of the river. In May, 1832, Brazoria became the capital of Texas. In June, 1832, its citizens led the Battle of Velasco, and when the revolution began, most of its men joined the Texas army. Nearly all the families had departed in the Runaway Scrape before General José Urrea burned the town on April 22, 1836. In the summer of 1836 it was the location of the provisional government and site of the signing of the Velasco treaties. Brazoria County was organized December 20, 1836; the creation of Fort Bend County in 1837 and of Galveston County in 1838 established its boundaries.

The town had six newspapers and a population of nearly five thousand. An intracoastal canal had been completed between Velasco and Galveston. The Houston Tap and Brazoria Railroad connected Columbia with Houston and with the Buffalo Bayou, Brazos and Colorado Railroad at Pierce Junction. The old Sugarland Railroad joined the Houston Tap and Brazoria at Anchor and the Buffalo Bayou, Brazos and Colorado at Sugarland to serve the vast plantations along Oyster Creek. The federal government was interested in improving the mouth of the Brazos for a deep-water port.

Brazoria had a well-established bar of good lawyers, and Temple expected to develop a practice rather slowly. On the other hand, it was a town where disputes were settled as often with guns as before a judge. His tactics and suave manners soon gained him a large criminal practice. In fact, his handling of criminal cases attracted such wide attention that the voters were soon willing to give into the hands of a boy the business of bringing law violators to the bar of justice, and they elected him county attorney before he was twenty-one.

He also fell in love with pretty Laura Cross. Born on her grandfather's plantation, Bayou LaFourche, in Louisiana, Laura had moved to Texas when still in her teens. With her mother and stepfather she lived on a plantation three miles from Columbia, and there she met Temple, at a dance.

"I saw him across the room, and he saw me," she said years later. "We literally ran into each other's arms"—as nearly as the decorous 1880s would permit. "It was love at first sight, all right, for we were both 'goners' then."

Temple was fond of music but "couldn't turn a tune to save his life." He did not dance, but there was "just enough French blood running through her veins to make him try." They became engaged on his twenty-first birthday.

Two weeks later—on August 25, 1881—nearly two

thousand people stood on a hill overlooking the Gulf at Galveston and got their first idea of young Houston's style as he delivered a eulogy at the unveiling of a monument to the heroes of San Jacinto:

Only a few decades back, the plumed and crested Algonquin roamed over magnificent Texas, sole Lord of its vast wastes save where a few isolated missions sought vainly to weave religion's silken fetters over the savage mind.

Yonder billows, blue and restless, dashed then as grandly against your level shores as now, but on their tossing bosoms floated not the freighted wealth of earth's nations. These same breezes, damp from dalliance with the waves, and laden with perfume stolen from the flowers, swept over our broad plains, but fanned not the cheek of civilized man.

Our silvery streams, rolling on to mingle their crystal waters with the stormy surges of the deep, murmured as sweetly and sparkled as brightly as now, but they moistened not the lips of the Anglo-Saxon, and turned not a single mill-wheel; nor cotton nor wheat field smiled in all their valleys.

The brown buffalo cropt undisturbed the green grass from our prairies, and the spotted deer rested unfrightened beneath the cool shade of our forest oaks.

Texas, lovely Texas, was as fair, as fresh and as beautiful as was Eden when God, delighted, gazed on the new-born world.

It was thus when came the men we today honor. These pioneers were the heralds of a new civilization—one that was born in the medieval convulsions of England, nurtured under the shadow of Virginia's mountains, and that flashed forth freed and panoplied from the struggles of the American revolution—a civilization whose fundamental principle was civil and religious liberty. Coming to Texas, it rested for a moment under the frown of Spanish civilization, which was developed on the glittering thrones of Europe, and in the torture chambers of the Inquisition. One idolized, the other abhorred civil and religious liberty. When the Anglo-Saxon settlements had attained a magnitude sufficient to invite governmental interference, the Mexicans adopted toward them an oppressive policy, typical of their institutions.

This ignited the spark.

Temple knew ancient history. Homer and Tacitus he knew

by heart. Byron was his favorite poet, and he could quote exquisite passages from Oriental poems, *The Giaour*, *The Corsair*, and *The Siege of Corinth*. Seargent Smith Prentiss, the Mississippi legislator famed for his three-day speech of great brilliancy and power on the floor of the United States House of Representatives during the administration of President Martin Van Buren, was his ideal of the lawyer, the advocate and the orator. But he revered the founders of the Texas Republic. He held as a consecrated heritage the free institutions they had established and the organic law they had written, and he warmed to the occasion:

The conflict of the opposite types of civilization for mastery of this continent was decided on the forest-fringed banks of a Texas stream. Never before in the history of the world were such gigantic results intrusted to so few....

Had that little band quailed before the might of invading despotism, our Pacific shores might yet be unknown; the golden wealth of California would yet sleep in her mountain gorges; the silver treasures of Mexico would now slumber, hidden in their caverned homes; the solitude of the Rocky Mountains would yet be a stranger to the shriek of the locomotive; the two oceans would not have shaken hands....

Sterner warriors or truer patriots than those who guarded the liberty of Texas, on that immortal day, never trod a battlefield. Their valor needs no eulogy.... for fame's clarion has sounded their praises, and earth is the only limit of their renown.

They will be here but a little while longer. Each year that passes thins their ranks. One by one the pale messenger is calling them across that river whose viewless farther shore is wrapt in the mists of doubt, the clouds of death.

While they are among us we feel toward them a devotion whose depth words can never tell. No minions cringe around them, no servile knee is bent to them, but the homage of a free nation is the more than loyal offering laid before them.

No ducal star glitters on their breasts, no shining coronet encircles their brows, but around their gray locks beams a glory by the side of which kingly splendors are dim.

Cling tenderly to these old men, for when they are gone nothing like them is left.

Tears fell down the cheeks of young and old alike. They called Temple "a true son of The Raven" and milled about on the hillside to shake the hand of "Old Sam's youngest boy." Excerpts from his speech appeared in the state press. At Austin, Governor Oran M. Roberts read them with interest. Perhaps he recalled the February 6, 1844, when General Houston, then serving his second term as president of the Texas Republic, had appointed him prosecuting attorney of the old Nacogdoches District.

A native of South Carolina and one-time Alabama legislator, Roberts had moved to Texas in 1841 and was practicing law at San Augustine. In 1846 he became district judge and in 1857 associate justice of the Texas Supreme Court. An ardent secessionist, he was credited with calling the convention of 1861 and with the authorship of the plan that had forced Old Sam to depose himself as governor. Yet he had always shown gratitude to and respect for the Houston family.

In 1862 he organized a regiment of Eleventh Texas Infantry, serving as its colonel until 1864, when he resigned to become chief justice of the Texas Supreme Court. Removed when the war ended, he served in the Constitutional Convention of 1866 and was elected to the United States Senate, but was rejected by Congress because of his secessionist activities. He practiced privately at Tyler and Gilmer until 1874. With the resumption of Democratic party control in Texas and, in 1876, the adoption of a new constitution, which finally became the fundamental law of the state, he again became chief justice of the Texas Supreme Court. In 1878 he was elected governor.

As a result of five years of war and nine of radical misrule and excesses in compliance with the congressional Reconstruction Acts, the state's finances were at a low ebb. Roberts adopted a pay-as-you-go policy and, despite strong opposition from the legislature and much public criticism, compelled all branches of state government, including the public-school system, to keep expenditures within the revenue. Texas was on the road to financial recovery.

The Rangers had been maintained on a haphazard basis before the Civil War and during the war had been in abeyance except for small forces guarding the Indian frontier. A state police system had been set up under the Reconstruction governor E. J. Davis, but it became so obnoxious that it was abolished with public celebration as soon as the government was returned to Texas citizens. In 1874 the legislature authorized the organization of two fighting Ranger forces. The larger one, the Frontier Battalion, consisting of six companies under the command of Major John B. Jones, was stationed along the western border to hold back and punish the Indians who still harried the settlements. Major Jones soon found that his main task was putting down white mobs, breaking up feuds, capturing murderers, and killing train robbers. The second force, the Special Force, under the command of Captain L. H. McNelly, policed the Mexican border, which bands of cattle and horse thieves kept in constant turmoil. By 1880 the Rangers had become an established institution and were well on the way to restoring order.

Texas still faced a serious law-enforcement problem on its extreme northwestern frontier, hence Governor Roberts's interest in Temple Houston. Until 1876 the Panhandle-Plains area—the region lying north of an imaginary line beginning at the southeast corner of present Nolan County and extending westward to New Mexico, and west of a line northward to Indian Territory and the southern border of the present Panhandle of Oklahoma—had been in the Bexar and Young territories. The 1876 survey and legislative enactment under authority of the new constitution divided the area into fifty-four counties and attached them to Jack and Clay Counties as part of the Tenth Judicial District pending arrival of a permanent population necessary to organized county governments. In 1879, after Wheeler County was organized with Old Mobeetie as county seat, the Tenth Judicial District included only the upper tier of twenty-six counties—a large, nearly square region designated as the High Plains—and Greer County between the Salt and Prairie Dog Town forks of the

Red River, in present Oklahoma. On February 15, 1881, the Tenth District "went south," and these twenty-seven counties became the Thirty-fifth Judicial District of Texas, with headquarters at Mobeetie.

Representative Avery L. Matlock of Montague, who introduced the bill in the legislature, and J. F. Evans, of the Panhandle Stock Association, who helped push it through, suggested I. N. Roach, of Weatherford, for district attorney. Roach had voted his county's instructions against Roberts in political convention, and the governor, refusing to buy his enemies, appointed instead James Nathan ("Jim") Browning, a noted lawyer and prosecuting attorney of Shackelford County, at Albany. But Browning soon resigned because the office would not support the manner of living to which he had become accustomed.

Governor Roberts had made a second choice, but this man, when informed of the wild acts of desperadoes of the region and told that to enter the courtroom unarmed was to take one's life in his hands, changed his mind. Familiar with Temple's handling of criminal cases in Brazoria County, the governor offered him the position.

Temple knew the ways of cow people from his boyhood experience on the Texas range. He was planning to be married but thought Mobeetie no place to take a bride.

"What do you think of my going?" he asked Laura.

"Do as you think best," she said.

"If I go, will you wait for me?" he asked.

"Yes—any number of years," she promised.

Temple took a train from Galveston to Fort Worth and thence on the Fort Worth and Denver City Railroad, called the "Texas Panhandle Route," to the end of track at Henrietta. There he boarded a mail and passenger stage, with his personal belongings and such records as the state had furnished, for the last lap of the journey along dim roads across unsettled country.

It required the better part of three days to make the trip, but if the new prosecutor was bored with any part of it, no one

James Nathan ("Honest Jim") Browning, first district attorney for the Texas Panhandle and Mobeetie lawyer. Courtesy of Panhandle-Plains Historical Museum, Canyon, Texas.

knew it. He was eager and pleasant and noted that the country had changed little since he had crossed it with the longhorn herd bound for Dakota. Temple carried a beautiful white-handled revolver in a stamped leather holster hung from a broad leather belt with a silver buckle, and as they plodded along the winding, dusty trail, he entertained his companions with a draw so quick the eye could not follow his hand.

Several times he would draw and aim, then suddenly draw and fire, and he seldom missed his target. It might be a jackrabbit bounding across the low hills, a rattlesnake slithering through the dried grass, or a prairie dog sitting on a bleak, dry hill and barking at the passing strangers. More often he picked something much smaller—a pod on a tall weed, the dead flower of a thistle.

Finally there were new targets to which he could point the gaze of passengers, signifying that Mobeetie was close at hand. The trail was strewn with empty whiskey bottles.

3

Canadian River Empire

The Texas Panhandle—embracing approximately fourteen thousand square miles, larger than Vermont, almost as large as Maryland and Massachusetts combined, and more than ten times the size of Rhode Island—was almost an empire within itself. In 1881, with Mobeetie the only town of any size and not a mile of railroad, it was little more than an eight-million-acre tableland of free grass.

For years cattlemen had circled this marvelous range country like hungry lobos circling a fat calf. Two obstacles stood in their way—buffalo and Indians. Buffalo by the hundreds of thousands swarmed across the region, south in summer and north in winter, and the Indians were always close behind.

The Medicine Lodge Treaty of 1867 had banned the tribes of the Southern Plains from hunting north of the Arkansas River. Then the Atchison, Topeka and Santa Fe Railroad built up the river valley through western Kansas. It reached Dodge City in 1872, and was extended to Granada, Colorado, in 1873. By that time buffalo had become scarce north of the Arkansas, and the long-haired hide men, firing deadly big-caliber Sharps rifles, swarmed across the Cimarron into the area the Indians considered their hunting domain. Indians by the thousands—Kiowas, Cheyennes, and Comanches—set the Panhandle aflame.

The Indians' first attack in force was on those they hated most—the buffalo hunters. At dawn on June 27, 1874, more than seven hundred warriors struck Adobe Walls, on the Canadian River, in a roaring torrent of flying arrows and carbine and smoothbore-musket fire. Their weapons were no match, however, for the long-range rifles of the handful of white men. The hunters wreaked havoc with their attackers. But the Indians caused such destruction to the post that the defenders were forced to abandon it and suspend operations. The tribes then separated and spread across the plains, pillaging and burning.

Federal military posts encircled the Panhandle. The Texas line of frontier defense extended from Fort Richardson at Jacksboro through Forts Griffin, Concho, McKavett, Territt, and Clark to Fort Duncan on the Río Grande. Between the Río Grande and the Pecos River stood Forts Stockton and Davis and Fort Bliss at El Paso. On the west, in New Mexico Territory, were Forts Stanton, Bascom and Union; on the northwest, Forts Garland and Lyon in Colorado. Fort Dodge, near Dodge City, Kansas, was the headquarters of the buffalo-hide industry. On the east, in Indian Territory, were Camp Supply and Fort Sill.

Quick-tempered, decisive General Philip Sheridan, commanding the Division of the Missouri, launched a vigorous pincer campaign. Lieutenant Colonel John W. ("Black Jack") Davidson was ordered west from Fort Sill. Colonel Ranald S. Mackenzie moved north from Fort Clark, at Bracketville, Texas. Colonel George P. Buell moved across from Fort Griffin. Major William R. Price came down the Canadian from Fort Union, New Mexico. Colonel Nelson A. Miles of the Fifth Cavalry, in immediate command of the troops in the field, left Camp Supply to converge on the Indians from that direction. By winter's end the marauding tribes had been subdued and forced back to their reservations.

To prevent the reentry of the Indians into Texas, the army established a new fort in June, 1875, on Sweetwater Creek in the area to be formed as Wheeler County. A few weeks later North Fork Cantonment, a temporary garrison set up near McClellan Creek in 1874, was moved to the new site, which was named Fort Elliott in honor of Major Joel H. Elliott, who had been killed on November 27, 1868, in General George A. Custer's Seventh Cavalry attack on Black Kettle's village on the Washita. The Indian troubles subsided, hunters completed the extermination of the buffalo, and settlers entered the Panhandle in reasonable safety.

Cattlemen pounced on the region. The business of trailing longhorn herds to markets outside Texas that had continued since the late 1860s was reversed. Colorado, Kansas, Missouri, and Louisiana herds poured into the Panhandle by the thousands. Scattered plazas started by Mexican sheepmen—some with as many as a dozen rock houses—already dotted the area. Sheepmen did not count; cattlemen either bought their meager improvements or ran them out, locating where they chose with a base near water, which, like grass, was a most necessary factor.

The first to arrive was Charles Goodnight. A native of Illinois who spent the Civil War years helping protect the Texas frontier, Goodnight made his start in the industry in Palo Pinto County and with his neighbor, Oliver Loving, broke the first trail to the markets furnished by army posts in New Mexico. In 1867 on one of these trails Loving fell to Comanche arrows while pushing ahead of the herd to drive an advance bargain with army officials at Santa Fe. But that was after the partners had blazed an extension into Wyoming, known as the Goodnight-Loving Trail, and established another ranch on the Apishapa, northeast of Trinidad, Colorado. In the next several years Goodnight laid off the New Goodnight Trail from Alamogordo Creek, New Mexico, to Granada, Colorado, taking time out for a trip to Hickman, Kentucky, in 1870 to marry his long-time sweetheart, Mary Ann Dyer. The reversals of the Panic of 1873 and overcrowding of the southern Colorado ranges prompted him to return to Texas. With sixteen hundred head of cattle he crossed three hundred miles of wilderness and in the fall of 1876 settled in the almost heart center of the Panhandle, forming a partnership with John Adair, of Rathdair, Ireland, whom he met in Colorado, and taking the latter's initials, JA, for the ranch brand.

Starting with twelve thousand acres (eventually increased

Charles Goodnight, first cattleman in the Texas Panhandle.

under his leadership to more than a million acres) and grazing over one hundred thousand head of cattle), Goodnight took every water hole up and down Palo Duro Canyon, beginning at Devil's Kitchen in Randall County and extending seventy-five miles to beyond the confluence of Mulberry Creek with Red River. At the foot of the Cap Rock in Armstrong County he built his headquarters of cedar logs cut in the Palo Duro. He chased mustangs and helped drive back the buffalo to prevent his stock from moving away with the wandering wild herds. He treated with the Comanche chiefs Satanta and Quanah Parker, who, despite efforts of the military, were at large and still marauding. In 1880 he organized the Panhandle Stock Association to prosecute rustlers and horse thieves and to fight general lawlessness. Goodnight would remain the dominating figure of the Panhandle for more than twenty years.

The second permanent ranch, the Quarter Circle T, was founded by Thomas S. Bugbee, a Maine Yankee who engaged in the freighting business in Idaho and Utah after the Civil War. In November, 1876, he drove a herd of cattle from Kansas to Hutchinson County, on the Canadian, establishing headquarters near Adobe Walls. In 1882 he sold out to the Hansford Cattle Company but soon reentered the ranching business with O. H. Nelson as his partner on Red River in Hall County.

The courage and vision of Goodnight and Bugbee attracted others. Early in 1877 two Bostonians, the devout W. H. ("Deacon") Bates and David T. Beals, a wealthy shoe manufacturer, brought their LX herds from Colorado to the Ranch Creek tributary of the Canadian River north of Amarillo. They increased their herds in 1878 and 1879 and in 1882 acquired 23,680 acres from a grant to the Houston & Texas Central Railway in northwestern Potter County. Some noted westerners drew pay from the LX: James H. ("Jim") East, second sheriff of Oldham County, who helped chase the impertinent William Bonney (Billy the Kid); Charles A. Siringo, cowboy detective and writer; and W. C. ("Outlaw

Bill") Moore, the manager who, many claimed, stole cattle faster than the LX could raise them.

In the fall of 1877, Leigh and Walter Dyer, two of Goodnight's brothers-in-law, drove four hundred head of cattle into the valley above the junction of Palo Duro and Tierra Blanca creeks, near present Canyon, Texas. The Dyers' only claim to the land was that of priority, which they sold in 1878 to Jot Gunter, W. B. Munson, and John Summerfield, surveyors for land companies on a partnership basis and among the state's outstanding purchasers of land certificates. Gunter, Munson, and Summerfield brought in their first herd, branded GMS, from Louisiana. In 1880 more herds were driven from northeast Texas. Summerfield sold his interest to Jule Gunter, Jot's nephew, in 1881, and the firm became Gunter, Munson, and Gunter. This firm branded Crescent G but still used the GMS. Then Jule Gunter brought in a herd from Indian Territory branded T Anchor; the ranch discontinued the other two brands and became known as the T Anchor.

The LIT Ranch was started by Major George W. Littlefield, a cowman of the old school who drove 3,500 head of mixed cattle into Oldham County from South Texas in 1877, first locating a headquarters on Pescado Creek, four miles below the Canadian, and later moving two miles north of the river on the Cheyenne (Magenta). The brand—L on the Left shoulder, I on the side, and T on the animal's hip—was taken from Littlefield's name. Before frost came, nearly 14,000 more head of cattle trailed in from the south were grazing on the luxurious range that extended from the Cheyenne twenty-five miles east to John Ray Creek in Potter County and embraced all lands for fifteen miles on each side of the river. In 1881, Littlefield sold 17,247 head, 250 saddle horses, and what equity he held in ranch improvements and equipment to the Prairie Land and Cattle Company of Edinburgh, Scotland. The major then transferred his operations to the Pecos Valley of New Mexico, where he started his famous LFD brand.

Before the advent of the LIT, Ellsworth Torrey, a former British sea captain with dreams of a ranching fortune and the backing of a Boston bank, moved into Oldham County with his wife, two sons, and two daughters, settling near Skunk Arroyo on the Canadian and the famous peaks that still bear his name. He had accumulated about 25,000 head of cattle in 1879 when he had his run-in with Billy the Kid.

Herds caught in the swirling blizzards of the Panhandle sometimes drifted as far southwest as the Pecos and the Río Grande. They were a welcome bonanza to the New Mexico renegades led by the Kid. Torrey had remarked that the Kid and his gang were ordinary thieves, unfit to associate or break bread with decent people. The Kid with four cohorts rode to Torrey's headquarters and demanded feed for their horses and a meal for themselves. The horses were fed, and when dinner was prepared, Torrey tried to serve the outlaws before the family ate. The Kid insisted that the family eat with them and, when the meal was finished, gave Torrey a severe tongue lashing and promised to kill him if he spoke disparagingly of his men again. For this reason, it is sometimes alleged, Torrey sold to the LS Company and left the plains.

The Kid was in custody from Christmas Eve, 1880, when he and the remnants of his outfit were captured by Sheriff Patrick F. Garrett and posse at Stinking Springs, until April 28, 1881, when he killed his two guards and escaped from the Lincoln County jail. He was shot to death by Garrett at midnight on July 14, 1881, in the bedroom of the Pete Maxwell home at Fort Sumner. It would seem Torrey had little to fear from the Kid, and the LS Company of W. M. D. Lee and Lucien B. Scott was not established until some time afterward.

Lee, a wealthy buffalo-hide merchant and post trader of Fort Elliott and Camp Supply, arrived in western Oldham County late in 1879 to form the LE Ranch for himself and his partner, A. E. Reynolds, who was then mining with his brother, C. F. Reynolds, near Creede, Colorado. They put a herd of Missouri Durhams on Trujillo Creek and located headquarters on the Alamocitos, in an old rock house purchased from sheepmen. In 1880 they acquired a second site from Dolores Duran, on Romero Canyon, which became the center of their activities. That same year Lee split with the Reynolds brothers, who took the west range, the cattle, and the LE brand. Lee kept the rock house, associated himself with Scott, a Leavenworth, Kansas, banker, and started the famous LS brand on Alamocitos Creek.

In 1881, J. F. Glidden, of DeKalb, Illinois, who invented barbed wire, and Henry W. Sanborne, of New York, who was to introduce and sell it, established the Frying Pan Ranch in Potter and Randall counties, surrounding the 250,000-acre venture with a four-wire fence. The wire was hauled from Dodge City at $2.50 a hundredweight, and the posts came from the Palo Duro and other breaks. The Frying Pan became the first fenced pasture on the High Plains.

Across the Panhandle to the east, other ranchers arrived on both sides of the Canadian. Josiah Morgan and Mose Harp brought a herd from Padre Island to Lipscomb County. The Turkey Track ran hundreds of horses and thousands of cattle from Adobe Walls to Indian Territory. Henry Whiteside ("Hank") Creswell drove a herd from Colorado, locating on Home Ranch Creek in Roberts County in 1877. He bought other herds and leased the right to range until his Bar CC covered more than a million acres in Roberts, Ochiltree, and Hemphill counties. The Rowe brothers—Alfred, Vincent, and Bernard—of England, started the RO Ranch, which spread through Collingsworth and Donley counties, with headquarters on Big Skillet Creek between the forks of the Red. There were nearly a score of lesser outfits.

Many of the cattlemen grazed herds, openly and otherwise, in the Cherokee Outlet east of Lipscomb and Hemphill counties, on the Cheyenne-Arapaho Reservation, and on the land of the Comanche Indians east of Greer. In turn cattlemen in the arm of Oklahoma known as No Man's Land, or the "neutral strip," maintained camps and grazed herds below its border from Wolf Creek to the Coldwater.

The Panhandle was big-ranch country, and its life-style would not change until the coming of the railroads. Nesters invariably found themselves in the heart of big ranches. Cat-

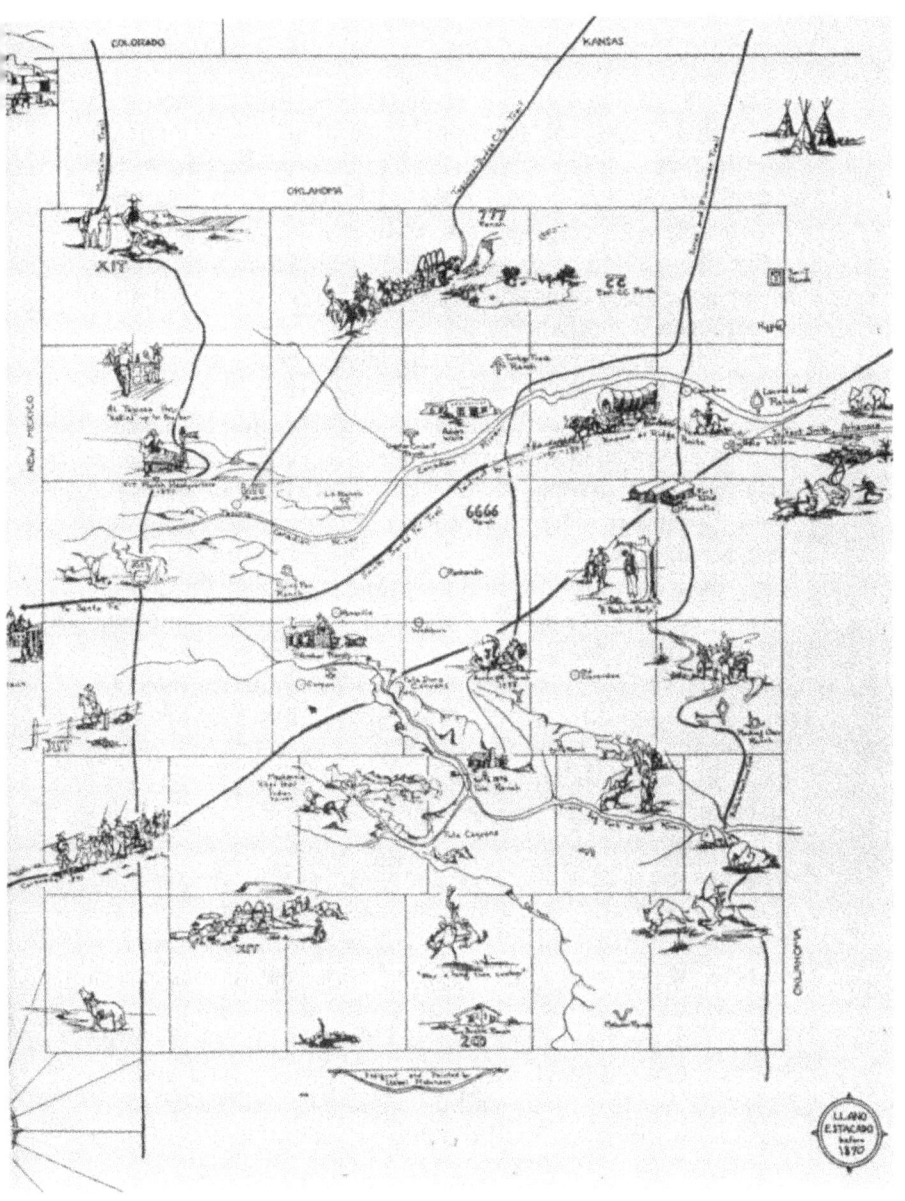

The Texas Panhandle in the 1880s, showing trails and ranch locations. Map by Isabel Robinson, for *Cattleman* magazine.

tlemen did not worry about them, for they had no money to fence their claims. A few found occasional employment on the ranches or killed coyotes and wolves for the bounty the cattlemen offered. Others gathered buffalo bones, scattered everywhere and bleached ash white by the wind and sun, piling them like haystacks and adding to them until a bone buyer came along or arrangements could be made to haul them to the nearest market.

Another money source was the many buffalo wallows and larger low places on the prairies, called lakes even when no water stood in them. Their dark-loam bottoms produced a tall, broad-leafed grass that was especially nutritious, and men baled and sold this hay to townspeople with livestock and to some cattlemen. The lakes were soon overgrazed, a few wet seasons raised the water level until the hay rotted, and the cash crop was gone. But these things sustained the settlers until they got some stock of their own or learned something about high, dry farming.

Fort Elliott was scarcely established when the scattered occupants of the surrounding country moved into the shadow of its flag and formed the nucleus of the first permanent settlement in the Panhandle. The fort, arranged in an east-west rectangle, sat about two miles southeast of the head of Sweetwater Creek and north of a major bend in the stream. Several natural elevations on the west and south were used as observation points; on the east a longitudinal ridge of sand hills provided a ten-mile field of vision. The north, unblocked by vegetation or harsh terrain, became the main entrance and exit for military parties. It was an excellent site with plenty of wood and grass available in the valley of the creek. Wild turkey, deer, pronghorn antelope, catfish, and sunfish abounded for the hunter and fisherman and, with wild plums and berries, supplemented the military diet. The Sweetwater had long been a camping place for Indians and soldiers, and when Major H. C. Bankhead, Fourth Cavalry, arrived with his troops to locate the post, a buffalo hunters' supply camp had been set up on the opposite side of a knoll on the south, called "Hidetown" because the hunters covered their picket houses with buffalo skins to shelter them from the severe winters.

The army had leased 2,560 acres for the fort's operations, and none but government men, teamsters, and post sutler were allowed on the post proper. The land had not yet been surveyed, however, and no one knew the exact boundaries of the site. Soon quite a number of other civilians were camped at Hidetown. The army made no objection until Henry Munson, a shoe cobbler, killed a young man. The post had been established to control the Indians, not to provide law and order for the white civilians, and the people were ordered out of the four-section area.

They moved around the bend of the creek about a mile away, remaining as close to the fort as possible. Others quickly followed—merchants, drummers, lawyers, real estate men, druggists, hotel and saloon keepers, professional gamblers, dance-hall girls, and Cyprians for the cowboy and hunter trade and to cheer the lonely boys in blue. Settlers came looking for homes and a fresh start. A few friendly Indians who pitched their tipis on the creek nearby were considered a part of the post village.

Population increased to 150, and they called the new town Sweetwater until Wheeler County was organized and a postoffice applied for in 1879. The seat of Nolan County had already been established as Sweetwater, so Mobeetie—the Comanche word for all soft, or "sweet," water—was chosen as the name. As the administrative and judicial capital of the Panhandle, situated at the junction of the military highways to Forts Griffin, Concho, and Sill and Camp Supply, and terminus of the Jones-Plummer Trail from Dodge City, Mobeetie became a thriving commercial center. It also was the stopping place for rough frontiersmen crossing the northeastern plains, and the pop-off valve for hurrahing cowboys from surrounding ranches and the fort's four to five hundred troops of Negro infantry and white cavalry.

The Jones-Plummer Trail, first a buffalo hunters' road, then

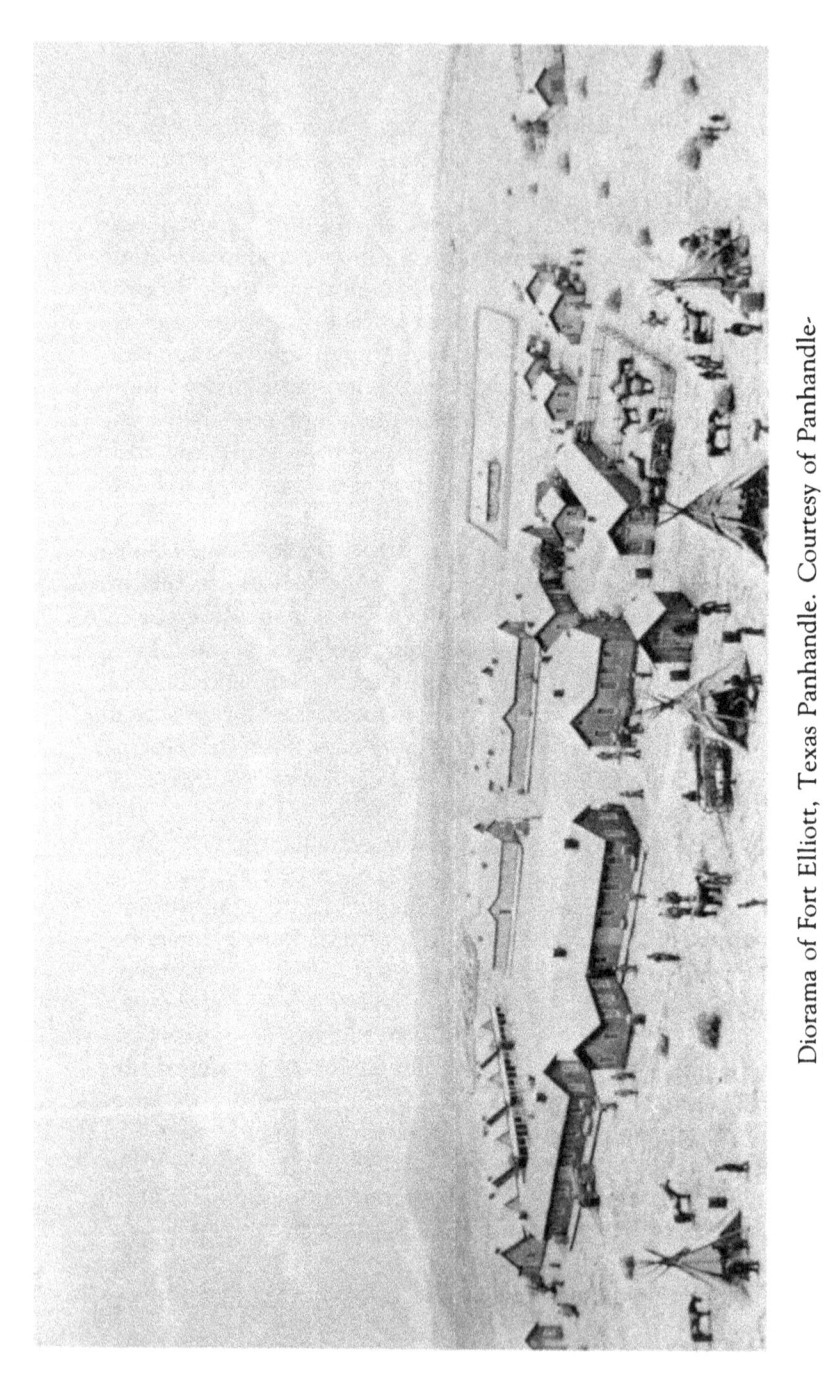

Diorama of Fort Elliott, Texas Panhandle. Courtesy of Panhandle-Plains Historical Museum.

a freight route, and finally a cattle trail, crossed No Man's Land at present Beaver, Oklahoma; crossed Wolf Creek near present Lipscomb, Texas; continued down the divide east of Timber Creek across the Canadian in Hemphill County; then led to Fort Elliott. After Tascosa, situated on the north bank of the Canadian 120 miles west of Mobeetie, developed into a trade center for that side of the Panhandle, a branch of the trail bore southwesterly from Beaver through Ochiltree, Hutchinson, and Moore counties, partly by way of the old trail to Adobe Walls, to the northeast corner of Oldham.

Stagecoaches and hacks provided passenger and mail service from Mobeetie and Tascosa to Dodge City, usually escorted by troops from Fort Elliott or Fort Dodge. Another mail line, originating at Vinita, Indian Territory, and advertised as the Lightning Express, had a tight schedule of fifty-nine grueling hours on horseback from Mobeetie to Tascosa, thence by hack or stage to Fort Bascom and Las Vegas, New Mexico. Freighters set up regular lines to Dodge City and Fort Worth, bringing in lumber, wagon wheels, saddles, harness, clothing, staple foods, whiskey, and whatever other necessities the merchants, saloonkeepers, cattlemen, and nesters ordered. A nester's visit to one of these towns was a family event. He brought his wife and children dressed in their Sunday best, as well as a wagonful of hay or buffalo bones to trade for work clothes, a bolt of calico, underwear, or a pair of shoes to fit the feet most in need. Here also many chuck wagons came to replenish their boxes before moving farther up the trails or off to the annual roundups.

Fifty miles southwest of Mobeetie, on a flat at the junction of Carroll Creek with the Salt Fork and east of Goodnight's trail from the Palo Duro, stood the dugout-tent beginnings of the Panhandle's third-earliest town, Old Clarendon—scoffingly called "Saints' Roost" because the Reverend Lewis Henry Carhart, representing the Northern Methodist Church with a pastorate in Sherman, Texas, had made an expensive attempt there in 1878 to settle a colony of more than twenty New England families who wanted to bring, along with material gains, God, education, and temperance to the frontier. Although its morals and spiritual ideals could not be made to harmonize with those of the Gentiles of the Plains, Clarendon would become seat of Donley County and the center of conflict in the struggle between cattlemen and farmers for possession of the territory until "free grass" was no more.

A wave of settlers was coming into the Panhandle. Mobeetie's population had increased by nearly three hundred, and it was a great hangout for one time buffalo hunters, discharged soldiers, horsethieves, and rustlers when Temple Houston arrived to assume his official duties in Wheeler County and the twenty-six others.

4
"A Baldheaded Whiskey Town"

Temple's initial view of Mobeetie must have activated the mental picture conjured from his studies in literature and history of the medieval towns of Europe. The rectangular fort, with stables and parade grounds attached, was an imposing sight upon the hill against the miragelike haze of a lowering winter sun, guarding like a castle of old the two-story rock courthouse and jail that occupied the top of one knoll, the residences scattered around the hillsides, and the business houses concentrated on a main street that ran generally three blocks east to west.

Starting on the north side, in the first block, his gaze must have swept past Frank Clampitt's livery stable and the Huselby House, a barber shop, G. W. Boynton's drugstore, C. L. Pendleton's Wholesale & Retail Whiskey Store, Charlie Rath and Henry Hamburg's Mercantile, a saloon, and F. M. Goodwin's store. In the second block stood Joe Mason's Cattle Exchange saloon, John Miller's wagonyard and blacksmith shop, and Thomas O'Loughlin's boardinghouse and restaurant, which he and his wife Ellen would shortly expand into the Grand Central Hotel. The entire last block was fenced in a picket corral for oxen and mule teams with a camp house and beer saloon inside as an accommodation for muleskinners and bullwhackers. On the northwest edge of town lay the restricted district of "fancy houses" known as Feather Hill.

On the south side of the street, his gaze moving back east, he saw old Negro Cindy Washington's town laundry, McKinney & Huffman's Hardware, onetime freighter Johnny J. Long's Mint Saloon and General Store, another saloon and gambling hall, a dance hall, John and Wiley Dickerson's gen-

Mobeetie, Texas, in the mid-1880s, looking east.

Bird's-eye view of Mobeetie in the late 1880s. Courtesy of Panhandle-Plains Historical Museum.

eral store, and Tom Riley's saloon on the corner. Then came E. L. Bennett's tonsorial parlor, Bert Clampitt's Palace drinking emporium, and the frame office building of Colonel William H. Grigsby, attorney-at-law. The postoffice on the southeast, Professor Newton Boles's dry goods, I. M. Brown's drugstore, another saloon, and Uncle Johnny Stroker's dance hall completed the business section.

Old-timers agree that at least eight saloons graced the settlement, though some claim eleven. George A. Montgomery, the first postmaster, who probably remembered correctly, listed thirteen. "Almost every other establishment is for the purpose of dispensing liquor," Temple wrote Laura. In a later note he described Mobeetie as "a baldheaded whiskey town with few virtuous women" but admitted that it was no worse than many others on the frontier "scissored from the same cloth." Typical bordermen, "dressed as you read of them in the dime novel, in high top boots, with large spurs and a brace of pistols," constituted the makeup of the population.

He found lodging at the Huselby House. Mark Huselby, the proprietor, had come to Fort Elliott as a cook in 1875 but had soon turned to the business opportunities in the new land. He had filed on some bottomland on the southwest, finding it profitable like many others to supply the fort with milk, butter, and vegetables, and laid the foundation for his ranch that eventually would include fourteen sections. His business in town centered on his hotel—a two-story structure of ten rooms at the front with an eight-room rock addition running to the back.

The hotel was usually a busy place. During court week, holidays, and other festive occasions, all rooms were full, and many guests brought their own blankets and slept on the dining-room floor. One unique feature was the buffalo robes on the beds, which Temple appreciated, arriving on a blustery afternoon.

That evening he met several of Mobeetie's leading citizens, among them lawyer W. H. Woodman and his pretty redhaired wife; Colonel Grigsby, who had formerly practiced at

Dickerson Brothers (John and Wiley Dickerson) general store at Mobeetie, built in 1882. Courtesy of Panhandle-Plains Historical Museum.

J. J. ("Uncle Johnny") Long's store at Mobeetie, 1886. Long, wearing vest, is in the center. Long also ran a private bank for the benefit of friends and customers. It was later the First State Bank of Mobeetie, and Long was its first president. Courtesy of Panhandle-Plains Historical Museum.

Henrietta, Texas, and won his title under the Missouri guerrilla leader William Clarke Quantrill; Jim Browning, who had stayed in Wheeler County after resigning as district prosecutor; County Judge F. M. Patton, a Civil War veteran and former buffalo hunter; and Mrs. Patton, who "came near being killed in bed one night by a band of drunken cowboys as they playfully shot up the town."

Scarcely a day passed that a dozen or more cowboys did not gallop in from their range work to revel in the town's pleasures until their heads were dizzy and their pocketbooks empty. Often they would ride right into the Exchange saloon and order drinks to be served to them on their horses, and then take in the metropolis. They seldom failed to notify the people of their departure by shooting out the lights.

Such celebrants, Browning told Houston, came from the Turkey Track; the Long S, owned by Ben Masterson and Robert Hamilton; Nick Eaton's U Bar U; Hank Creswell's Bar CC; and other nearby ranches. Most of the time they were harmless and did not mean to give trouble. When sober, they were steady citizens of this western frontier country.

John Decker, one saloon bartender, had not been as lucky as Mrs. Patton, however. One day Charlie Norton was riding up and down the street, firing his six-shooter and raising hell in general, when one of his bullets went through the saloon door and struck John in the hip. They stretched Decker out on a billiard table. His hip was split open, and he was bleeding so profusely that nobody thought he would make it. But someone got the doctor from the fort, and Decker was soon up and about again.

Gamblers and their shooting scrapes over the games also made for a hot time. One evening when Tom O'Loughlin was away on a hunt, a fight broke out at the Cattle Exchange, and Mrs. O'Loughlin became so uneasy that she put her two children under the bed and piled extra mattresses and bedding against the door and wall next to the street to check any stray lead.

Another time Grainger Dyer, one of Goodnight's brothers-

Mark Huselby, hotel proprietor and a leading Mobeetie businessman. Courtesy of Panhandle-Plains Historical Museum.

in-law, was playing poker with a drifter named McCabe. Both men were drinking, a quarrel ensued, and the game broke up. Dyer left the saloon and strode over to O'Loughlin's restaurant, where he took meals when in town. Still angry, he waited inside the door until McCabe appeared on the street, then drew his pistol and opened fire. McCabe fell, and Dyer, curious to know if he had killed him, poked his head out the door. McCabe, only wounded in the knee, was ready for him. His ball struck Dyer in the breast. Dyer was rushed to the fort hospital, too late to save his life. McCabe stood trial for the killing, but was acquitted.

Negro troops at the fort were no problem. They tended to stay away from Mobeetie and the taunts of the gamblers and cowboys. A. G. Springer operated a bar-ranch-restaurant enterprise for travelers along the trail several miles north of the post; he catered especially to soldiers, and the black ones found A. G.'s a place of refuge and fellowship. But white troopers sought the town dives, and many fights occurred between them and the less desirable citizens. The saloon girls and ladies of Feather Hill were the cause of much trouble and many shootings, not to mention the flotsam and jetsam from the east coming to this place of little law.

School for Mobeetie's fifteen to twenty pupils was conducted in an upstairs room of the courthouse, with one teacher for all grades. Church services were held in any convenient place that a minister appeared with courage enough to deliver a sermon. All the attorneys and most of the county officers lived on "Tony Ridge," an elevation in the south part of town.

On the bank of the Sweetwater Creek, Henry Fleming, the Panhandle's first sheriff, had built a two-room stone house with ceilings so high that they could not be reached by standing on a chair and long, narrow windows high enough from the ground to afford excellent protection from the flying lead of rowdy passersby. The structure was the nearest thing to an old southern mansion in a town where most people lived in low-ceilinged frame and adobe houses.

Sheriff Fleming was a tall Irishman, a professional saloonkeeper and gambler of the Hidetown days, but a man of strength and purpose whose word was as good as his marksmanship. The day after Houston arrived, Fleming introduced him to the court and other members of the Wheeler County bar: Moses Wiley, special prosecutor for the county since 1879; veteran attorneys C. M. Stephens, Lucious Dills, and L. D. Miller; A. L. Neal, of Alabama, the first lawyer granted a license to practice in the district and lower courts of Texas by the Wheeler County commissioners; and District Judge Frank Willis.

These older men, experienced in the ways of the frontier, scorned the idea that a mere youth could cope with conditions in this untamed land. Judge Willis, a man of keen sense and ready wit who weighed nearly three hundred pounds, was surprised because Temple looked so much like a boy. But word had spread that he was handy with a six-shooter, and all were willing to recognize anyone capable of protecting himself in a country where often vigilance was the price of life.

Despite their age difference, the judge and the young prosecutor found much in common. Willis had been born in Alamo, Montgomery County, Indiana, in 1840. His parents had settled in that portion of the county southwest of Crawfordsville early in the nineteenth century. His father, Benjamin Franklin Willis, traced his origin to England, where one illustrious antecedent, Sir John Willis, serviced for His Majesty George III. Nevertheless, the family had espoused the American Revolution and the American cause just as their Texas counterparts had rebelled under the iron heel of Mexico.

Like Houston's, Willis's mother had also died when he was little more than a babe in arms. Farming was hardly a lucrative business, and the large number of brothers and sisters made the going rough. What education he obtained came through the public schools and his own private reading. To make ends meet, he got a job as a teacher. A college education seemed beyond his reach. He borrowed law books and read them at

Lucius Dills, Mobeetie Lawyer.

Frank Willis, judge of the Thirty-fifth Judicial District. Courtesy of Panhandle-Plains Historical Museum.

home after teaching all day. Whenever possible he accompanied lawyers to court to learn how they conducted cases, and at every opportunity he attended entire court terms. Admitted to practice in 1869, he put out his shingle first at Liberty, Kansas, then at Independence, where he served a term as district attorney. In 1872 he married Eva Boles, a daughter of Professor Newton Boles, finally moving to Montague County, Texas. There he had prospered materially and won the esteem of such noted lawyers as Jim Browning and Avery L. Matlock, who served the Panhandle region in the Texas House of Representatives and had been instrumental in securing him the judgeship.

Whereas Houston's ideal of the lawyer was Seargent Smith Prentiss, Willis admired Daniel W. Voorhees. Voorhees, one of the most brilliant statesmen of his day, had practiced at Covington, Indiana, was United States district attorney for Indiana from 1858 to 1861, was a member of Congress during the Civil War and again from 1869 to 1871, and since 1877 had served in the United States Senate. His greatest oratory, in Judge Willis's opinion, was in defense of John Cook during the latter's trial for participation in John Brown's raid at Harper's Ferry.

Another prominent figure influencing Willis as a youngster was General Lew Wallace. Wallace, who had begun his military career as a second lieutenant in the First Indiana Infantry in the Mexican War and his professional law practice in Covington and Crawfordsville, was completing his term as governor of New Mexico, where he had sought to convert Billy the Kid and published a new book, *Ben Hur*. Temple had "devoured" *The Fair God* a few years before. Both Wallace books graced the small personal library he had brought to Mobeetie.

Temple's advent in Wheeler County was somewhat less exciting than the coming of Judge Willis. Willis, accompanied by his father-in-law and their families, had moved overland by wagon from Montague to Mobeetie the last week of June. The evening of his arrival a windstorm ripped off half the roof of the rock jail and courthouse. On July 4, the county commissioners, meeting in called session, decided to put on an asbestos covering as quickly as possible. They also decided to have a well dug, install water closets and hitching posts for the convenience of courthouse patrons, and appoint a foreman for the so-called public works. At a second meeting in August they considered ways and means to pay for the material and labor and authorized an additional guard for the prison.

It was a case of closing the barn too late. In the interim all the prisoners escaped. The noise of repair and construction had concealed the work of a saw on the metal plate lining the jail cell. The schoolteacher and pupils remembered hearing the sawing but thought nothing of it. The children had been curious to see the prisoners. The prisoners asked the children to bring some chalk and diverted their attention by drawing pictures on the cell walls until the opening was large enough to squeeze through. A few had to shed their clothing, and one prisoner left a generous portion of his skin on the rock wall, which they also had to remove. Jim Beard, an employee of the Rowe outfit, jailed for being drunk, went to the ranch headquarters on Big Skillet Creek and sent word that he would be back when court set. He kept his promise and was given a light sentence. The other escapees were still at large.

A Wheeler County grand jury investigating the matter reported to Judge Willis on August 9, 1881, that

> we find our County Officers have endeavored to do their duty, according to their best understanding. That there has, however been some loosness [sic] open to censure. We do not think that there is any excuse for the escape of prisoners of notorious bad character, when the county has provided a strong jail for their detention....
>
> In reference to the latter we suggest that it has not been built with sufficient regard to ventilation. A strong malarial smell impregnates the cells, liable to produce contageous (sic) diseases. The attention of the Sheriff and Commissioners is invited thereto that sanitary precautions may be taken to prevent sickness among prisoners confined therein.

The jury's inquiry into offenses brought to its attention was more significant:

We have found indictments in all cases where we have deemed it expediant [sic] to do so taking into consideration at the same time the present thinly settled condition of the country and general lack of knowledge as to what constitutes a violation of the laws of the state. We have for that reason ignored many offenses which we think may be more properly prosecuted upon complaint or information than by indictment. We think also that until the country becomes more thickly populated and more urgent demand for the enforcement of law relating to public and private morals arises that it would be better to enforce those laws which are intended to surpress (sic) the grave crimes and we think by so doing a greater respect will be engendered for the law and the court than by dealing with offenses which as yet would be frivolous in this community.

With such recommendations the tone for his actions, Temple began his work without favor or hesitation. Jurors and witnesses came from Mobeetie, Clarendon, Tascosa, and the farflung ranches and "nester layouts" throughout the Panhandle. He found it extremely difficult to serve process where "each man took his wagon, buggy, or pack horse and camp outfit and slept where he could find a place to unroll a bed." Yet nearly all members of the December, 1881, grand jury were summoned from a distance beyond Wheeler County. They included men like Goodnight and found sixty-five true bills, the largest number ever presented at a court setting of the Thirty-fifth Judicial District.

Reporting to Judge Willis on December 8, the jury admitted that

a large number of bills have been found which, no doubt to a great extent interfered with the business of many people in the town [Mobeetie]... nevertheless we must say that at all times, before and since the session, we have been treated with unfailing courtesy. If we have done aught against the interest of parties residing here it has been through a sense of duty as to the proper enforcement of law [which] we believe the people understand.

The county prison and circumstances surrounding the wholesale break were reexamined:

We are of the opinion that the jail is lacking in furnishings necessary for the comfort of the prisoners... during cold weather. The floors are of iron and prisoners are not provided with mattresses or anything to shield them from contracting rheumatism or other diseases liable to be contracted by reason of sleeping upon a cold iron floor. We therefore recommend that the Commissioners provide mattresses for the use of prisoners occupying the jail. We think that the County Officials in charge of the jail are justly entitled to severe censure for their negligence in permitting the escape of prisoners confined therein for felony of high grade. The jail has been strongly constructed at a great expense to the tax payers of this and adjoining counties and we think that with due care, on the part of those in charge... an escape therefrom would be almost an impossibility. We suggest therefore those in charge be held to a more strict accountability for the proper discharge of their duties [and] have ignored finding a bill on this occasion for the reason that we believe the escape occurred more through want of experience on the part of the officers than through any criminal intent.

They also disagreed with the previous jury, demanding that

better order be kept on the public streets in regard to the behavior of prostitutes; that the town is now improving and changing very radically the character of its population. Many respectable families reside here at the present time....

While we have no desire to prosecute or oppress women of this character in their unfortunate and fallen condition yet we think the plying of their vocation and wanton bad behavior on public streets and in broad daylight is something which common decency alone calls for a suppression.... We expect in the future that County Officials will take notice and arrest at once any woman misbehaving in public, especially in the business portion of the town or in a manner to excite public attention.

Wheeler County dockets show that early cases dealt mostly with assaults, stock theft, and murder. From December, 1881, however, there was a marked increase in the "lower" violations—gaming or keeping and exhibiting gaming tables and banks, prostitution, and vagrancy. During the first three months of 1882, forty-seven such cases came before the district and justice courts, thirty-two resulting in conviction with jail sentences or fines and costs from ten to twenty-five dollars.

Some gamblers claimed to be employees and only partly interested in the business and were pronounced not guilty, especially where the owner or employer paid a fine. Others pleaded guilty as partners and were fined jointly and then separately on other charges. A few asked that their sentences be suspended since this was their first offense, and the requests were granted. Allegedly, those unable to pay or obtain a suspension were jailed during the day but allowed to go down to the saloons at night and watch the games.

On the vagrant-and-prostitute ledger appeared such picturesque names as Belle of Mobeetie, Little Queen, Little Phebe, Betsy Nan, Patsy Starr, Prucilla Hunter, Liddie Cole, Corinda Johnson, Red Nellie, Spotted Jack, Willie Riggs (alias Wild Bill), Frog-mouth Annie (so called because she always held a piece of tobacco near the corner of her mouth, which kept it stretched), Ella Brown, the Diamond Girl (who never appeared in public except gowned in black satin with diamonds glittering everywhere), and Dolly Varden. Dolly managed the fancy house that gave the town's northwest district its name. There two women fought over a cowboy who wore his spurs in bed. During the quarrel his spurs ripped open the feather ticking, and feathers were scattered all over the hill. Dolly lived with a handsome blade named Ed Butts, whom she kept well dressed and supplied with ready cash. Butts was booked as a professional gambler and pimp, and he finally left Mobeetie.

The Diamond Girl provided the romantic story that the town would tell in years to come. After being charged with vagrancy in December, 1881, she took the name Ella Holmes. When she was again incarcerated some time later, a cowboy named Jim Brady paid her fine, and they lived together in a house just north of the jail. Then Ella fell in love with a young lieutenant from the fort. Brady, in a jealous, drunken state, killed her and fled to Collingsworth County. He finally was apprehended, convicted, and sentenced to fifteen years.

Most of the women charged were dance-hall girls who found justice more lenient than the jury. They were given token fines and released. There was a growing opposition to prostitution on the frontier, but most of the people still considered it a "necessary evil." Five cases of fornication were dismissed for "insufficient evidence." The woman simply would claim that she was keeping house for the man or that he was her boarder, and that ended the matter.

Despite grand jurors' suggestions that the Panhandle become law-abiding, many agreed with Judge Willis and Houston that it must be gradual. There was not as much improvement as the better element felt that it had a right to expect, and the grand jury that convened in April, 1882, with Hank Creswell as foreman, took another tack:

> In regard to the violation of the gaming and vagrancy laws, we find that a number of parties were indicted at the last term of the court but that the proper officers saw the law violated from time to time without any attempt to suppress it. We have thought best to go near the real head and indict the said officers for neglect of duty in allowing said vagrants to congregate in public places and for allowing gaming to go on in open violation of the law.

Five bills were brought against the sheriff, constables, and justices of the peace. The cases of the justices and constables were *nolle prosequi* on April 10 for absence of evidence necessary to obtain conviction. Fleming was found not guilty of neglect notwithstanding that he had been shrewd enough at cards to win a herd of eight hundred cattle one night at the gaming tables but quit in disgust because his integrity had been questioned.

On July 1, 1882, the iron-handed Ranger captain, George W. Arrington, filed his resignation to become effective August 31. During the eight years he had patrolled the Panhandle—Fort Elliott, Tascosa, Fort Griffin, Doan's Cross-

George W. Arrington, "Iron-handed" Ranger captain of the Panhandle, who became sheriff at Mobeetie. Courtesy of Panhandle-Plains Historical Museum.

ing and all the rest—he had dreamed of owning a ranch, and finally he invested his savings in a strip of land above Mobeetie on the Little Washita River. A strict disciplinarian who took the shortest course to accomplish his purpose and ended his expeditions by jailing his prisoner, he had made bitter enemies but many staunch friends. The August 10 issue of the *Mobeetie Panhandle* observed that

> the section of wild and reckless border over which the vigilant and intrepid Arrington stands guard with his company is one of the most peaceful in the whole state.... There ought to be some way to hold the captain to the work he has done so well, and for which he is so eminently fitted in every respect.

The people agreed and practically drafted him to run for the office Fleming had vacated. He was elected by a large majority as the new sheriff of Wheeler and the fifteen counties (including Greer) then remaining under its jurisdiction.

On a voters' petition approved by Wheeler commissioners as required by law, Oldham County had been organized in November, 1880, with Tascosa as county seat. Its first officials, elected on December 6, took their oaths on January 12, 1881, and ten western counties of the Thirty-fifth District—Dallam, Sherman, Hartley, Moore, Potter, Deaf Smith, Randall, Parmer, Castro, and Swisher—formerly attached to Wheeler, were attached to Oldham for judicial purposes.

This portion of the Panhandle was no longer subordinate to the capital on the east. Cattlemen and other residents of these counties could record their brands and papers at Tascosa, and Judge Willis, like the assize judges of England, journeyed with District Attorney Houston and assistants the 120 grueling miles from Mobeetie over narrow trails and unbridged streams to try their "west-side" cases.

5

The Bloodiest Place in Texas

Tascosa had its beginnings in 1876, when Don Casimero Romero, a well-to-do sheepman from Mora County, New Mexico, brought his large household and three thousand woollies to the springs on Atascosa Creek where it joins the Canadian. It was the same year that Charles Goodnight pushed his longhorn herds onto the Cap Rock and down the Palo Duro. The site had long been used as a favorite camp by the Comancheros in their trade with the Plains Indians. One of Romero's neighbors, Agapito Sandoval, and his family came with him. In 1877 the Trujillo, Garcia, Valdez, and Sierna families followed, settling near Romero and Sandoval. Then Mariano Montoya established a sheep ranch near the confluence of Rita Blanca Creek and Puento de Agua, soon to be joined by the Tefoya family.

The colonists tended their flocks, dug irrigation ditches to water garden patches, ground meal, baked tortillas, hung bright-red garlands of pepper to the roof timbers of adobe huts, and in the evenings about their doorways sang love songs to guitars and chatted in liquid Spanish. *Bailes* and *fiestas* added zest to their lives, and on saints' days *muy caballeros* rode madly in the hazardous rooster race, *corrida de gallo*. A permanent plaza was established in a wooded mote along the creek and christened Atascosa—meaning "boggy"—for the treacherous quicksands of the Canadian bottom. It was the only easy crossing for cattle for miles in either direction, and with freight being accessible at this point three hundred miles northwest of a railroad and Texas's line of settlements, the drowsy village soon filled with new activity and strange faces.

The first Anglo resident was young Henry Kimball, a carpenter and blacksmith who came in 1876 to work on Romero's hacienda and built a shop for his forge and anvil. Early the next year the two-room adobe store of G. L. Howard, prominent Elizabethtown, New Mexico, merchant, and his partner, Ira Rinehart, a German Jew and former sheriff of the inland mining empire, was standing beside it. Rinehart soon sold his interest to Howard, acquired forty-one acres of the townsite south of Main Street, and established a store of his own. In the spring of 1877, James E. McMasters, searching for a trading-post location, drove his wagon loaded with merchandise from Taos to the Canadian Valley and became Howard's new partner. Then Howard and McMasters bought twenty-four acres on the north side of Main Street, comprising most of the remaining townsite, built a large adobe storeroom, and stocked it with everything from spurs to sorghum molasses freighted by ox and mule teams from Dodge City, Kansas, and Springer, New Mexico. Charley Cummings started a restaurant nearby. Henry Kimball's business grew in such proportions that a more centrally located shop was needed; he moved to Main Street and erected a two-room adobe building. By 1878 the big cattle outfits were overrunning the sheep paradise; Atascosa became a trail and supply station for the JA, LX, LS, LE, T Anchor, and LIT—brands known from the Río Grande to Montana.

The need for a new postoffice was called to the attention of Romero and his friends. Postal authorities in Washington replied that there were already a town and county called Atascosa in southern Texas. The problem was solved by simply dropping the initial *a* and calling the new supply center Tascosa.

The prospects attracted John Cone, a wealthy Big Spring merchant, and his brother Will, who had come west from Kansas City for his health. Their quest for business lots, however, was coldly received by Howard, McMasters, and Rinehart, who owned all the desirable business property and did not care for competition. Not to be thwarted, the Cones moved down the creek a short distance, bought a block of land

James McMasters's store in Old Tascosa. Masters is standing at the post in the center. Left to right with horses: LS cowboys Tobe Robinson and Frank Valley.

from Casimero Romero, and opened a combination saloon, hotel and general store. This was soon surrounded by a motley collection of buildings that housed saloons, gambling rooms, and dance halls for the benefit of the hardy souls who came to town to have a good time. By tacit agreement, the town was divided into Upper and Lower Tascosa, but people who opposed disorder shortly called the lower section "Hogtown" because its inhabitants behaved like swine, and visitors always came away hog-drunk.

Dolores Duran, the Spaniard who sold his holdings on Romero Canyon to the LE, became the Cones' partner. Romero, impressed that his old village was on the threshold of being a great distributing point for the cattle country, established a freighting business between Tascosa and Dodge City. The Cone-Duran enterprises were more strategically located, so Casimero decided to haul for them. His decision proved a wise one. He soon accumulated enough money to move his family to Dodge and build a hotel, the St. James.

The die of competition was cast. On Valentine's Day, 1879, H. A. Russell, with his wife and four children and old friend Charles Terry, arrived from Groesbeck, Limestone County, in two wagons en route to La Junta, Colorado. Instead they swelled Tascosa's population, for Russell promptly made a trade with Cummings for his restaurant, provisions, and equipment. He afterward paid Howard and McMasters one hundred dollars for a corner lot at Spring and Main streets, on which he erected a hotel. An itinerant painter executed a cow's head over the sign and the notice "50¢ for a meal—50¢ for a bed."

Two LX cowboys, Marion Armstrong and Cape B. Willingham, lived with their families in a rock dugout on Bonita Creek. Early in 1879 they were given key jobs with the Lightning Express. Armstrong managed the mail line between Tascosa and Mobeetie; Willingham rode shotgun on the run to Fort Bascom and Las Vegas. In August both men moved their families to Tascosa, and the Armstrongs leased Russell's vacated restaurant for a home. Jack Ryan, the LX wagon boss

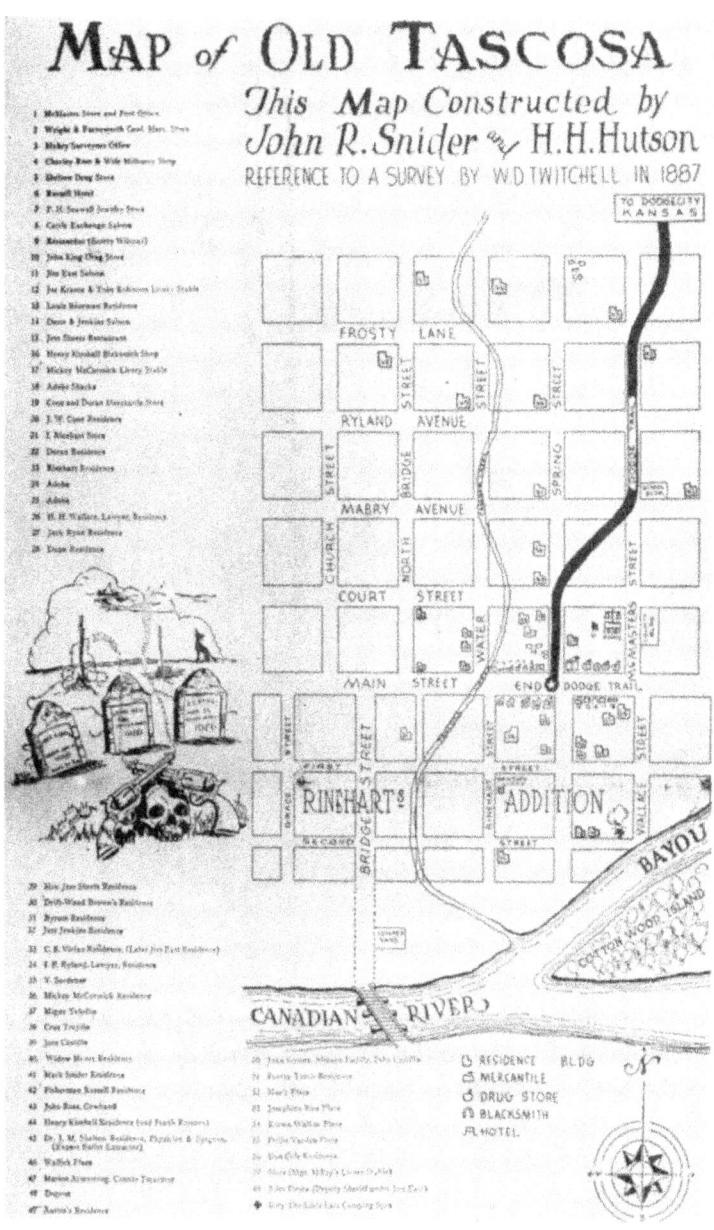

Old Tascosa.

The Equity Bar in Old Tascosa. The man on horseback is Jim East, second sheriff of Oldham County.

in 1878, had managed to save $160, and with a man named Frank James (no kin to the notorious Jesse) bought a lot west of the hotel and opened a saloon. Their sign read: "The Equity Bar."

This started a real estate boom. Saloons in Tascosa proper increased to five. But the most popular ones were in Hogtown. Some of the reigning belles were Sally Emory, Mustang Mae, Ole Buck, Santa Fe Mol, Jo Rice, Rocking Chair Emma, and

Frenchy, the wife of Tascosa's Irish gambler and livery-stable proprietor, Mickey McCormick.

Frenchy (her real name is not known) was a beautiful girl with a devilish look in her eyes. Allegedly she was born near Baton Rouge, Louisiana, ran away from a convent at age fourteen, and went to Saint Louis, where she earned her living dancing on the burlesque stage and in bars. Wild tales of adventure in the cowtowns took her to Dodge, thence to Mobeetie to entertain the soldiers and hordes of buffalo hunters from the plains. In Mobeetie she met the witty McCormick, who had hauled a lawyer from Tascosa to Fort Elliott, and went back to Tascosa with him to preside over his gambling interest. That was in 1880, at the height of the conflict between Billy the Kid and his new lieutenant Dave Rudabaugh and their counterfoils Pat Garrett, Jim East, and Charles Siringo. Frenchy knew them all—soldier, hunter, outlaw, lawman, the cowboy close at hand and those who came with the trail herds, and sometimes remittance men of noble English blood. She remained Tascosa's lone resident after the town died, with only memories of its pageantry, its gaiety, and its twenty-six graves of men who had died with their boots on.

Tascosa bloomed as the "Cowboy Capital of the Plains." After it became county seat, more people moved across the cattle and Indian trails to help make the liqour flow and six-guns roar, and Cape Willingham, the first sheriff, charged G. L. Howard with the first homicide since Oldham's judicial growth began. Witnesses proved self-defense, and the victim, a thirsty cowpuncher named Bob Russell, became the first occupant of Tascosa's famed Boot Hill Cemetery.

Other officials elected in 1880 were James E. McMasters, county judge; C. B. Vivian (a one-armed man with a good sense of humor who married Mrs. Willingham's sister), county clerk; Marion Armstrong, justice of the peace of the Tascosa precinct; and five commissioners. W. H. Woodman, who with local attorney H. A. Lewis had presented the petition for Oldham's organization at Mobeetie, was appointed legal adviser at fifteen hundred dollars for one year. Henry Kimball was employed as interpreter.

The sheriff of Oldham and the nearly sixteen thousand square miles of attached territory was by far the most important officer, and the first commissioners' court, which assembled on February 14, 1881, authorized one deputy. Although familiar with the tranquilizing effect of his sawed-off shotgun on would-be road agents while working for the Lightning Express, Willingham had been too busy making a living for his family to learn about using a handgun expertly and seldom wore one. His tools had always been a rope, a saddle, and a good horse, but this was a different breed of cattle. It was a rough, hard country, and Tascosa was a violent town. He needed a fast gun to back him, and he chose Henry Newton Brown.

Brown, a square-jawed young man with whitish-blue eyes, was too deadly with a six-shooter to be pushed very far. He had fought at the side of Billy the Kid in the Lincoln County War but parted with him, still the best of friends, at Tascosa the winter of 1878–79. Two more of the Kid's warriors, Fred Waite and John Middleton, had also decided to forsake the outlaw life and had gone to Indian Territory. Brown stayed at Tascosa, working for George Littlefield until the fall of 1880, and then trailed horse thieves for Campbell & Goodwin-Austen, a British outfit on the Rita Blanca. He was surprised at Willingham's offer but welcomed the job of fiery troubleshooter.

Right away one whiskey-logged cowpuncher, in the habit of riding roughshod over Tascosa citizens, shot up the town. Apprehended by Deputy Brown, he was ordered to report to the justice of the peace and pay his fine. The man pretended to do so but instead mounted his horse and dashed off to Rica Creek. Later in the day Brown told another rider going that way to tell the man to come back and pay his fine or he would kill him. Familiar with Brown's notorious past, the offender returned and went directly to Armstrong's makeshift courtroom. He paid his fine and an extra one for contempt, but he angrily protested the deputy's "mongrel" methods and called the community "a pile of adobe huts."

Brown slammed his pistol on a chair and stepped back the same distance as the red-faced defendant. "There's my gun," he said. "You're as close to it as I am. Put up or shut up."

The cowboy stared transfixed. He wanted to grab the weapon but realized that being a second too slow meant death. His nerve failed him.

Brown picked up his gun and holstered it. "All right," he ordered, "see how damned fast your horse can swim the Canadian!"

Although it was a victory for the law, Sheriff Willingham felt compelled to reprimand his deputy for allowing a little criticism to get his mane up.

Despite McMasters' election as county judge, there was no county court during the first years of Oldham's existence. All cases over which a county court had jurisdiction were tried in the justice court. On May 2, 1881, the first district court grand jury convened at Tascosa and returned several indictments for theft, murder, and embezzlement.

Working together to maintain peace through these courts—but by revolver, rifle, and sawed-off shotgun if necessary—the law-and-order team of Willingham, Brown, Armstrong, Kimball, Rinehart, Howard, and McMasters agreed upon a signal that would bring swift, coordinated action in event of big trouble. That trouble came on a June afternoon in 1881.

Young Fred Leigh and several cowboys were bringing some cattle from South Texas to the LS Ranch. Finding the Canadian too high to swing the herd across, they herded the longhorns onto the knee-high grass in the valley under light guard. Leigh and a half-dozen riders swam the stream on their horses and galloped into Tascosa to belly up to Ryan's bar. Willingham informed them they were not to wear their guns in town. Noticing that the sheriff was unarmed, Leigh demanded to know whether he was setting an example.

"You might say so," the unruffled officer replied. He explained that Tascosa was now a court seat and asked their cooperation in the maintenance of order.

The cowboys guffawed. They downed a round of drinks, ignoring his request completely, then walked their horses down the street to Howard and McMasters' store counter for a keg of raw whiskey to take back to camp and dashed off to the river yelling like Comanches.

Later in the afternoon, the whiskey consumed, the crew decided to risk driving the herd across the river. When the cattle were safely on the other side, Leigh, who had a drink or two the better of his comrades, gave his profanity a greater poignancy in denouncing the new order of things in Tascosa. The cowboys voted to tree the town and get on a "hilarious drunk." Dashing down Spring Street on the Dodge City Trail from the north, they sighted a pregnant Mexican woman standing in her yard feeding some tame ducks. Leigh fired at one of the birds, blowing its head off. The woman screamed and fainted, and word flashed through the village that she had been shot.

Willingham and Armstrong were unloading supplies in the stockade behind Howard and McMasters' store. While Armstrong gave the prearranged alarm, the sheriff crossed behind the Russell hotel to the rear of Ryan's place, where he kept his sawed-off shotgun. By the time Leigh and his whooping cowboys had turned west on Main Street and ridden half a block to the saloon, the law-and-order group was converging on the scene.

Leigh dismounted, holding his reins in his left hand, his free hand still on the horn. Cocky and angry, he never saw the sheriff until Willingham stepped from behind the saloon with shotgun raised and ordered him to surrender his weapon. Leigh made no reply but leaped back into the saddle without touching the stirrup. As he hit the saddle, his right hand flew to his holster. It was his last act in life. The double charge of buckshot from Willingham's greener struck him in the side and chest, blowing him off his horse. The animal bolted in terror and dashed down the street. So did Leigh's companions when they saw Deputy Brown jump from the saloon door, McMasters and Kimball coming up by the hotel, and Armstrong and Rinehart striding from the opposite direction armed with Winchesters. Armstrong held an inquest on the spot, and Boot Hill cemetery had its second tenant.

The great disadvantage for the authorities was lack of a proper place to confine their prisoners. Oldham's commissioners had authorized construction of a ten-by-ten-foot rock jail, but it was months before anyone got around to building it. Hard cases had to be transported to Mobeetie for safekeeping; minor offenders were haphazardly chained to hitching posts or locked in one of the small storerooms about town until the justice court could hear their cases. Too often businessmen had reasons for not wanting their storerooms used, and the problem was compounded by the miserable winter of 1881.

In December, Willingham arrested Jack Martin for public drunkenness and fastened his prisoner to a pillar supporting the cottonwood beam in the ceiling of Ryan's saloon. A roaring fire was built in the grate, and the prisoner was left to sleep anywhere on the floor within the radius of his chain. During the night he became thirsty. Unable to reach the bar, he tore up one of his blankets, wove himself a lariat, and managed to ring a bottle of brandy. Very much encouraged, he persevered. When Ryan opened his establishment at dawn, he found Martin corralled in empty bottles and blissfully asleep in the arms of Bacchus.

The temporary jail was in use, and a contract had been let to construct a $16,000 two-story stone courthouse and jail for Oldham when Temple Houston arrived to try his first murder case the spring of 1882. Henry McCullar, mean as hell and in the habit of pistol-whipping anyone who incurred his displeasure, was one of a number of toughs who had left Mobeetie and made their way to Tascosa. One April night he tangled with Mexican Frank Larque, a monte dealer in Hogtown, whom he caught cold-decking. Mexican Frank knew about McCullar's cowpuncher shampoos and was in no mood to have Henry cut up his scalp with a six-shooter. He had no time to draw his own pistol but simply lifted the holster and shot McCullar through the stomach. The wounded man crawled out of the saloon with no one offering to help him and reached the home of a sporting woman he lived with named Jenny. Jenny summoned a doctor, but McCullar died a few days later and was buried on Boot Hill.

Mexican Frank grabbed a fast horse and headed for the New Mexico line with Sheriff Willingham and his new deputy, Louis Bousman, in pursuit. Brown had by this time drifted on to further adventures as city marshal of Caldwell, Kansas, and his eventual demise at the hands of a Medicine Lodge mob.

Willingham and Bousman soon reached the Alamocitas ranch headquarters, where the fugitive had taken breakfast and departed, confident that he could reach the border before anyone overtook him. He had not reckoned with Cape's superior knowledge of the country, in which he had hunted stray cattle for years. Cape took a short cut, circled around him, and hid in an arroyo beside the trail. When Mexican Frank rode up, Cape stepped out of the mesquite brush with a cocked shotgun pointed at his midsection and returned him for trial before Judge Willis.

Hundreds flocked to Tascosa to witness the proceedings. C. B. Vivian was clerk, W. H. Woodman defended, and Houston prosecuted vigorously. Larque was convicted and sentenced to twenty-one years.

There was a heavy docket, and court was in session for two weeks. One night a group of buffalo hunters still seeking the few animals scattered about the Panhandle stopped at Hogtown's combination store, saloon, and hotel. A big poker game was soon underway and which lasted until after daylight the following morning. One of the hunters, a man named Keyes, was playing opposite a Mexican. An argument developed over a certain card in Keyes's hand, and the Mexican, infuriated that he had been cheated, drew his pistol and shot Keyes across the green-baize-topped table. Before he could kill another player, Bill Yandell, a cowboy standing behind Keyes watching the play, drew his gun and, firing between Keyes's body and arm, killed the Mexican. Houston nollied Yandell's case on grounds that he was defending life rather than exhibiting murderous intent.

This was after Temple and Judge Willis returned to Tascosa for the fall term of court. By that time Boot Hill cemetery had received two more victims. Bill Gibson (whose name proved to be an alias) appeared in town with a considerable sum of money, took on a load of booze in the Captain Jinks Saloon, and passed out in the room of one of the dance-hall girls, where he was found several hours later, pockets empty and shot through the head. Suspicion centered on John Maley, the bartender, but the murder went unsolved. No one knew that Gibson's brother, Ed Norwood, cowboyed for a nearby ranch. After the burial Norwood rode into Tascosa with a tremendous thirst. He hung around the saloons for several days, learning much about his brother's death through bar talk, and displayed a large roll of bills to Maley. He even courted the girl whom he believed had been in on the killing for part of the money and then feigned drunkenness and was allowed to go to her room and sleep in the same bed. Laying awake all night was a great disappointment, however. No one came to murder and rob him, so he returned to the saloon and shot Maley dead. The bartender was buried beside Gibson.

Norwood was promptly arrested and jailed pending action by the grand jury. Before Houston and Judge Willis arrived to deal with his case, Norwood's cowboy friends flocked into town. They started a mock battle at the lower end of Main Street. The sheriff and his deputy rushed down to stop it. During their absence a hole was torn in the back wall of the rock jail big enough for a horse to jump through, and Norwood fled to parts unknown.

If Temple thought Mobeetie a bald-headed whiskey town, he found Tascosa the bloodiest place in Texas.

6

District Attorney, Texas Style

While Tascosa rivaled Dodge City in hospitality (food, sex, and liquor dispensed all day and into the night), it was most famous for its gambling. Hotels, stores, and even livery stables had gaming rooms, and every saloon had faro, monte, and poker tables. Almost every man in town gambled, and professionals came from other western cities to challenge the local talent to be reckoned with in any company. Some games lasted for days and equaled the fastest and biggest play of the mining capitals of Tombstone and Denver, as participants backed their luck and skill with great stacks of silver dollars and twenty-dollar gold pieces. Houston commented years later, "It would have been impossible to enforce Texas' gaming statutes without arresting the entire populace."

Gaming was a way of life in this section of the Panhandle. Many of the card sharks run out of Mobeetie had flocked to Tascosa. Businessmen took the sport seriously. A classic example was Jack Ryan. Ryan had been called to serve on a jury in a murder trial. After deliberating all night and well into the next morning, eleven men stood for acquittal, and Ryan stood alone for conviction. He insisted that the defendant have his neck stretched, or else he would "hang" the jury. The others cajoled him, argued vehemently, and nearly fought him. But Ryan refused to give in. At this juncture his partner, Frank James, tapped on the window of the jury room. James whispered that the biggest poker game ever seen in Tascosa was in progress at that very moment in their saloon, and the players were about to break the bank. Ryan peeled several hundred-dollar bills off his roll and gave them to James with orders not to let the game break up but to keep things

Temple Houston, district attorney of the Thirty-fifth Judicial District of Texas at Mobeetie.

going until he got there. Then he turned to his fellow jurors and told them that, while he still believed the defendant guilty, he was forced to admit that human judgment was fallible. A verdict of acquittal was returned at once, and Ryan hurried over to the game.

Visitors and cowboys on the trail told of many wild happenings there, and Tascosa was often featured in lurid stories in magazines and the metropolitan press. One tale accepted by latter-day historians concerns a marksmanship match in which Temple Houston bested the famed Bat Masterson and Billy the Kid. The target, some claim, was a tin star removed from a plug of chewing tobacco and stuck on a post behind a Hogtown saloon where it caught the sun. Others say that Masterson did not participate but arranged the affair between Houston and the Kid. At twenty paces, his gun hand moving with amazing swiftness, Temple drew and shot the tin star out of the plug of tobacco that Bat had flung into the air. It brought a roar of applause from the crowd and congratulations from the Kid himself. "Quien lo haja mejor? (Who could do better?)" he asked, and good-naturedly refused to continue the contest.

Houston never mentioned having met Masterson or the Kid. In fact, when Temple first saw Tascosa, Bat Masterson was pursuing his twin professions as a peace officer and a gambler in Trinidad, Creede, and Denver, Colorado, and the Kid had been ten months in his grave. Temple did, however, enthusiastically inject himself into the pageantry that kept the town in a constant state of expectancy. When a session of court adjourned, lawyers, clients, and court officials would gather in a saloon and drink at the same bar and engage in a game of poker or in story-telling bees that became traditional. Drinking, like gambling, was an integral part of life and not considered a law violation. Temple enjoyed these drinking and story-telling bouts. Informed on current topics and thoroughly conversant with history and literature, he quoted pages of poetry, excerpts from the most famous speeches, and the outstanding parts in Shakespearean plays. He seldom played poker, but he participated in a number of shooting matches for money stakes.

He also delighted the populace by appearing on the street in startling but beautifully tailored buckskin attire brought from Old Mexico. The trousers, open to the knee and faced and fringed with narrow ribbon in all the bright colors of the Mexican flag, matched the pepper-red band on his hand-woven Mexican sombrero of exceedingly wide brim and adorned with an eagle of silver spread against the high crown. He wore his white-handled revolver strapped outside around the waist and referred to it as "Old Betsy." Admirers who saw him knock down target after target swore that he could out-shoot any gunslinger in the West. Thieves and cutthroats gave him a wide berth. The streets teemed with cow ponies, oxen and mule teams, buggies, buckboards, wagons, sun-tanned plainsmen, bone-pickers, and homeseekers of many nationalities, and he would stand at night for hours watching the carousing and listening with penetrating attention to the talk, laughter, and snatches of song that floated about him. In the next moment he might ride off with a posse to catch a wrongdoer he later prosecuted.

Stock theft and assault were the crimes most often tried at rip-roaring Tascosa. Murder was murder if the victim had been given no chance to draw. Jurors would usually yield to their sympathies and allow the criminal to go free, but convictions could be obtained. Temple, walking in short, nervous steps, auburn hair flowing, gray eyes snapping, and head dropped forward in a romantic appearance of lugubrious preoccupation, spoke in a voice tuned to play on their heartstrings. When he arose to plead a case, even imposing legal talent like W. H. Woodman, L. D. Miller, and Jim Browning, who frequently opposed him, felt helpless to alter the effect of the young district attorney's suggestive oratory.

By the summer of 1882, Temple had become a familiar figure on the streets of Old Clarendon. "Saints' Roost," through the Reverend Mr. Carhart's advertising and persuasion, had acquired a substantial population. More than three hundred immigrants came from New York, Washington, Wisconsin, Ohio, Indiana, and Illinois. Several were retired ministers; a few were civil engineers; many were graduates from Harvard, Yale, Princeton, and the University of Virginia. For the most part all were well versed in the fine arts and law. And they came to stay. The women were charming, their homes comfortable and extending gracious hospitality. Dodge City supplied the settlement, but the high cost of transportation made importation of lumber prohibitive, and the first buildings were constructed of native materials—rock, adobe, sod, and picket saplings. Two of the most pretentious homes, built on secluded sites along Carroll Creek, belonged to Tom Morrison, operator of the Baby Doll Ranch, and J. H. Parks, a surveyor from Illinois. The colonists, however, did buy enough lumber to build a church with a stone foundation and brought from Philadelphia the first church bell to be used in the Panhandle. The bell, originally used in a Quaker settlement on the Delaware River and a prize exhibit at the 1876 Philadelphia Centennial where Carhart first saw it, was donated to the cause of missions in the Southwest.

Carhart had business contacts in Sherman, Texas, and he started stores, a blacksmith shop, a boot and shoe shop, and a wagon yard. A rock hotel was constructed, and stagecoach communication was established with Mobeetie and Tascosa. A branch supply house was opened by Major Van Horn, the sutler at Fort Elliott, and the Sanger Brothers, the oldest mercantile firm of Dallas, sent their representative, Morris Rosenfield, with goods and fixtures to open a new outlet. Rosenfield swapped merchandise for buffalo bones and hooves, which he sent ten thousand pounds at a time to eastern markets to be made into buttons, fertilizer, glue, inkwells, and ornaments. On the west, south, and east lay the Bar O, Diamond F, JA, Spade, and RO ranches, and farther south on Red River were the Mill Iron, Diamond Tail, and Shoe Bar. Clarendon also became their supply and social center.

But the town sought to attract only people of education and strict adherence to the Methodist faith, selling lots with the proviso that the purchaser would never operate a saloon, gambling house, or dance hall on that bit of ground. Owing to this social rigidity, Clarendon showed little of the color of its sister settlements and probably deserved its appellation.

In 1880, Carhart took a pastorate in Dallas, leaving management of his burgeoning financial interests to his attorney brother-in-law, Benjamin Horton White. When he returned to the Panhandle in 1883, he established the Quarter Circle Heart Ranch on 343 sections previously claimed and surveyed, extending north from the JA holdings to McClellan Creek, in the center of which lay Clarendon. In 1884 he went to England and sold stock in the operation, which he renamed the Clarendon Land Investment and Agency Company. He resigned from the company and left the Panhandle for good when the Quarter Circle Heart brand went the way of many others on the plains after the severe drought and cattle industry crash of 1885–86.

Meanwhile, Benjamin White provided Clarendon with effective leadership. Better suited to the task by training, experience, and temperament than the promoter-preacher, he was generally liked and respected, and he solicited the support of Charles Goodnight, rough, swearing man that he was, to combat the bad men. Goodnight realized that, although they preferred books and pianos to firearms and bowie knives, the colonists were no weaklings. He honored their freedom to worship as they pleased and their aloofness from what they considered sordid surroundings, and he regarded them as allies in keeping gambling and drinking places from being conveniently accessible to his riders.

One day a messenger galloped up to Goodnight's ranch in the Palo Duro with the distressing news that a man named McCarney had arrived from Mobeetie with wagons loaded with whiskey and gaming paraphernalia, determined to set up a dive in spite of every saint in the roost. Unarmed as usual, Goodnight accompanied the messenger back to Clarendon and rode down to the wagons of sin. He told McCarney to hitch up his teams and get out.

McCarney was breaking no law, and he resented this dictation. As other members of his entourage gathered around, he demanded to know why a saloon could not be opened. The cattleman explained that the people simply did not want one there.

McCarney allowed they would find out after they were open. Goodnight pointed toward Carroll Creek and a row of cottonwoods with a lot of good limbs, stating that it would be easy to throw a rope over them. McCarney argued, cursed, and threatened. But he decided that it was healthier for him to return to Mobeetie.

Again, when White called Goodnight's attention to the fact that a number of colonists and ranchers had children of school age with no provision for a public education, the old cattleman discussed the matter with the Panhandle Stock Association and obtained enough money from its members south of the North Fork to provide a school and maintain it for two years. In May, 1881, Clarendon citizens asked for and were granted by Wheeler commissioners a school community to embrace all of the territory in the unorganized county of Donley.

Shortly afterward, because of continuing trouble with rustlers and the great distances that had to be covered by the officers of Oldham and Wheeler, Goodnight suggested that those members of the association occupying range below the Cap Rock might be better served by a judiciary center nearer than Tascosa and Mobeetie. As a result, in February, 1882, Tom Morrison and 189 other Donley citizens applied to the Wheeler commissioners for organization with Clarendon as county seat.

Lawyer Neal represented the large ranchers, who generally opposed the move because of attendant complexities, such as herd law and taxes. Moses Wiley, Woodman, and Browning stood for Donley County. Organization was granted, an election was set for March 22, and the first county officers were sworn in on April 11—G. A. ("Gyp") Brown, a local attorney, county judge; B. H. White, county clerk; W. D. Kimball, treasurer; J. H. Parks, surveyor; James T. Otey, a

Clarendon merchant and the first postmaster, tax collector; and J. D. Wilson, sheriff. Morrison, S. B. Nall, Leigh Dyer, and Charles Goodnight were the first commissioners, with Goodnight as chairman. Clarendon became the third district-court seat in the Panhandle, and the swing for District Attorney Houston and Judge Willis was now from Mobeetie to Tascosa to Clarendon and around again.

Traveling by hack and buggy across country was dangerous enough, not to mention holding court at Tascosa, where there was always the possibility that the friends of an outlaw on trial might come to his rescue. Goodnight's ultimatum and the Christian colony's stand against cards and whiskey south of the North Fork aroused the animosity of saloonkeepers and gambling-house owners. No one had been killed, but saloons were started near Clarendon, and desperadoes roamed the country, offering bribes. Saloons were legal, but bribery was not, and Temple prosecuted the cases brought to his attention. Court assistants went armed with shotguns and rifles; Temple relied on the Texas statutes and Old Betsy.

After Clarendon became county seat, the rock hotel was converted into a courthouse, and a new two-story hotel was built of expensive lumber freighted from Dodge. It was painted white and B. H. White, who supervised its construction, assumed the managerial responsibility; therefore, it was called the "White House." White served as resident manager until 1883.

At one time or another every celebrity in the Panhandle, many cowboys, and even bone-pickers slept in the White House beds. During court week and festive occasions tents were set up on its grounds to accommodate all who attended. The district-court party took quarters there. The lack of saloons left lawyers and officials without the usual gathering place during court recesses, and so a room was provided upstairs in which everyone concerned, the accused included, could partake of a hot toddy mixed in a large pitcher.

Another meeting place was Rosenfield's store. Besides boasting the most extensive and varied stock of merchandise

81

for perusal, it was a firearms depository. Most visitors wore guns into town, but carrying them was prohibited in the colony, and on some days the long counter at the back of the store was piled so high with rifles and six-shooters that it looked like an arsenal. The plump, curly-haired, sympathetic, enterprising Jewish merchant also provided games of chance and other amusements in which the lawyers and officials participated. Sooner or later everyone went to "Rosie's."

Sometimes these sessions went beyond the bounds of ordinary sociability. Old timers recalled how Houston, Willis, Woodman, Colonel Grigsby, Jim Browning, and L. D. Miller came to Clarendon to hold court, as smart a bunch of lawyers as one could find anywhere. All were heavy drinkers, except Judge Gyp Brown. One night they schemed to get Judge Willis drunk. Since he was a big man, they decided to take him on one at a time. Houston took the judge first, downing his whiskey and a shot of acid phosphate to keep from getting too intoxicated. Then another lawyer would take his turn, until the judge had drunk them all down and was waiting for them when they came back.

Few real felonies were tried at Clarendon. Early dockets show mostly cases of perjury, bribery attempts, and charges of practicing medicine without a license, indecent exposure, taking and using "estray mules," sequestration of a yearling, unlawful fencing and grazing, and gambling. Most of the inhabitants were connected by birth, marriage, or denominational interests; the rest were cowpunchers in the employ of the big ranches, and it was practically impossible to obtain an impartial jury. It was even more difficult to find twelve men legally qualified, for in the entire district there were no more than seventy landowners and freeholders.

At one term of court, when range roundups made jurors scarcer than usual, the proceedings seemed blocked. One more man was needed on the jury. A young fellow named Sterling Buster was literally picked up on the street and dragged into the courtroom for duty. Thinking to free himself from a very distasteful task, he explained to the judge that he lacked six months of being twenty-one. The judge looked him over quietly and then in his most serious, dignified voice declared him, with the consent of the court, to be of legal age and ordered him to get to work with no more foolishness.

The antics of the lawyers with whom he associated greatly influenced Temple. He admired them all; a few he imitated, patterning a style of his own. He loved Colonel Grigsby's tales of the Civil War and the growing-up years of the five Grigsby boys in Montague County; the colonel's early cases at Henrietta; the property he owned there and in San Antonio; his ranching experience in Shackelford County, where he had first known Jim Browning; his ambition to become a supreme court judge.

Jim Browning would expound on how he had migrated from his native Clark County, Arkansas, to Cooke County, Texas, in 1866, to become a cowboy at age sixteen. In 1867 he had gone into the cattle business with his brother, Joe, at Fort Griffin when it was wildest and by choice took up the study of law. Elected to the bar at Albany in 1876, he had served first as justice of the peace, then for two years as county attorney, fighting gambling and other frontier vices. A rabid reformer, he spent Sundays teaching Scripture to the girls in Mobeetie, although Houston knew that he was the best monte player in the county. The rougher element resented his evangelical efforts, but even threats against his life did not soften his zeal. Large of stature and a popular orator, he led the "free-grass" element and opposed the large acreage leasing of Panhandle school land to stock raisers. In 1882 he was elected representative from the Forty-third District in the Texas legislature.

A German singing teacher came to Mobeetie. His English was very broken, and Browning, Houston, and Judge Willis decided to celebrate his talent. They bought a large tuning fork, got the teacher on the platform, and presented it to him. Temple made the speech, closing by saying, "The Old World had her Chopin and her Mozart, but it remains for the Panhandle to have this genius."

Temple admired Judge Patton for his unusually high character, but he delighted in Moses Wiley's clever attacks to impeach a witnesses. Uncle Johnny Stroker, who ran the dance hall across the street from Clampitt's livery, was a fiddler and gave a dance every night, Sunday included. No fighting or drinking was allowed; however, this was not the case when certain individuals came down from Feather Hill—so Clampitt testified in court. Wiley was certain that Clampitt's statements were fabrications. He could not prove perjury, but to get his point across, he put on a witness from Dodge City.

"Have you seen and heard liars?" the lawyer asked.

"Yes, sir," was the answer.

"Done a little lying yourself, haven't you?"

"I am an experienced liar," the man admitted.

"Then you should be able to speak with authority. Would you think from appearance that Clampitt was lying?"

"He looks like the biggest liar I ever seen," was the convincing reply.

Clampitt strongly objected. "To hell with such a court," he shouted. "I'm getting out of here." And out he went.

While L. D. Miller was counted crude, and people often laughed at points in his court arguments, few attorneys were better human-nature readers. Miller seldom failed to pick a jury to suit his purpose. Temple thought him a better bronc rider than a lawyer, however.

Miller loved horses, kept a corralful of them, and traded often. Cowboys brought him their renegade ponies, and he would break them. Once he saw a horse that he liked. He was fresh out of cash but had two sections of land, and the owner agreed to take one of the sections in trade. After Miller drew the papers, the man looked them over and remarked, "Something wrong somewhere—I traded for *one* section and you're trying to put off *two* on me." Miller offered to amend the contract, but the man backed out.

W. H. Woodman held Temple's greatest respect. Faultless in dress, with expressive face, keen blue eyes, and jet-black hair worn in a long, straight bob, he depended on his eloquence to sway jurors. At some time he had taken voice lessons, and it was rumored that he had been a Shakespearean actor, for he sang like a professional and acted equally well. If tears were necessary, he could weep a bucketful; if biblical verses were advantageous, he could quote Scripture till the sun went down. Whatever the source of his formal schooling, he claimed to be Englishman by birth, Virginian by education, and Texan by the grace of God.

Some thought that he had practiced for a time at Henrietta before coming to Mobeetie in 1879. But his tales were of the early buffalo hunters and first sheep and cattle ranches along Yellow House river on the lower Estacado and how the stream was named for Indian cave dwellings in the yellow-tinted bluffs above Yellow House Lake, called Laguna de las Casa Amarillas by Spanish explorers traveling its dry canyon bed to water at Buffalo Springs. Because he had no partner, Woodman called himself the "Lone Wolf of Yellow House Canyon."

He denied owning or studying law books. Arguing a case one day, he remarked that he needed a book containing a certain precedent and sent a cowboy over to his office to get it. Everyone was astonished, for Woodman had no library. The cowboy returned shortly and reported that he could not find the volume. Woodman arose, apologized for the delay, adding that the fellow was undoubtedly a prevaricator; he had only one book, and it was lying in the window.

Judge Willis provided some of the more colorful moments. Crossing the Canadian with its treacherous quicksands was exciting enough, but on one trip to Tascosa there was quite a head rise. The court party, already late for the opening of the term, decided that it was safer to "wash" across and bring over their suitcases and double horse rigs when the water went down. A rider went ahead, feeling the way past the quicksands. Then the lawyers stripped to their underwear, carrying the rest of their clothing, and waded in. Woodman carried the only volume of the 1879 Texas statutes in the Panhandle. About midstream they hit deep water, and it became necessary to swim. Judge Willis was no swimmer, and his weight made his predicament serious. Houston and Browning, tall, sturdy men able to fight the swirling current that had surprised them, hoisted the judge on their shoulders. Woodman, floundering behind, saw the law book torn from his grasp and swept away in the reddish torrent.

"Save the statutes of Texas!" he cried.

And Judge Willis's deep voice boomed across the water in reply, "Let the law go, Woodman, and save the district court!"

Another incident involved Mose Hays, a Hemphill County ranch owner who was a member of the Mobeetie jury and failed to show on time. Jurors often were late because of the distances they sometimes had to travel. Judge Willis grew impatient and told the clerk to assess him seventy-five dollars for defaulting. Another man was pressed into service, and the proceedings began. About noon Mose came in, but it was late evening, after court adjourned, before he had an opportunity to talk to the judge. Willis sternly informed him that he had been fined seventy-five dollars. Hays protested that it was too much. They left the courthouse together, the cowman imploring the judge to remit it and offering every apology for his tardiness. Willis was adamant and advised him to take it up in regular order.

The cowman, following him downtown, continued his appeal, but his honor had turned a deaf ear. As they approached Tom Riley's saloon, with the familiar clink of glasses and aroma drifting from inside, Hays asked the judge if he could buy him a little drink.

This time his honor was listening. Turning, he slapped the suppliant on the back, and exclaimed, "Now, Mose Hays, you've said something!"

He never mentioned the fine afterward.

Willis also had his way of addressing his friends during proceedings. Sheriff Armstrong was "Wash" Arrington; J. N. Browning, "Jasper Newton": A. L. Neal, by his deeds, "Lykergus Neal"; W. H. Woodman, "William Hiddjo"; and L. D. Miller, "Lorenzo Dow". Houston, whom the judge considered a "quick tempered yet very fearless man," was "Tempo Firgit."

Personalities aside, it was Judge Willis's almost sole responsibility to interpret and apply the laws in this open-range country where the individual was wont to vaunt his freedom. Too strong an interpretation and too rigorous enforcement might be met with open defiance, and such men as these understood the real spirit of the west.

Still Judge Willis insisted that every attorney conduct himself with dignity. Following one recess on April 18, 1882, when Temple reappeared in court showing the effects of having imbibed too much from the flowing bowl, Willis fined him ten dollars for drunkenness in office. Again, on December 6, while having a round with Woodman, Houston was fined five dollars for improper language in court, and Woodman was assessed five dollars for loud talking.

Even after Oldham and Donley counties were organized, Mobeetie remained the chief seat of justice for this section and the social and entertainment center of the Panhandle. Its legal lights formed a nucleus of the town's most substantial citizens, because their profession carried a certain prestige and they represented law and order. The officers at Fort Elliott and their families also helped give a cultural tone to the free, careless spirit of a people better schooled in the stern realities of frontier life. The two groups spent many evenings together at card parties, musical and dramatic clubs, and other forms of social pastimes and developed a fraternal relationship that gave Mobeetie a sophistication and elegance not found in Clarendon and Tascosa.

A rock schoolhouse was built, and Mobeetie had its first long-term school. Funerals, Halloween masquerades, and church, when an occasional itinerant preacher came through, were held there. Two chaplains supervised the spiritual well-being of the Fort Elliott garrison. Weddings were celebrations of considerable importance. Those involving military personnel took place at the post. Swimming became a popular recreation of the garrison and townspeople after a pool was dug in Sweetwater Creek, and there was skating in the winter. Thanksgiving and Christmas were festive occasions, with post hunters bringing in wild turkeys and deer for the holiday tables. Lawyer Woodman, comical from a bit too much cheer, played Santa at the annual Christmas tree.

The Fourth of July was a two-day affair. Young ladies from the settlers' shacks and the big ranches came in buggies and organdy dresses to the marathon sessions at the Mobeetie courthouse. The young men, impeccably dressed, held silk handkerchiefs in their hands while dancing to keep from ruining the women's new dresses with perspiration. They brought picnic baskets, ate hokey-pokey ice cream, and drank lemonade cooled by one-hundred pound blocks of ice and prepared in brand-new cattle tanks purchased for the occasion.

The great event was court week. During sessions of district court at Mobeetie, people came from throughout the judicial area for unadulterated fun. Many brought camping outfits and stayed several days. It was well worth the loss of time from farming or range work to witness the many frivolous cases wrangled over and to see "Old Sam's boy" perform. The more insignificant the issue the more entertaining Temple Houston. He "without a doubt got more enjoyment out of being prosecuting attorney than from obtaining conviction after conviction." He would bait and torment his opponent until the latter was ready to explode and then pour the right potent oil on the fire in words most disarming. At the conclusion of the day's hearings the fun began. There were horse races, wild horse riding, roping contests, and dancing night after night, climaxed by the finest of equestrian sports, "Tournament Day."

Tournaments drew the largest crowds and were preceded by a barbecue. The track was a quarter mile long. Posts with arms extending four feet were set fifty feet apart, and rings were hung on the arms. The spears were eight feet long and two inches thick. The marshal of the day was an imposing figure, well dressed with a broad sash and a three-cornered hat and mounted on the finest steed he could procure. The Knights of the Lance were gorgeously attired and their mounts caparisoned in the manner of the knight they had chosen to represent. At the marshal's signal the men would ride at breakneck speed, and the one "spearing" the most rings was declared the winner. A substantial prize was awarded—a fine watch or a hand-tooled saddle. In addition, a young lady was crowned queen of the tournament and escorted that evening by the winning knight to the Tournament Ball.

Houston was prominently present at every event. Never ostentatious but always ready to discuss a subject dear to the hearts of men of leather—guns—he spiced these semiannual affairs with his own sideshow. Target shooting was a popular diversion, as was trapshooting at tomato cans and whiskey bottles. The sport always drew a crowd, especially when his contestant was a woman.

Mollie Quillin was a tiny woman but of a warrior nature like her brother Tom, a young daredevil arrested at Mobeetie in 1880 for discharging firearms in a public place and a key witness in the Zack Stucker murder case in 1881. Mollie wore her hair in a thick braid that reached below her knees. She had been born at Red River Station and knew Judge Willis and Colonel Grigsby at Montague. Her father, William W. Quillin, was an Indian tracker; her grandfather had served with General Sam Houston at the Battle of San Jacinto. She had come to Mobeetie in 1882 to visit her brother and a month later married the postmaster, George A. Montgomery.

Rated an excellent shot, Mollie hunted coon, deer, and antelope with local sportsmen, and she challenged Temple to a pistol match. A nickel was thrust into a crack atop a fence rail. Mollie took the first shot and hit the edge. Then Temple rested Old Betsy and hit it dead center. Mollie kept the coin as a souvenir until her death at Hobart, Oklahoma, in 1940.

Temple fit admirably into the scene and scheme of his new activities. His auburn hair now swept his shoulders. At Mobeetie his dress was a mixture of legal dignity and western informality—a white Stetson, a black frock coat that tended to accentuate his slender height, and shop-made boots with square toes and riding heels that made his feet look sizes smaller. He wore a black cravat and a miniature gold saber tiepin that had belonged to his father.

The men respected him. His elaborate and courtly manners made him a favorite of the ladies. He could have given the young swains of the district much competition, but his thoughts were of Laura Cross.

During a slack period shortly after New Year's Day, 1883, he made the long journey back to Brazoria County. On February 14, at the Waldeck plantation three miles from Columbia, he and Laura were married, and afterward Temple referred to her as his "Valentine."

7

War on Cattle Thieves

Their wedding trip to Mobeetie, while not extraordinary in light of today's transportation, was full of interest. With frequent stops for lavish entertainment provided by friends and relatives along the way, they reached Wichita Falls, the new terminus on the Fort Worth and Denver City Railway. This left 189 miles to be made by stage, but, Laura recalled, Temple

obtained a hack pulled by two horses. We forded the streams in February and March.... one evening we camped on Red River and Mr. Houston pointed across to where there were some Indian tepees. He said the Indians were on the warpath and we had better move on as soon as we ate supper. I never saw it so dark after we got started and we lost our path. Mr. Houston got out and walked and led the way and I followed him until we found the trail again. We drove until two o'clock in the morning, then made down our bed on the prairie. At daylight we heard cow bells and found that we had camped a short distance from some freighters. We passed a log house in Greer County which had been abandoned because of a different and better road. It looked mighty good to me to get under shelter once more and (we) slept.

One day we were driving along and our horses fell headlong over an embankment and broke the breast yoke. Mr. Houston had to go in search of help. He was gone from 9 o'clock until three. He happened to see John Pope ride away from a dugout (a line camp of the McAnulty & Pope Cattle Company). If Mr. Pope had not ridden away from the dugout, Mr. Houston probably would not have seen it, as it had come a light snow and the ground was covered. Mr. Pope's cowboys came to our assistance, and we were soon on our way again.

One evening Mr. Houston pointed ahead and said, "See the

buffalo bones on those hills yonder?" When we came closer, I saw that instead of buffalo bones it was Mobeetie.

The rough cattle town gave Temple and his beautiful and aristocratic lady a rousing welcome:

> Mr. Houston was twenty-three and I in my 'teens. We had to walk right down through the streets of sand in our silks and satins. The sand got in my slippers but I didn't mind. A cowboy galloped past, shooting a pistol with one hand and taking a drink of whiskey from his bottle with the other. Then a group of cowboys rode down the street by twos, shooting and yelling as loud as they could. They were good riders, too, but there was a Negro who was the best rider of all. This was much different from what my life had been in Brazoria, but I had no fears....
>
> I am of French and Scotch-Irish blood.... I met a French noble there who had a mail route. He was a spendthrift and his parents refused to allow him to spend their money. He had to work for himself. His hands all struck on him once and he had quite a time. He could speak English. When Mr. Houston introduced him, I spoke to him in French and I thought he was going to hug me.
>
> We spent the first night in Mobeetie at the stone house of Henry Fleming.

The next day Temple moved his bride into a frame house he had prepared for her on Tony Ridge. Laura remembered:

> The town had several frame residences, a few sod buildings and even tin-can buildings. These were tin cans nailed on frames. Some of them had no floors while some did. Some were nicely furnished. My furniture was ordered along with that ordered for the Fort and it was nice.

Thereafter the couple became a familiar sight in the Panhandle capital, especially in the early evening when it was their custom to walk hand in hand from one end to the other of the veranda which ran the length of their cottage.

Reared on a plantation with servants of all kinds, Laura found Mobeetie

> no picnic, but I had lots of fun.... Fort Elliott was as gay a post as could be found on the frontier. Most of our friends were at the

post—Mrs. Dr. Appel and Lula Godfrey—her sister and Major Godfrey, Lt. Collins who married a Miss Beach of New York. There was also a little Texas girl from San Antonio but I cannot recall her name. Capt. Leggitt was a widower. He was killed with a rifle, accidentally. Lt. Day was a great friend of Mr. Houston's—also Lt. Breaton [John J. Brereton] who was a brilliant Lawyer and Mr. Houston's bosom friend.

In town Fannie Boynton, daughter of Dr. Boynton, the druggist, was

one of my dear friends. Fannie married Frank Hoffer, a ranger in Captain Arrington's old regiment. We had good times. . . . There were cowboy dances once a month. We went; Mr. Houston did not dance, but it was so much fun to watch the cowboys do the quadrille and schottische in their boots and spurs.

We also had card parties and rehearsals. There was Mrs. Woodman and her sister, Hannah Nations. Hannah came to Mobeetie to be with Mrs. Woodman and married Bee Hopkins (part owner of the old Shoe Bar and later manager of the Laurel Leaf brand). Others who took part in the rehearsals were Mrs. Newman, Mrs. Will Isaacs and Mrs. Arrington. Captain Arrington was sheriff. The lower floor of the jail was arranged to house the sheriff's family, and they lived there.

After taking office, Arrington had joined Goodnight and the Panhandle Stock Association in the continuing war on cattle rustlers. The driver of a Spur trail herd, in passing, killed a JA calf to feed his crew. In accord with the association's policy of prosecuting "big" thieves, Arrington arrested the man seventy-five miles up the trail and hauled him back to Mobeetie for trial. A roar went up over the country. This handling of a big cattleman like an ordinary cow thief rankled some old-timers who saw no harm in eating a neighbor's beef. Houston presented the case to a Wheeler grand jury. Though no indictment was found, the action had a marvelous effect in showing that the fight on theft was to proceed from the top.

There were no objections when the government butcher at Mobeetie was caught killing Laurel Leaf and Bar CC cattle and burying their hides in a ditch. This time Houston obtained an indictment. In his closing remarks to the trial jury he quoted Lord Nelson's injunction to his men before Trafalgar: "England expects every man to do his duty," and implored them, "Texas expects the same of you!" His eloquent plea sent the butcher to the penitentiary.

Another case involved John Petrie, who managed the Rowe Brothers ranch on the Salt Fork in Collingsworth and Donley counties. Petrie was a good cowhand and a gentleman, except for frequenting the Hogtown saloons and gambling halls at Tascosa. His neighbors claimed that he headed a shrewd band of rustlers. The Rowes refused to accept the allegations or fire him, and they were summoned by the association's executive committee to show cause why they should not be expelled under its bylaw prohibiting employment of a known cow thief.

Owing to the difficulty of obtaining convictions, several members had for some time favored forming a vigilance committee, but cool heads like Goodnight's and President Evans's prevailed. While the association was in executive session on the Rowe matter, a rumor that such a committee was being organized swept the Panhandle. Within thirty-six hours, two dozen well-known rustlers left their haunts and were never found. Evans's detective, however, gathered enough evidence to jail Petrie and four of his men at Clarendon pending action of a Donley County grand jury.

The evening before district court convened, two wagonloads of their Hogtown friends, with plenty of whiskey and a couple of lewd women, arrived from Tascosa and camped on the hill across the creek from the courthouse. During the night they decorated the streets of Clarendon with shameful caricatures of Judge Willis and made veiled threats on his life. Next morning Goodnight rode in with his JA outfit and other men from the Spade Ranch and Shoe Bar. Judge Willis met him on the street and excitedly told him what had happened, that the bunch on the hill meant business, and that he did not think it safe to hold court.

Goodnight replied that he had eighteen men—all sharpshooters with rifles and pistols; the judge should hold court, and if it became necessary, he would hold the hill.

The hearing proceeded undisturbed, though tension was great. Both sides were playing for high stakes. Veniremen were scarce. Willis properly ruled that association members could not serve because they were paying for the prosecution, so cowboys were deeded town lots to make them eligible. Even with the jury completed, the cattlemen realized that its members, through either sympathy or fear, were with the defendants. They were bluffing but determined to bring as many indictments as possible to break each defendant financially, if not convict him. No one knew better than Petrie that the plan might work. He proposed that if the cases were dropped he and his men would leave the country. The association accepted, and the first formal judgment of banishment in the history of the state was entered upon the records of Donley County:

We, the undersigned, do solemnly swear, that in consideration of certain cases now pending being dismissed, and the further consideration that no more . . . shall be filed against us, we each of us hereby agree to leave the Panhandle of Texas within ten days, and never voluntarily return.

But the things Goodnight said to Petrie and his cohorts to speed them on their way as they strode to the hitching rack for their horses were too warm to be recorded.

On the other side of the Plains, Outlaw Bill Moore (David Beals's and Deacon Bates's LX manager, who had killed his brother-in-law in California and his black coachman in Wyoming and was a fugitive from the law of both states) had mavericked enough company cattle and neighbors' calves to start his own brand at Coldwater Springs, in No Man's Land. After he was replaced on the LX by the stocky Scotchman John Hollicott, Outlaw Bill disposed of his Coldwater interests for $70,000 and established a new ranch in western New Mexico, where he soon shot and killed two more men and fled with a large reward on his head. David Beals was off negotiating with the Gunter-Munson-Summerfield surveying and land company of Grayson for another 100,000 acres that would extend the LX range from Palo Duro Canyon to Chalk Hollow north almost sixty miles into Moore County. During his absence, Deacon Bates apparently tried to make up the LX deficit by gathering strays himself.

The first hint of his operation came in the summer of 1883, when a trainload of LX cattle were driven from the Cherokee Outlet to Caldwell, Kansas, where the inspector cut nearly one-fourth of them as strays. Association detectives went to work and determined that, during the winter when hair was long and brands hard to read, Bates had trailed the LX beeves into the Outlet, picking up strays along the way and, after fattening them in the spring, shipped them to market. Further investigation turned up another seventy-two head with eastern Panhandle brands in Illinois that had been unloaded outside Saint Louis and driven across the river.

This caused a minor explosion among Panhandle ranchers. They promptly swore out warrants. The Deacon, hearing that he was being sought, lit out for Boston. Houston prepared the proper papers to bring him back to Texas, handed them to Sheriff Arrington, and said: "Cap, go get him. We can't let that rich son of a bitch get away with this!"

Arrington promised, "One way or another, I'll bring him back."

The former Ranger captain traveled to Massachusetts and took Bates into custody but soon found that extradition was necessary. He was kept running from pillar to post several days by Bates's political friends and lawyers in an attempt to secure the needed document. His real trouble lay in getting to the governor. It was only when he became angry and bulled his way past statehouse guards that he was able to reach his office.

The governor happened to be Benjamin Butler, the Lowell, Massachusetts, criminal lawyer and politician who had risen to the rank of brigadier general and distinguished himself during the Civil War first as commander of Baltimore and eastern Virginia and later as military guardian of the mouth of the Mississippi after New Orleans surrendered to the naval forces under Farragut. A member of Congress from 1866 to 1875, he had advocated the impeachment of President Andrew Johnson, and in 1882 he was elected governor of Massachusetts. Butler read the papers Arrington presented to him, and a look of pleasure crossed his face.

"Well," he mused, "the Deacon finally got himself into hot water." He reached for his pen. "Mr. Arrington, this man is an old personal and political enemy of mine. I sign this extradition order with gratification and will render any assistance you may need in getting him back to Texas."

Arrington thanked him and hurried Bates toward the Panhandle, changing trains frequently in a zigzag course to avoid losing him through *habeas corpus* and other legal dodges already set in motion by the rich man's lawyers. A few days later Arrington recounted the difficulties of his trip to Houston, ending with his favorite laconic expression, "I calaboosed the prisoner."

Bates's hearing was set for November. In the meantime Houston resigned to run for the Texas Senate; Lucius Dills was appointed district attorney to fill out his term; Bates paid the Panhandle owners for their cattle; and Judge Willis dismissed the case on Dill's motion that there was no longer evidence to sustain any allegation in the indictment and that the ranchers would "exonerate" the defendant. In 1884, Bates and Beals sold the 187,141 acres they owned (not counting 250 sections of school land), 40,000 cattle, and 1,000 horses to the American Pastoral Company of London.

Texas's conservative Constitution of 1876 had provided for a senate of thirty-one members and a house that might be enlarged to 150 members as the population increased. Senatorial terms ran four years, with biennial sessions and salaries at five dollars a day for the first sixty days and two dollars a day for the remainder of each session. In 1882, John Ireland, a former member of both the house and the senate, succeeded O. M. Roberts as governor but continued somewhat Roberts's policy of economy. In 1883 the Panhandle was redistricted; Wheeler and its fifteen attached counties, with Hale, Floyd, and Motley added, became the Thirty-first Judicial District instead of the Thirty-fifth, and Houston decided to run for this district seat in the legislature.

Temple proved as vigorous a campaigner as he was a prosecutor. Son of the Raven, lordly in bearing, and master of the courtly bow to ladies and mannered courtesy to men—none forgot him.

At Gainesville in October, at an old-fashioned barbecue and statewide rally of Democratic candidates held on the banks of Elm Fork of the Trinity river, speeches were delivered by United States Senator Samuel Bell Maxey of Paris; United States Congressman from the Third District James W. Throckmorton of McKinney; former Congressman D. C. Giddings, delegate to the Democratic National Convention; Representative Avery L. Matlock, candidate for the Texas Senate from Montague; and Barnett Gibbs, who represented Dallas and Kaufman counties in the Texas Senate in 1882–83, now candidate for lieutenant governor.

That night Temple spoke from the steps of the courthouse. His countenance was immobile in repose, but when he began talking his clear gray eyes moved over the thousands of people before him, and his intellectual face became illumined so that he seemed transfigured. His speech was a simple tribute to the Texas pioneers, but those who listened thought that human lips never uttered anything of the kind more chaste, eloquent, and beautiful.

Gibbs and Matlock won their posts easily. John Ireland was reelected governor with 212,234 votes, against 88,460 for the Greenback party nominee advocating "easy money," and 25,557 for the Republican.

Temple Houston's star never shone more brightly. In what seemed little more than the natural course of events, he was chosen by acclamation of voters of his district, who loved him to idolatry.

8
Texas State Senator

Temple served in two sessions of the legislature at Austin—beginning in January, 1885, and in January, 1887. There, as in Brazoria County and the Panhandle, he attracted wide attention with his eccentric dress and dynamic personality.

Claude Weaver, Oklahoma congressman in 1913-15 and a Temple Houston biographer, wrote:

> I was a student in the Texas University at Austin in 1887 and saw much of Houston. I was often a spectator at sessions of the Senate. Houston seldom spoke. When he did speak on pending legislation, he wasted no words, attempted no flights of fancy, but spoke with a sententious clearness.
>
> On occasions where oratory was appropriate, his style was very different, and his speeches embellished with rhetorical figures and poetic imagery, rich and strange.

Well versed on issues and always ready to do battle for his constituents and the state, Temple seemed imbued with the spirit of his father. He was the author of a number of important bills, chief of which provided pensions for the children of the Texas martyrs.

At various periods since the annexation of Texas to the United States, the ruins of the Alamo had been claimed by the city of San Antonio and the Roman Catholic church. During the Civil War the Confederates used the grounds and building for quartermaster purposes. After the war the United States government leased the Alamo from the church, making some improvements, and used it until 1876. In 1883, Texas purchased the church property and placed the Alamo in the city's care on condition that the city maintain it and furnish a

Houston at the time he was senator in the Texas State Legislature, 1884–88.

custodian. Little effort had been made to restore it, and Temple introduced a bill providing for its restoration as a public shrine. Framed and hanging within its hallowed walls are his portrait and a copy of his eloquent appeal of patriotism to the old building presented to the Alamo Museum.

He maintained a private practice at Mobeetie and spent as much time as possible between legislative sessions with his family. His wife had borne him a son, Temple, Jr.

Laura recalled:

We had a terrible blizzard in 1885. Mr. Houston was gone. He had piled me a lot of wood inside one of the rooms of our house. It was a good house, but it got so cold I had to keep the baby wrapped up in the bed to keep him warm. This blizzard lasted a whole week. Mr. Houston had asked Mr. Grigsby to look after me while he was away. Mr. Grigsby had the only coal stove in town. He took me home with him and we all lived together for a week in one room.

The same year a daughter, Louise, was born. Temple was away again in 1887 when the child died of *cholera infatum*. Mrs. Johnny Long, a Montague County buffalo hunter's daughter who had married the Mobeetie saloon- and storekeeper when she was seventeen, remembered, that when the little girl died, she washed, dressed, and laid her out. Except for this tragedy, Laura fared well with friends like the Longs, the Grigsbys, and the others.

E. B. Spiller, Wheeler County's first surveyor, assisted Temple in his Law and Land Office operation. Colonel Grigsby's new sign read: "Att. at Law and Gen. Land Agency." Jim Browning, serving his first term in the House of Representatives, operated a Law and Land Office with Surveyor Jno. O. B. Street. A. L. Neal was county prosecutor, Arrington was in his second term as sheriff, and L. D. Miller had replaced Lucius Dills as district attorney. Arrington's and Miller's activities—with a dozen or more reward notices in each issue of the *Mobeetie Panhandle* ranging from $250 to $1,500 offered by owners and managers of various ranches for the arrest and conviction of anyone illegally branding or stealing their horses and cattle—kept lawyers Dills and Woodman defending in the courts of Mobeetie and Clarendon.

Temple's popularity brought him considerable criminal practice at Mobeetie and Tascosa. Much of his time, however, was spent on land matters.

The highly optimistic 1880 report of Clare S. Read and Albert Pell, members of the British Parliament who were sent to study ranching in America, and such pamphleteering as General James S. Brisbin's *The Beef Bonanza*, published in 1881, had brought so much Scotch and English money to compete with eastern capitalists in acquiring herds and range rights that the industry, originally an individual enterprise usually managed by the owner, had become a corporate operation with nonresidence and hired managers. Of Texas's some eighty million acres of public domain, including lands set apart for schools, the elevated plains of the Panhandle were supposedly the most favorable for profit. By the end of 1886 at least five companies in England and eight in Scotland of the more than sixty corporations organized in the British Isles between 1880 and 1890 had invested in the region, with titled nobility, members of Parliament, and army officers prominent on their boards of directors.

Besides the Prairie Land and Cattle Company of Scotland, which brought the LIT from George W. Littlefield, and the American Pastoral Company, which bought the LX Ranch from Bates and Beals, the Ranche and Cattle Company, Ltd., owned Hank Creswell's Bar CC; Jule Gunter, having become sole owner of the T Anchor in the spring of 1885, sold the 275,000-acre property and some 24,000 head of stock to the Cedar Valley Land and Cattle Company of England; the Matador Land and Cattle Company, Ltd., ran 60,000 cattle under the Matador V brand on approximately 300,000 acres acquired in Motley, Dickens, Cottle and Floyd counties; the Francklyn Land and Cattle Company, a New York-based firm financed by England's wealthiest subject, Lord Rosebery, and by Williams, Deacon and Company of the Bank of London, owned the White Deer Pastures embracing 637,400 acres in

Hutchinson, Roberts, Carson and Gray counties; and the Capitol Freehold Land and Investment Company, Ltd., of London, had underwritten the XIT, established by a Chicago syndicate in 1885, with some 110,721 cattle valued at over a million dollars and more than 3 million acres covering parts of nine counties: Dallam, Hartley, Oldham, Deaf Smith, Parmer, Castro, Bailey, Lamb, and Hockley.

In 1883 the Texas Legislature had created the State Land Board to classify lands that had been surveyed and set apart for the University of Texas, common schools, and eleemosynary institutions as to agricultural, pasture, or timber usage; to lease or sell them in blocks of not less than 640 acres; to maintain jurisdiction of the mineral rights retained by such sales or leasing; and to employ qualified persons to execute the land acts of 1879 and 1881. This board proved to be somewhat partisan and inefficient, creating an unpleasant conflict between the cattlemen accustomed to free grass and the board demanding four cents an acre a year for state pastures, and between the board and the homesteaders claiming the right to file and settle on school lands.

Both sides brought strong pressure on the Texas Legislature. In Temple's district it became a burning political issue that resulted in the defeat of E. B. Spiller by Jno. O. B. Street as county surveyor. Spiller had made the survey of the Francklyn Company lands; Street represented the settlers. However, most of the competition and litigation among cattlemen and between cattlemen and settlers arose from their efforts to prove title and establish correct boundary lines.

The land records for Northwest Texas were first set up when Jack County was organized with Jacksboro as county seat in 1857, after the region was detached from the Old Bexar, or San Antonio Department, to become a separate political unit. Jack County became disorganized during the Civil War, and its records were moved to Henrietta, the county seat of Clay County. In 1873 the twenty-six counties of the Panhandle were attached to Clay, then to Wheeler County when it was organized in 1879. A number of surveys had been made by the

Clay County surveyor, but the matter remained dormant until the 1880s, when land speculators and settlers began disputing Panhandle land titles on grounds that the Clay County surveyor had no jurisdiction.

Many first locations had been made for railroad companies through district surveyors. To encourage railroad development, the Texas Legislature of 1854 had given these companies sixteen sections out of the public domain in West Texas for every mile of track built in the state. Parties who had made relocations filed protests against the patenting of lands under these first locations, and the chief clerk of the Land Office and some of his assistants filed a number of relocations and protests on large segments of land—a strategy generally regarded as blackmail—thinking the parties against whom they had filed protests would pay them something for their claims.

The railroads finally obtained an injunction from the United States Circuit Court at Dallas, and all parties to the suits gave up the fight. Until then the questions involved were new and undecided by the courts and provided much work for attorneys.

Other prophetic movements and crucial events in the Panhandle also provided much legal business for Senator Houston and his fellow lawyers. Cape Willingham had become manager of the Hansford Land and Cattle Company and the vast Turkey Track Ranch, with headquarters near Adobe Walls. Jim East, the LX wagon boss who had accompanied the Panhandle expedition into New Mexico and helped Pat Garrett track down Billy the Kid and his gang the winter of 1880–81, was the new sheriff of Oldham. East took his oath of office at Tascosa on New Year's Day, 1883, and vowed to change the face of the bawdy cowtown.

While Willingham had rendered good service, he had countenanced the sharks and tinhorns from the Mobeetie overflow. The Panhandle was undergoing change, and Oldham County, adopting a firm policy in keeping with the times, had proceeded with a bond election to finance its proposed courthouse. A school district had been created and a church established in Tascosa, and it was the consensus of the hitherto demoralized populace, now daring to prosecute, that the town no longer serve as a hole up for camp followers and outlaws.

Despite the work of the Panhandle Stock Association and the six-shooter battalions of the corporation outfits, rustling continued. East joined hands with Sheriff Arrington at Mobeetie and sent a warning to larceny-minded nester cowboys and professional maverickers to keep their irons off herds in his district. Most of his problems stemmed from the Cowboy Strike of 1883.

Pioneer ranchers like Charles Goodnight had shared the hard, rough work of the range with their cowpunchers and had allowed them to run a few cattle or horses of their own on the premises and even to place their own brand on unmarked strays that drifted into their territory. As the ranches moved to corporate and foreign ownership, these privileges were denied. The big cattle companies extended their ranges chiefly by taking advantage of a lease-law provision that stated that if a lessee had built as much as one hundred dollars' worth of improvements he might hold the land without danger of having it leased or purchased by someone else. This provision was complied with simply by building an occasional dugout or a few corrals. In many instances they merely bought the water claims or headquarters of squatter outfits. Most nesters were ignorant of the correct status of the public domain or unable to travel to places where the information could be obtained. Many dared not interfere with or question the practices of the corporations. Owners of small herds were increasingly shut out from participation in spring roundups, thus missing an equal chance to brand strays. And the rules and restrictions for punchers working for the large operators became so stringent that the once independent cowboy, on his twenty-five dollars a month, found it increasingly difficult to be anything more than a hired man on horseback.

Chafing under capitalistic methods, the independent boys

began banding together. On March 24, 1883, Tom Harris, wagon boss for the LS Ranch, J. W. ("Waddy") Peacock for the LIT Ranch, and Roy Griffin for the LX Ranch, who operated floating outfits that followed drift cattle, camped with their crews at the LS supply depot above the mouth of Frio Creek in southeastern Deaf Smith County. They enjoyed a meal of beef, corn, tomatoes, molasses, and sourdough biscuits and, after voicing the dissatisfaction prevalent over the Canadian range, drew up the following ground rules for the first cowboy strike in American history:

We, the undersigned cowboys of Canadian River, do by these presents agree to bind ourselves into the following obligations, viz:

First, That we will not work for less than $50 per mo. and we further more agree no one shall work for less than $50 per mo. after 31st of Mch.

Second, Good cooks shall also receive $50 per mo.

Third, Anyone running an outfit shall not work for less than $75 per mo.

Anyone violating the above obligations shall suffer the consequences.

After sending to each ranchowner a copy of the proclamation and a demand for the time-honored right to a few cattle of their own on the open range, the cowpunchers took the wagons and went into camp on Alamocitas Creek, in Juan Dominguez Canyon west of Tascosa.

By April 3, according to the official records of the Federal Bureau of Labor Statistics, 325 cowboys from seven ranches had accepted the strike ultimatum. Actually the only ranches involved were the LS, the LE, the LX, the T Anchor and the LIT—five rather than the alleged seven—and the cowboy union grew to about two hundred.

In the Palo Duro, Charles Goodnight received the news without apprehension. His men were out of range of current talk that might sweep them into the strike. But the affair puzzled him. No workmen were more faithful to their employers than cowboys, and he could not understand why Tom Harris wanted to organize them and demand more money when he was already drawing one hundred dollars a month, twenty-five dollars more than the price demanded for range bosses. Harris claimed to be sorry for the puncher who drew only twenty-five dollars a month and board.

The syndicates reacted to the strike ultimatum in various ways, all negative. The LIT offered its cowboys thirty-five dollars and bosses sixty-five dollars a month to continue working. The offer was refused. So the ranch separated the boys from their horses. Afoot they were allowed to hang around the chuck wagon and take their meals. The LE cowboys were fired on the spot, while the LX just waited to see how things would develop.

Down at the T Anchor, Jule Gunter stockpiled buffalo guns after six of his men left for the Canadian and word filtered back that the strikers planned to attack his headquarters. An adobe blacksmith shop near the ranchhouse offered the only protective cover for an attack, and Jule decided to prepare for them. He and his men dug a hole in the middle of the dirt floor, sunk a keg of blasting powder that had been brought in to build roads in the canyon, set a keg of nails on top of the powder, and covered the trap with all the refuse they could find. A fuse was strung from the ranchhouse to set off the powder mine. Goodnight sent Gunter word to let him know if he needed help to clean up the riffraff, and Jule had a man with an extragood horse stand by to do a Paul Revere ride to the JA.

His efforts proved unnecessary. Only two of the strikers appeared at the T Anchor. Captain Harris, they said, wished to know what Gunter intended to do about the demands the boys on the Canadian were making. Gunter met them in the yard, feet braced apart and chin thrust forward, and asked if they could take a message, word for word, as he said it—that if they could to tell their Captain Harris to go to hell. Afterwards Gunter called in all his men from the line camps and outer ranges and remained prepared for any eventuality.

Tom Harris and his boys pulled their wagons into LS headquarters on the Alamocitas. J. E. McAllister, the LS general manager, tried to compromise by offering the men forty dollars a month. Harris and his boys stuck to their demands, so McAllister notified LS owner, W. M. D. Lee, at Leavenworth. Lee boarded a train to Dodge City, took a rig out of Dodge, and arrived at the Alamocitos within thirty-six hours.

Between eighty and ninety cowboys were camped in the ranch yard. Lee interrogated Harris in the ranch office. Harris admitted that he had set his own price when he went to work for the company and had not asked for more money. He also admitted that many of the cowpunchers working for the ranch were nester boys not worth fifty dollars a month. Lee then offered to pay fifty dollars for every man Harris would recommend as a top hand. Harris shook his head, stating that he would stay with the boys.

Lee fired him. Then he walked outside, fired every striker in the camp, and cut them off the LS chuck line.

This left the ranch shorthanded. Some of the better cowhands who had not joined the strike took over the spring roundup. Veteran cowboy Jim Mays replaced Tom Harris as wagon boss; Duncan S. ("Dunk") Cage, Sam Buford, and Tobe Robinson ran outfits; and Lee offered Kid Dobbs, of the Campbell & Goodwin-Austen outfit on the Rita Blanca, seventy-five dollars a month to boss a fifth LS wagon, which Dobbs accepted with Campbell's blessing. Dobbs had been a rider for Cape Willingham on the Lightning Express mail line between Trujillo and Fort Bascom for thirteen months in 1879 and 1880 and had been a member of the first expedition sent from the Panhandle in the fall of 1880 to scout for the Billy the Kid gang in the vicinity of White Oaks, New Mexico.

Harris and his strikers set up a new base of operations on a creek above Tascosa. Within a week Harris sent Dobbs word that if he wanted to keep a whole hide he had best quit the LS at once. Dobbs sent back word that he worked for whomever and wherever he damned well pleased and challenged Harris to name his own ground and weapons. When Dobbs and Ed King, another LS rider, ran into Harris a few days later at

Trujillo, the matter was dropped with an exchange of pleasantries.

Word spread rapidly throughout the cow country of job openings on the big Panhandle ranches. Young men pulled up stakes in Kansas, Colorado, South Texas, and New Mexico and headed for the Canadian. Many were no more than farm boys, but they were already accustomed to long hours and hardships and sufficiently adept at riding, roping, and branding that ranchers had little trouble hiring hands for the work they had to do. For instance, the LS branded ten thousand calves that spring and trailed five thousand mixed cattle in two herds to Dodge City. Before the season ended, 150 men, most of them new faces, were riding for Lee and Scott.

Without a shortage of cowboys as leverage against the cattlemen and without a way to resist strikebreakers, Harris and his followers had only money in their pockets and time on their hands—a bad combination, given the proximity of the attractive oasis Tascosa. For about six weeks Jess Jenkins's Hogtown drinking, gambling, and dancehall facilities enjoyed a booming business. Then the one and only cowboy strike fizzled. Without money or jobs many of the cowpunchers tried to return to the syndicates at the old wage, only to find that they had been blacklisted.

Harris went up the Canadian to Liberty, New Mexico, and established the Bar WA (connected). With the help of Jess Jenkins he sold shares to nester ranchers in the Panhandle and organized a cattle pool, which some referred to as the Get Even Cattle Company. Several cowboy friends with small herds settled on land as his neighbors. It was a difficult country, a hundred miles from the county seat at Las Vegas, and the Mexicans cared little that organized bands of rustlers preyed on Texas ranchers. Outlaw Bill Moore bought cattle or horses wearing any brand, until he fled from New Mexico with a price on his head, finally to die in Alaska at the hand of the sourdough gunman Soapy Smith.

Most blacklisted cowpunchers refused to leave the Panhandle, declaring they had as much right to the range as the big ranchers, and took up homesteading adjacent to their former bosses, determined to get into the cattle business one way or another. Brands were designed and registered that could easily be burned over existing brands. At least a dozen were devised for altering the XIT. One turned the XIT into a Star Cross. Every unbranded or weaned calf belonging to the syndicate became fair game for revenge-seeking maverickers, despite the danger they eventually faced in the courts. The cattlemen were relentless in their charges and employed lawyers to help prosecute them. Temple Houston frequently represented the big cattle companies, aiding the county attorneys of Oldham and Wheeler and District Attorney Miller.

One maverick brand was shifted to various owners, first as the Steeple Bar, then as the Hackamore, and finally as the Hondo, to escape the cattlemen's inexorable justice. The T-48 altered the LS. Unable to confiscate it, Lee and Scott finally bought the brand for fifty dollars and retired it. The most notorious design resembled a rectangular block with four legs, called the Tabletop, owned by Bill Gatlin. Almost every Canadian River brand except the XIT could be changed into a Tabletop.

The LS was blamed for breaking the strike, and the mavericking operation seemed pointed to ruin Lee and Scott—at least the LS suffered more than its share of depredations, two of which ended in bloodshed.

Gene Watkins, a blacklisted cowboy who had found work at Jess Jenkins's saloon, was in the habit of slipping LS horses out of the pasture at night to hustle mavericks, returning the horses before daylight. A Mexican wrangler, Jermo Martínez, caught him and threatened to report him to headquarters. The two men quarreled bitterly, but a fight was averted.

One evening Martínez ambled into Jenkins's saloon and gambling hall. Jenkins was dealing monte, Sally Emory was paying off, and Watkins was tending bar. The Mexican paused at the table to watch the game. Watkins yelled, "Get that son of a bitchin' greaser out of here!"

Martínez went for his gun. Watkins drew and fired first, but Martínez killed him. Then someone shot the Mexican. The explosions snuffed out the lights, and two men, presumably friends of Watkins's, ran outside into the darkness.

The only witness to the murder was an Indian named Pisquah, who hung around the saloon begging drinks. He happened to be cold sober at the time, and the two men apparently figured that he might talk. A few nights later Pisquah was found face down in a mud puddle where some workmen had been making adobes, his body full of lead.

Kid Dobbs always believed that it was the same gang of thieves that later rounded up the LS horses and drove them out of the country. John Brophy, a deputy brand inspector and no man to tamper with, told McAllister that he would just bring his remuda back. McAllister warned him not to be a fool, that the gang would shoot him on sight.

But caution was never one of Brophy's virtues. In about ten days he returned with the horses, their brands altered, from New Mexico. Asked by the amazed cowboys if he had killed anybody, John replied that he had just tracked till he found them and had no trouble getting them back. That was all he ever told about his horse hunt, but the rustlers sent word to the LS that they intended to kill him.

One night Brophy attended a Mexican *baile* at Liberty. A man approached him on the dance floor and said that there was a friend outside with an important message. Tom Harris had been selling more beef from his corrals and to butcher shops than should come from his own herds, and Brophy had been to his ranch to inspect some hides, which proved to be his. Brophy was expecting further information on Harris's activities, but he thought of the rustlers' warning and sidled the length of the room with his back to the wall. The moment he stepped through the doorway, a bullet from the darkness struck him in the chest. As he toppled inside, a second bullet struck him in the back. His assailant, apparently believing Brophy to be dead, rode away into the night and was never identified. John was taken to Las Vegas, where he survived his wounds. When he was able to travel, two cowboys drove a wagon from Alamocitas to Las Vegas and brought the invalid home.

The big companies of the region—LS, LX, LIT, Frying Pan, Turkey Track, T Anchor, LE—and the PPP and Bell brands in New Mexico united in retaliation. They sent for Pat Garrett, with whom they had worked successfully a few years previously. Garrett had been succeeded by John W. Poe as sheriff of Lincoln County. He agreed to work for the ranchers for one year if they would obtain his appointment as a captain in the Texas Rangers. The ranchers took up the matter with Attorney General John D. Templeton and Governor Ireland, who authorized a company of "Home Rangers" with Garrett in charge, the ranchers to pay all wages and expenses.

Garrett arrived in the Panhandle in the spring of 1884 with George Jones and Barney Mason, his brother-in-law, who had helped in his fights with Billy the Kid. He set up headquarters at the LS Ranch and recruited from the range guards additional triggermen like Kid Dobbs, Ed King, Lon Chambers, Bill Anderson, Johnny Lang, Albert Perry, and Charley Reasor. Reasor, a half-Cherokee, was made tracker, and Perry, who had been working as a cattle detective, was made sergeant of the corps.

Garrett's first move was to encourage the commissioners' court to list all brands regarded as maverick brands in Oldham and the unorganized counties under its jurisdiction and outlaw them. Next he obtained a proclamation from Governor Ireland making it illegal for cowboys to wear six-shooters. The order went into effect on April 17, 1884.

Jim East, though respecting Garrett's situation, objected. This was tantamount to labeling the little owners as rustlers, disabling them from fighting back, and driving them out of the Panhandle. When advised that the commissioners were talking about removing him from office for failure to enforce the law, East blandly agreed to cooperate. But he and his deputies would ride with the "Rangers" on all arrests, and they would be made under his authority as sheriff of Oldham.

During the summer Garrett and his men went from wagon to wagon, notifying as many as two hundred men in one day of the order. Those who protested were asked to read the proclamation and advised to see the judges or their attorneys in Tascosa. This usually ended the argument. The proclamation proved unenforceable, however. The cowpunchers rigged up scabbards and carried their six-shooters under their arms instead of in belt holsters. Winchesters carried on saddles were not prohibited.

Garrett and his men also familiarized themselves with every cow camp and cattle herd up and down the Canadian. When the Oldham grand jury convened in the fall, it found 159 bills charging theft of one kind or another. The indictments were the legal papers Garrett needed, and in the two months that followed, he and East ran down rustler after rustler. That winter, with a blizzard howling over the prairies, they captured seven men and their leader, Bill Gatlin, for whom warrants had been issued, in an old rock house at Red River Springs, on the Canadian.

Meanwhile, the Oldham Commissioners' Court ordered all strays or mavericks wearing burned brands rounded up and turned over the the county. Cattle whose ownership could not be proved would be handled as the court saw fit. In this operation McAllister and his LS cowboys gave Garrett and his men full support. Thirty-three head of Tabletop cattle were brought to Tascosa and thrown in with other mavericks. Most of them ended up in Scotty Wilson's meat market. When the court later sought compensation for the animals, Scotty laughed and said: "The boys steal 'em, the county steals 'em; by God! I butcher 'em for the hungry hundreds." He refused to pay for the cattle.

Gatlin hired H. H. Wallace, Tascosa's most famous attorney. Wallace, a tall, stately, polished Virginian typical of his contemporaries, also conducted Episcopal prayer services in Tascosa and preached most of the funerals. He was known as the little man's lawyer, and the corporations would not employ him. Wallace threatened to file a twenty-five-thousand-dollar damage suit against Oldham County and criminal action against the commissioners for overstepping their authority in outlawing brands.

Temple Houston advised at least two big cattle companies that consulted him, and it was the opinion of W. H. Woodman, now the new district attorney of the Panhandle, that the commissioners could neither escape criminal responsibility nor defeat the damage suit against the county. The big cattlemen called Wallace into a conference. Wallace agreed to settle for eight hundred dollars. Afterward the big outfits became friendly with him. Wallace announced for county judge and won easily over his opponent, Theodore Briggs.

The county's illegal dealing in cattle, the banning of six-shooters, and the range surveillance of Garrett and his men (whose presence in the valley was considered unnecessary and generally resented as gunmen hired to help the big outfits gain possession of the open range rather than to stop rustling) developed hard feelings. Everybody began to take sides, especially in Tascosa. The businessmen and saloonkeepers in Upper Tascosa favored the big ranchers. Hogtown favored the little men under the leadership of Tom Harris, Jess Jenkins, and three or four gamblers suspected of helping the maverickers.

The Home Rangers were disbanded under the weight of contempt from both factions. But several nefarious characters had the daylights scared out of them. When district court convened in the spring of 1885, much of the tougher element and most of the men whose honesty had been questioned had left the country. There were only a few convictions on the many grand-jury charges brought against the small ranchers and homesteaders.

The Get Even Cattle Company also found the going rough. One after another its shareholders withdrew, leaving Jenkins largely in control. Jenkins and Harris quarreled for three days, and pistols were drawn before they reached an agreement. When the pool was closed out, Jenkins lacked seventeen head of having enough cattle to settle all accounts. Harris never got over the failure of his venture. One evening he was found dead in a wagonyard. One hand clutched a note saying, "I'm tired of this, put me away," and an empty bottle of morphine.

After the ranger company disbanded and Garrett returned to New Mexico, most of its members worked for the LS in camps up and down the river, riding bog and continuing their vigilance against mavericking and cattle theft. Ed King and Johnny Lang, with cowboys Frank Valley, Fred Chilton, Bud Turner, and W. W. McCurry and a cook, Felix Martinez, were camped at Jerry Springs. They would ride into Tascosa after supper, enjoy a gay evening, and return by midnight.

McAllister frowned on the practice, and told them to stay out of town until things settled down but that if they did go to stay on their side of the street. The boys had never backed away from trouble. King, Lang, Valley and Chilton considered it their freeborn right to go wherever they pleased, and they walked any street and visited any dive that struck their fancy.

Finally the Hogtown enmity, sparked by the two reigning belles, Rocking Chair Emma and Sally Emory, erupted into a private but vindictive war. Sally was the sweetheart of Lem Woodruff, a former LX cowpuncher and now bartender at Jenkins's saloon, but they had fallen out because Sally began keeping company with Ed King. Woodruff took up with Rocking Chair Emma at Captain Jinks' Hogtown dancehall, which miffed Sally no end. She asked King to get Woodruff for her, and King, with the gallantry of the times, and perhaps because he had gained some repute as a gunfighter, promised to accommodate the lady.

One night in early March, 1886, Woodruff, Emma, and Captain Jinks were sitting in a building fronting Main Street when hoofbeats and yelling came from outside. Woodruff stepped to the window and saw King, accompanied by Valley and Chilton, riding past the house. King, well tanked, shouted, "Where is that goddam pretty Ed?"

"Pretty Ed" was a cognomen King had manufactured to humiliate Woodruff. Woodruff returned from the window and, sitting down again, burst into tears. He knew that King, Valley, and Chilton intended to kill him but decided he would rather be killed like a dog and buried in Tascosa than have anyone say they ran him out of town.

Woodruff rallied Charlie Emory (no relation to Sally) and Louis Bousman, former deputy of Cape Willingham, as bodyguards. They were soon joined by John B. Gough, an unprepossessing youth whose peculiar eyes had earned him the sobriquet "Catfish Kid." Gough was of the type most despicable in frontier days—an imitation badman who usually shot when the other man was unarmed or at a disadvantage.

No one ever knew the contents of the note Sally Emory sent Ed King at Jerry Springs late the afternoon of March 20, for King burned it in Felix Martinez's cookfire as he, Lang, Valley, and Chilton hastened to clean up and eat supper before departing for Tascosa. McCurry, suspecting a showdown, took Turner aside and suggested that they stay out of town; there was no reason to get mixed up with this locoed bunch. Turner had not planned on going anyway, and later, when King urged them to come along, they told him that someone ought to keep Felix company.

King and his three pals loped away on the trail at sundown. Reaching Tascosa, they stabled their horses at Mickey McCormick's, a half block east of Jenkins's saloon. Their activities the next several hours have not been accounted for accurately. There was a Mexican *baile* in the hall of the old Romero home, and the quartet were there the early part of the evening, dancing, talking, and drinking a few beers. Afterwards they apparently drifted up Main Street seeking the pleasures more suited to each man's fancy. The four finally met again in the Equity Bar, where Dunk and Hays Cage, alarmed by the news that the Jerry Springs boys were on a spree, found them after midnight having a fresh round of drinks.

The brothers tried to persuade them to return to camp, but Valley and Chilton wanted to sit in on a poker game that was starting, and King spoke of keeping a date with Sally. Dunk told Hays that they would not listen to anybody now, and the brothers started for home. It occurred to Lang that King should not make the Hogtown visit; he even volunteered to go to McCormick's livery stable after the horses. King decided to go with him. Valley and Chilton would wait for them in the saloon.

King and Lang angled east down Main Street, crossed Spring Street, and passed Jenkins's saloon, Jesse Sheets's restaurant and Kimball's blacksmith shop on the right. It was now almost two o'clock in the morning, and nothing seemed to be stirring. A few minutes later they rode back toward the Equity Bar, leading the other boys' horses and unaware that from the low wooden porch in the shadows about Jenkins's saloon Lem Woodruff, Charlie Emory, the Catfish Kid, and Louis Bousman watched their every movement.

Then Sally stepped into view, walking north from Spring Street, and approached King. Surprised, King quickly dismounted and handed the reins of the horses to Lang. Lang did not hear what Sally whispered to King. If it was a warning, King took it lightly, for he embraced the girl and playfully slapped her on the backside, telling her to go home and that he would come to her place shortly. Then he walked back to Jenkins's saloon and stepped up on the porch.

There was a gun flash in the shadows, an unexpected roar. Ed King spun half around and fell face up near the saloon door. He never knew what hit him. As he lay there with blood gushing from his mouth, Lem Woodruff rushed out of the darkness, placed the muzzle of his 45-70 Winchester close to King's throat, and pulled the trigger. The burning powder scorched King's chest and his hickory shirt. Then Woodruff and his pals ran into the saloon, turned out the lights, and barred the doors. Sally fled screaming down Spring Street, and Lang, snapping out of his momentary paralysis from the sudden attack, galloped to the Equity Bar. He burst through the batwings, yelling at Valley and Chilton, "Come on—them bastards have killed Ed!"

The three men, rushing to where King was lying in the street, met a fusillade of lead. They spread out, Valley taking the center, and charged the saloon, pouring a stream of bullets through the doors and windows. Woodruff was hit twice during the onslaught—in the bowels and in the groin. Charlie Emory received an ugly leg wound. He managed to drag himself out back and into the shelter of the blacksmith shop. Woodruff retreated to his sleeping quarters, a small square adobe at the back of the saloon. Valley and Chilton, dashing through the passageway between the saloon and restaurant, rounded the corner in time to see him close the door.

Jesse Sheets, who was sleeping in the back room of his establishment, had heard the shooting. He pulled on his pants and shoes and stepped from the rear door to see what it was all about. Valley spotted him standing in the dark, took him to be Louis Bousman, stopped short, rested his gun against the saloon wall, and fired. Sheets died instantly with a bullet in the forehead.

Valley cried that he had got one of them, and rejoined Chilton, who was approaching Woodruff's adobe.

They pumped five shots into the pine door and sod walls. The house leaked lead like a sieve. Realizing that he would be killed like a rat in a trap, Woodruff made a desperate resolve. He limped to the door, threw it open, and fired pointblank at Frank Valley. Valley fell in a heap with a bullet in the brain. Chilton dashed for the shelter of an old water well fifteen yards distant, firing as he went. Before he could reach cover, someone behind a nearby woodpile with a Winchester drilled him through.

Lang, who had taken his stand on the opposite side of the saloon, spattered the woodpile with bullets. Gun empty and left alone, he began a dangerous retreat diagonally across Spring Street. Every step he took was to the accompaniment of singing lead. Even though he was a moving target, his escape was miraculous. One bullet ripped through his coat sleeve as he rounded the front of the Cone and Duran store. Another bullet shattered a window in the Exchange Hotel across the street, and a woman watching from the window fainted.

After reaching Main Street, Lang was joined by friends from the Equity Bar. Lead still whistled through the night. Sheriff East and his deptuy, L. C. Pierce, had reached the scene of action. As Pierce approached the woodpile, a stooping figure dashed toward the river.

Pierce ordered him to halt.

The man did not stop. Pierce's .45 boomed. The Catfish Kid tripped and fell into the mud pit of an adobe maker, and the bullet whizzed over his head. As Pierce ran up to him, he rolled his weird eyes sightlessly toward the stars, choking and groaning as if dying. Assuming that Catfish would not last more than a few minutes, the deputy raced off to find others involved in the fight. Catfish jumped up and fled.

East rushed to Louis Bousman's house on Tascosa Creek. Bousman was in bed. He denied having a part in the battle but could not explain why he still had his clothes on or the hot barrel of a Winchester leaning against the wall. As more citizens ventured onto the streets, Charlie Emory was found lying in the doorway of the blacksmith shop, suffering terribly. Lem Woodruff had vanished.

The citizens were horrified at the sight of King, Valley, Chilton, and the restaurant owner dead and distressed that only two of the gunmen were in custody. Lang claimed self-defense and was not arrested. East and his deputy had enough to do to prevent further trouble and keep bystanders from touching the bodies pending the arrival of Dr. J. M. Shelton and E. C. G. Austen.

Austen remembered:

> I had been recently appointed Justice of the Peace, but had not qualified... so was forced into it as there was to be an inquest. All this occurred on Sunday morning. H. H. Wallace came to my house about 2 A.M., calling to me, "Get up quick, there are four dead, and don't know how many wounded." I got up and went down town. Things looked threatening.

The officials noted the positions of the bodies, probed wounds, and recovered some of the bullets and the shattered teeth of Ed King. Then the bodies were brought out on Main Street, laid on a stone terrace, and covered with a tarpaulin until funeral arrangements could be made.

The entire populace stood about in small groups, wondering what would happen next. Johnny Lang, leaning on a hitchrack in front of McMasters' store, told his version of the battle a dozen times. Turner, McCurry, and Martinez arrived from Jerry Springs; Tobe Robinson and his boys rode in from an LS camp on the Rita Blanca. Sheriff East deputized several men to search for Woodruff. Turner and Robinson rode upriver and circled as far north as present Hartley looking for the Catfish Kid. They returned to Tascosa in late afternoon to learn that Catfish had come in and surrendered and Woodruff had been captured.

Not knowing how many of King's friends might be after him, Woodruff, weak from loss of blood and using his rifle as a crutch, had dragged himself down to and across the creek. After hours of painful crawling over the prairie, he managed to reach the Theodore Briggs home three miles west on the Rica. Here, according to Austen,

he was found by Deputy Pierce after taking in a boy who was riding to a saloon in town for a bottle of brandy, as he said, for Mrs. Briggs who was supposed to be sick. Pierce took out the medicine himself and found Lem not expecting to live, but he did.... Dr. Shelton patched him up as well as he could, and he was removed to the Tascosa jail.

Friends of the slain men wanted to lynch Woodruff. Cowboys had ridden in from every direction—nearly five hundred men paraded the streets, all armed and siding with one faction or the other. The strategy and cool nerve of Sheriff East and other town leaders prevailed. But there was the greater fear of wholesale revenge by the LS, settling the fight between the big and little men once and for all.

Dunk and Hays Cage were about half a mile from town when they heard the exploding guns and rode back to stare at their friends' bodies in disbelief. Hays remained at the scene and told Dunk to get all the boys from the camps and go after Mister Mac.

Mrs. J. E. McAllister, in a 1938 *Amarillo Globe-News* interview, gave the best wrap-up of concluding events.

I was out on the ranch with Mr. McAllister, twenty-five miles from Tascosa [and] remember yet how I felt when awakened that night. Ordinarily, sounds never bothered me, but I heard hoofs striking the rocks for the longest time. I awakened Mr. McAllister, "Listen, something is wrong," I said.

"Yes, that horse is about run down," he answered as he got out of bed.

We were up and dressed when Dunk Cage burst into the house after he had jumped off his exhausted pony.

"Oh, Mr. Mac, it's terrible," he cried. "They are shot—Fred and Frank—and Ed. They are dead, down in Hogtown. Mr. Sheets got killed, too."

Bit by bit we got the story from him. . . .

Of course, I went in with Mr. McAllister. They were our boys, and there were things to be done. We started out in the buckboard long before daylight. Lon Chambers and Kid Dobbs went with us [as] bodyguards for Mr. McAllister because they were afraid there might be more trouble.

When Tascosa was reached, I was left at the home of Mrs. C. B. Vivian while the men went down town.

Mrs. McAllister told how her husband chose several dependable LS men to keep the rest of the outfit in line. McAllister himself joined Sheriff East, Deputy Pierce, and several prominent Tascosans in maintaining peace and order, and wherever he appeared on the street, Kid Dobbs and Lon Chambers walked by his side. He ordered the bodies removed to a vacant room in a nearby adobe house and then tried to determine who started the fight. Everyone seemed to have a different version. Even E. C. G. Austen was unable to unravel the twisted details of the battle in which at least fifty shots were fired:

I was sworn in as Justice of the Peace, a jury summoned, and off we went. There were forty-two witnesses examined by H. H. Wallace, and as far as I am able to judge, it was the most wonderful inquest ever held. Deputy sheriffs all around, armed to the teeth, but everybody else disarmed. Gus Fritchie, bookkeeper at the Wright and Fransworth store, was clerk and to save time had a list of the witnesses and headed all the papers with 'So and so being sworn deposeth and saith, etc.' When it came to Louis Bousman... brought to the bar and told to tell all he knew... he did and a lot more. Being a prisoner he should not have been sworn, but told the evidence he gave would be used against him in the trial. But I had forgotten some things, as when a lawyer for the defense asked me if I had sworn him (Bousman) I could not remember and the evidence was thrown out, it was so contradictory. He made two opposite statements, and could not be believed.

Two indisputable facts stood out: Ed King had been shot down without a chance to draw his gun, and Jesse Sheets had not been a participant.

Mrs. McAllister continued:

All that Sunday hammers and saws were busy. Lumber from an old barn was taken down, planed, and fitted together to make four coffins. Mr. McAllister and I saw to it that they were padded smooth and soft, and lined with white cloth. Mr. McMasters opened his store [and] we went down and bought three black suits, the best he had. We got everything nice, including white shirts. After the bodies were dressed and placed in the coffins, the LS cowboys watched over them until time for the burial service.

When poor Mrs. Sheets learned that four graves were being dug side by side on Boot Hill, she requested that her husband not be buried alongside the gunmen. Jesse's grave was dug some distance from those that were to hold King, Valley, and Chilton.

Monday morning the three coffins were placed in a wagon and driven up the stony hill. The McAllister buckboard, with Dobbs and Chambers riding on either side, followed the wagon. More than seventy LS cowboys, riding two and two, came next, with Tascosa citizens and other friends bringing up the rear. H. H. Wallace, selecting an old Anglican version of the Twenty-third Psalm, began the service with: "The Lord is my shepherd; therefore can I lack nothing. He shall feed me in a green pasture, and lead me forth beside the waters of comfort." Afterwards he read the Episcopal Service for the Dead. As he uttered the awesome words, "Dust to dust," C. B. Vivian stooped and gathered loose dirt to throw on the coffin lids. A group of ladies closed the service with two hymns. As the strains of "Rock of Ages" died away, the Sheets cortage arrived, and many of the people moved from the cowboys' graves to pay their respects to Jesse.

Mrs. McAllister concluded:

There was still a difficult task for me, however. I always got the home address of every man who worked for the LS. Ed King, Fred Chilton, a native Texan, and Frank Valley, whose home was in Missouri. Writing letters to the families of those boys was the hardest thing I ever did. We sent their saddles and all their things home, too. . . . received three letters in a short while thanking us for what we had done. It was a long time before the pall lifted from the ranch.

The Oldham grand jury indicted Woodruff, Emory, and the Catfish Kid for the murder of Ed King; Bousman turned state's evidence; Lang was indicted for complicity in the slaying of Jesse Sheets; and the cases were removed to Donley County for trial. For defense of his friends Jess Jenkins secured the services of his attorney brother Charles, of Austin, who had earned a considerable reputation as one of the lawyers who defended the notorious John Wesley Hardin at Comanche in 1878 for the killing of Deputy Sheriff Charley Webb, of Brown County. Charles Jenkins's skillful handling of the cases at Clarendon in July, 1886, resulted in a hung jury, and the retrials were transferred to Wheeler.

By the time district court sat at Mobeetie in November, the important witnesses, including Sally Emory, had left the state. Only Lang appeared for the prosecution. Woodruff was unable to make the trip from the Tascosa jail. His doctor pronounced that to take him would risk his life and that longer confinement in his present condition would be fatal for the prisoner.

This occasioned a postponement, and Woodruff, Emory, and the Kid were granted bail.

Meanwhile Johnny Lang, supported by the LS owners and defended by Temple Houston, stood trial to clear himself of any wrongdoing. Temple maintained the accusation was unjust, that the indictment, besides charging his client as an accessory, must charge the principal (the deceased Valley) with the offense committed, and the complicity of an accessory, under the Texas code, must occur after the commission of an offense.

"My client," Houston thundered, "was *forced* to join the fight in an attempt to apprehend parties who had shot down a friend. He arrived at the back of the saloon only after Jesse Sheets had been slain."

The jury acquitted Lang. He soon left the Panhandle and settled in Oregon, where he later served several terms in the state legislature and enjoyed a successful life.

Following Lang's departure the cases of Emory and the Catfish Kid were dismissed. They returned to the gambling dives of Tascosa, where Catfish murdered and robbed an inoffensive old German from Springer, New Mexico, who was sleeping in a wagonyard. Catfish was convicted and sentenced to sixteen years in the penitentiary at Huntsville. He died there before his term expired.

Woodruff stood trial alone for the King murder. Houston aided District Attorney Woodman in the prosecution; Jenkins and L. D. Miller defended. With Louis Bousman's contradictory statements the only evidence, the trial soon reached the wrangling state. There were several bitter clashes between the prosecution and the defense, and also with Judge Willis. Woodman was charged with carrying a pistol, and he and Miller were fined twenty-five dollars for using abusive language toward, against, and concerning each other, each of them guilty of contempt of court. Miller apologized and his fine was set aside. Woodman offered no regrets; he had twenty-five dollars. He went free.

Charles Francis Rudolph, editor of the *Tascosa Pioneer*,

reported the proceedings. He had also covered the earlier trials at Clarendon and Mobeetie. On June 12, three weeks before the cases began in Donley County, the first issue of the newspaper appeared to tip its beaver to the good people of the great Texas Panhandle and empire of free grass.

Rudolph had come to Texas from Ohio in 1882 to publish a weekly paper at Saint Jo, Montague County. By 1885 it had become a successful daily. But the stories of the Panhandle began to fire his imagination, and anticipating the development that the proposed new extension of the Fort Worth and Denver City railroad would bring, the twenty-seven-year-old editor moved his publishing business to Tascosa.

In the initial issue he introduced his editorial policies in forthright terms:

> We are not here expecting to paw up the earth, to stir up young cyclones, nor to obliterate old landmarks that were here ahead of us, but simply... to publish a paper that shall be democratic so far as its politics goes, or in its criticisms liberal and considerate enough toward all men and all business; and to all labor for the good of the best town of its size on the continent.

He had launched two crusades: to bring the railroad into Tascosa and to build a wagon bridge across the Canadian River to give access to the rapidly developing country to the south. While having no hostility for any lawful interest or industry, he had gone on record as championing the idea that, although livestock interests in the Panhandle far outshadowed every other pursuit and should be fostered, the farm would eventually and inevitably crowd the ranches of Northwest Texas.

Like most frontier editors, Rudolph was not one to sit on the fence while others took sides. For instance, he was unalterably opposed to the Prohibition movement and said so often. Nothing pleased him more than to be presented a bottle of good whiskey by one of the local saloonkeepers. He was noted for his marvelous ability to consume the liquid flame and for a lingual deficiency that some termed a lisp.

Following Woodruff's acquital, and according to the custom

of the day, he retired with Temple Houston and the other lawyers and officials to a local saloon to drink and play whatever game attracted them. As the evening wore on, Temple saw companion after companion succumb to fatigue and slip off to bed. The only person to stay with him was the editor of the Tascosa newspaper.

Sometime after midnight, when the saloon was practically deserted, the pair grew hungry. Sitting down at a table, they ordered some crackers and tin-can delicacies from the saloon pantry. After feasting a while, still in an expansive mood, they began to discuss their favorites.

The editor casually remarked, "Houston, this swimp is pretty good."

"That's not 'swimp'; it's 'shrimp,'" replied the senator, ever meticulous in enunciation.

Slowly the editor's hand came from under the table, and Temple stared into the depths of his steely eyes and the cold round bore of a six-shooter. "By God, I say it's 'swimp,'" the editor pugnaciously asserted.

"And by God, I say it's 'swimp,' too," Temple hastily conceded, and the incident was closed with another round of drinks.

Shortly after Christmas, Temple hurried to Austin for the January, 1887, session of the Texas Legislature, where Charles Goodnight and Judge Frank Willis were in serious trouble.

9

The "Grass-Lease" Fight

Goodnight's difficulty stemmed from the legislative act of 1883 creating the state land board and providing for competitive leasing of school sections at not less than four cents an acre. Each range, whether owned in fee or still part of the public domain, was held by the cattlemen by mutual good will and understanding. Infringement on another's grazing area was tantamount to war and rarely practiced. Hence when the board advertised for bids, no rancher tried to lease range from under his neighbor but merely applied for the area he already controlled at the minumum rate prescribed by law.

The Land Board—composed of the governor, the attorney general, the comptroller, the treasurer, and the commissioner of the general land office—held that such applications ignored the competitive intent of the land act. Influenced somewhat by the growing conviction in the older part of the state that the cowmen were becoming wealthy from the public domain, and because the colonization-minded legislature began to support the farmers' efforts to wrest the grasslands from the cattle operators, the board refused the cowmen's tender of four cents and arbitrarily resolved to lease no more land for less than eight cents an acre.

Many of the cowmen, caught on the verge of a depression by the backwash of the boom in the cattle business and struggling under high interest levies and tremendous outlays for fencing to establish permanent ranches, were unable to pay the doubled rate. Some did not bid at all, but most of those in the eastern Panhandle joined Goodnight in sending Temple Houston to Austin to maintain their original tenders of lease.

The land board continued to refuse, declared the cowmen

trespassers, and proposed that the state send the Rangers to tear down the fences. Governor Ireland, uncertain of his constitutional authority, demurred but intimated that if the county sheriffs took no action he would order out the military. The cowmen stood their ground and threatened action against the board for revising, without legislative authority, provisions of the act it was created to administer.

In December, 1885, Attorney General Templeton notified District Attorney Woodman to bring suits against the cowmen for "unlawful fencing and herding on public lands," adding:

It might be necessary to resort to extraordinary means in some cases to hunt up evidence.... Send someone, not as a spy or detective, but openly, for the purpose of seeing and ascertaining that there is an illegal enclosure or that there is line riding so that he can go back and testify before the jury to that fact.

He also thought that "the Land Board, and perhaps the Governor, would take steps to furnish the assistance."

At the same time Templeton wrote Judge Willis that, "though the validity of the law has been gravely questioned," if a conviction could be had in the lower court, "the court of appeals will sustain it." He also pointed out that "a question of such gravity should be left to the court of final resort." Willis did not answer.

Templeton forced the issue, and in January, 1886, Woodman asked the grand jury convened at Clarendon for indictments, saying, "The state will have them whether or no." Determined to have the law clarified, the jury, composed mostly of cowmen with Goodnight as foreman, found seven true bills against Goodnight and sixty-nine more against the Rocking Chair, Rowe Brothers, J. F. Evans and Company, Clarendon Land and Investment Company, Hansford Land and Cattle Company, American Pastoral Company, S. R. E. Land and Cattle Company, Cedar Valley Land and Cattle Company, Glidden and Sanborn, Lee and Scott, the Prairie, and others that had done fencing on a total of about three and a half million acres. Nine of the twelve jurors, like Goodnight, indicted themselves. After the clerk spent several days writing up the bills, Goodnight brought them to court in a basket, and the jury was discharged.

Meanwhile, Grass Commissioner W. T. Gass dashed about the country compiling evidence and contending that the cowmen's tender of lease money had been made for the purpose of giving them a supposed favorable standing in the courts. At the same time Goodnight sought opinions from Congressman Throckmorton of McKinney; Silas Hare, former criminal judge of the district of Dallas, Collin, and Grayson counties; and William M. ("Buck") Walton, Confederate Army colonel and former attorney general of Texas who was then practicing law at Austin and promoting his recently published book, *Life and Adventures of Ben Thompson, the Famous Texan*. Announcement of the unofficial opinions of this counsel that the land board's action was insupportable by law caused Governor Ireland to suggest that they reduce the lease to four cents. Treasurer F. R. Lubbock and the comptroller remained undaunted, however, and felt that they should go forward with Templeton in court at Clarendon.

Goodnight employed for his defense Thomas Jefferson Brown, a prominent Sherman attorney, soon to represent his district in the legislature. Brown suggested that Goodnight also retain Colonel Grigsby and Representative Jim Browning (despite the latter's standing with the Panhandle nesters), and the cowman deferred to his wishes. Owing to the scarcity of qualified residents the trial jury was made up mostly of cowboys in the employ of the men indicted. This situation upset Attorney General Templeton. Immediately upon arriving at Clarendon, he sat down on a convenient log with Goodnight to discuss the impending litigation. Apparently Templeton was more interested in political support for his friend Jim Browning, who was aspiring to the office of district judge, for he offered to drop the fight if Goodnight would back Browning against Willis. As Goodnight thought of the fifty-two cowmen involved in the fight with him, the "tender of exception" made his blood boil. He said bitingly: "I know nothing about law, but I do know if I have committed a crime you can't remit it. Now I have two guns, you have none—an outlaw comes up here and shoots you down and I just sit here. What does it mean for me?"

"It would make you an accessory to the crime," answered Templeton.

"You're mighty right—and if I compromise with you, I have incriminated fifty-two men who have disobeyed no law. Four cents was the minimum."

"Then there is no hope of compromise?" asked the attorney general.

"Not a damned bit!" snorted Goodnight. "I'd see you in hell first, farther than a wedge would fall in twenty years." And the conference ended.

According to the *Clarendon Northwest Texan* of January 25, the Goodnight cases were "ably prosecuted by the eloquent W. H. Woodman" and defended "ably, exhaustively, and successfully" by Brown, Browning, and Grigsby. The attorneys contended that the defendant had bid four cents for the enclosed lands, the leases had been awarded by the county surveyors designated by the land board to receive bids for both sale and lease of public domain, and the lessee had tendered the money and had kept up such tender yearly. Judge Willis ruled that if this was found true the jury should render a verdict of not guilty, and the jury did, forthwith.

Woodman, though fully appreciating the amusing situation, took occasion to excoriate the jurors individually, saying that he could have expected no more from a bunch of cowboys. After the trial, when the jurors rigged one of their members to whip him for this seeming injustice, Woodman laughed him down, asking if he did not know that it was all for the benefit of the attorney general.

Case followed case without a single conviction of a cowman. Finally Judge Willis, citing as his reason that every case on the docket was so similar that acquittal was inevitable and that there was no need in further wasting state funds, dismissed the remaining suits.

This infuriated Templeton. In his biennial report of 1885–86 he stated, erroneously, that the Panhandle country is hostile to the idea of paying for the use of lands. The sentiment controls in the election of the officers. . . . it goes with the juries into the jury box, it is present with the grand jurors in their deliberation, and while the judge may preside over the court, this sentiment presides over the judge.

A grand jury finding bills against itself and cowmen being tried by their own cowboys he labeled a "ridiculous spectacle," and he charged "intimidation of court, incompetency on the bench, and collusion between the accused and those sitting in judgment."

Here was vindication for the land board's arbitrary action. Willis's political fortune was at stake. Templeton hoped to dispose of him through the combined support of the beleaguered administration and the considerable free-grass element around Mobeetie and Tascosa who opposed the big cowmen and had petitioned the legislature against leasing.

Goodnight rode to Mobeetie and asked Browning not to make the political fight an issue. He was hardly diplomatic. He accused Browning of charging him three times more for his counsel at Clarendon than the distinguished Thomas Jefferson Brown, who had traveled all the way from Sherman, and, despite acceptance of the cowman's fees, Browning's sympathies remained with the other side.

Goodnight swore out a mandamus to force the state's agent to accept his tender of lease at Clarendon, but the official departed in the night without having the writ served. Browning was employed by the state to assist against Goodnight in a similar mandamus proceeding at Colorado City. On May 5 he and Templeton secured a temporary injunction enjoining Goodnight from line riding and maintaining his original fence on JA lands, but it was discharged in July, and Goodnight was awarded costs against the state. Templeton and Browning excepted to Judge Willis's action and appealed to the state supreme court.

Goodnight went to the board at Austin and offered to take all school lands in his range at four cents from the date of his application in 1884. Lease tenders were made in cash, so he and W. B. Munson, of the T Anchor, with Attorney Buck Walton, went to Colonel George W. Brackenridge's bank and drew $72,000 for the JA and the amount owed by the Munson firm. Loading more than $100,000 in a wheelbarrow, they strapped on their six-shooters and marched up Congress Avenue to the land office. Treasurer Lubbock refused to accept the money, but when Walton (a fiery warrior who mixed his law with a judicious amount of liquor) thrust a receipt under his nose, he obligingly signed it. The cowman then returned to the bank and paid $175 for use of the money.

Browning decided not to run for district judge, but Colonel Grigsby entered the race. Goodnight supported Willis. So did Sheriff Arrington. Both Grigsby and Arrington were rabid southerners—Grigsby a Quantrill man, Arrington one of Mosby's guerrillas. Grigsby rebuked the sheriff for supporting a damned Yankee. To add insult to injury, Arrington made a list of Yankees and prohibitionists in the district, telling the first that Grigsby was a rank rebel and the latter that he loved his whiskey. It was not an impressive block of votes, but it was sufficient to return Willis to office.

Most state officials connected with administration of the public domain were defeated in the 1886 election. Lawrence Sullivan ("Sul") Ross, a popular hero with almost legendary experiences as an Indian fighter and a Confederate veteran, became governor, taking office on January 18, 1887. James Stephen Hogg, a crusading editor at Quitman and Longview who had gained statewide fame for his fights against railroad subsidies, lawlessness, and corruption in the state and national government and had served as Wood county attorney from 1878 to 1880, was elected attorney general. Hogg inherited from Templeton the fight with Willis and Goodnight.

On January 21, Willis appeared before the legislature, requesting an investigation into the truth and justification of the charges against him in Templeton's report. And Goodnight, in the *Galveston News* of January 24, flouted Templeton's assertion that a fourth of all school lands were in the Panhandle, paying no lease:

> I would like to know why something is not said about the other three-fourths not leased. ... it is singular that one-fourth in the Panhandle creates so much concern. If the board had allowed the law to stand, the Panhandle would have paid a 3 years lease by this time. At least 4,000,000 acres were applied for and wanted, and tender of rent money made. The board refused $160,000 per annum, or about $500,000, and the Democratic party holding them to account for the loss, turned them out of office. Now they want to make a scapegoat of the Panhandle cattlemen and a victim of... the district judge.

By early February, a special committee was considering impeachment of Willis. Goodnight sent Buck Walton to appear before it. Walton read a letter Willis had received from Silas Hare at Sherman, stating that Grass Commissioner Gass, who had been instrumental in bringing the charges, had told him that there was little basis for them but that he was going to the Panhandle and hunt up proof to show that Judge Willis was in collusion with Goodnight. Walton requested that Gass be called and dealt with; Attorney General Hogg agreed, but he was for vigorous prosecution of the charges against Willis.

Willis knew that Representative Browning was hostile to him, and he was uncertain what Temple Houston's attitude might be in the senate. Without the backing of the Panhandle's own representatives, he felt that he would be slaughtered, and he entreated Browning and Houston.

Temple told him that he would ask to be excused from voting. Browning agreed to take a neutral ground, but he warned Willis that there were only a few lawyers in the house, the balance were grangers, and he stood about as much show as a stump-tailed bull in fly time.

As the investigation moved forward, Goodnight, Woodman, Arrington, Cape Willingham, O. H. Nelson of the Bar Ninety-Six bull ranch on Red River, and other prominent men appeared in defense. County Judge H. H. Wallace testified for the state that while Willis's conduct of his court was always regular, dignified, and eminently proper in its sittings at Tascosa, he was considered a partial judge. Jess Jenkins said that it was the belief among Tascosa's working class and his friends in suburban Hogtown that Willis leaned toward the big cattlemen. Much was also made of a barrel of whiskey that Bruce McClelland, Clarendon's stuttering surveyor, kept in his office, and Hogg elicited an admission that all the court officers had found solace there during the trials. McClelland addes, "Y-y-y-ee-s s-s-i-r. A-a-n-d-d t-the A-a-ttorney G-g-g-en-r-ral———"

"Stop, sir!" shouted Hogg.

"... d-d-rank mo-more th-than an-anybody!"

The committee room roared. After McClelland left the stand, he told Goodnight, "I-I-d of c-c-amped th-there t-t-ill spring, or g-g-ot it out."

On February 18, the attorney general arraigned Willis before the committee on two counts: his conduct and actions were collusive, fraudulent, and farcical; they were "irregular and invalid as the defendants," but "estopped the State." If the judge was knowingly responsible, Hogg argued, then he was corrupt and impeachable for a high crime—if he did not know, then he was guilty of criminal negligence, an official misdemeanor. Buck Walton argued the defense; Hogg wound up in rebuttal with a scathing denouncement of Judge Willis as a man who should no longer disgrace the judicial ermine of Texas and vowed that if the legislature should fail to impeach he would prosecute corruption in office if it took every dollar in the state treasury.

Sentiment was against Willis and the cowmen. In East Texas, where granger votes were heavy, Goodnight was looked upon as usurper of the children's grass, a feudal baron, an arch bullionaire. And the *Galveston News* of February 18 predicted:

> If Mr. Willis ever gets into the Senate its goodby John. That body is composed of lawyers. They will have no mercy with carelessness, looseness or ignorance ... go its length toward putting the ermine

away from anyone's shoulders who doesn't wear it with grace. His hope is among the non-professional men in the House . . . who don't like quirks and quibbles in the administration of the law . . . but will insist that the bullionaire is not a lord. He is the victim of an unwise policy, which bearing the worst fruits, will continue to bear them till it is cursed out of existence—a policy of allowing a few men to organize a county and run it to suit their own convenience.

The committee drew up a statement of facts, formulated charges, and presented its report to the house. Again Buck Walton spoke in defense, the attorney general for the state. Upon conclusion of Hogg's speech—despite the minority report by two of the committee of five who found no fault with Judge Willis's administration of justice and recommended that he be fully exonerated—a resolution for impeachment was adopted sixty-seven to twenty-two. Browning, as promised, declined to vote. Although the vote lacked four of being the constitutional two-thirds required for impeachment, the resolution was declared passed.

According to the resolution Frank Willis had been district judge for six years, with 6,156, 549 acres of public domain in his jurisdiction, about 1,300,000 of these unlawfully enclosed and occupied by cowmen who owed the state $.04 an acre, or $123,353. The Panhandle Stock Association, composed mostly of men unlawfully occupying these lands, had employed the sheriff of Donley at $1,000 and District Attorney Woodman at $1,500 a year as a bonus over and above their legal fees of office. Goodnight and other cowmen sat on the Clarendon grand jury in January, 1886, and several of the petit jurors were Goodnight employees—not only partial but parties to the violations. This jury remained practically unchanged in fifty-six trials that took place in four days and returned a verdict of not guilty and a judgment in full and due form in each case. The judge was tampered with in his charge to the jury, and some of the defendants were tried and acquitted in one day without their knowledge or even presence. Willis knew of the salaries paid the sheriff and attorney and made no effort to suspend these unusual proceedings unprecedented in form, farcical in effect, and subserving the interests of the cattlemen who were violating the law.

On the basis of these findings Willis was charged as having been guilty of criminal neglect and oppressive in office and, by reason of influence wielded over him by the cattlemen and corporations, of having willfully obstructed and prevented the state of Texas from collecting the just revenues due. He was now in the senate for trial, and, as the *Galveston News* of February 18 had predicted, it looked like "goodby John."

The trial began on March 14. Defending himself, Willis, in a general demurrer, asked for dismissal of the charges on the constitutional grounds of a two-thirds vote. The house proceedings were ruled legal and right, the demurrer refused, and additional testimony taken.

The trials of the absent defendants, Willis explained, had proceeded upon agreement of counsel; it had never been his policy on the frontier to require a defendant's presence in misdemeanor cases. As for not changing venue and suppressing the "farcical" proceedings, he knew of no law by which a judge could, on his own motion, change venue in misdemeanor cases or suppress a trial where both parties were demanding it.

The most bitter points of contention—and those upon which the state primarily rested its hopes of impeachment—were the subsidization of public officials and the reason why Willis had permitted a grand jury to indict itself and a partisan petit jury to try the defendants at law. Addressing himself to the latter, Willis replied that the scarcity of property holders in the Panhandle made it almost impossible to draw a jury without stretching the statutory requirements. He related how, in 1884, when thirty men were charged with cattle rustling at Tascosa, a qualified panel could not be found to try them. County Attorney J. G. Murdock testified that, had the cowboys been removed, a jury could not have been formed in Donley or its attached counties for the trials at Clarendon. Of a possible sixty qualified jurors in the district, twelve were on the grand jury, eighteen on the petit panel, and the others scattered over 10,000 square miles of territory lacking railroad, telegraph, and telephone. The alleged collusion among court, counsel, jury, and offenders did not exist, nor did the not-guilty verdicts give the offenders, as the state claimed, a "favorable standing in the courts of higher resort." The former attorney general, not the cowmen, had forced the issue that resulted in acquittals, and it was Templeton, playing politics, who had raised a "stink" to befoul the cowmen and their courts and thereby divert the real issue with the land board from public scrutiny.

Turning to the subsidization of public officials, Hogg placed upon the stand a member of the house committee who had heard O. H. Nelson also testify that Temple Houston, during his term as district attorney at Mobeetie, had demanded and received the sum of six hundred dollars from the Panhandle Stock Association as a bonus above the fees of office. Temple, remaining aloof from the fight until now, took umbrage at this statement. He arose to claim "that chastity of honor which feels a stain like a wound," and asserted that the six hundred dollars was an independent fee.

Then he thundered:

I will not stand upon this floor and in this high presence, and bend my privileges to the abuse of any man, but I say, sir, that anything contrary to what I have said, is utterly, unspeakably and abominably false... and he who feels himself wronged may right himself how and where he chooses. I hold myself personally responsible wherever I may be, either in or on the outside of this hall. Less than this I should not speak; more than this I could not say.

Colonel B. B. Groom, an English rancher from Carson County who was present and heard the challenge, left the hall in a sweat. Knowing Houston's reputation as a fire-eater, he rushed to the Driskill Hotel and sought out Nelson.

"O. H.," he exclaimed, "you had better run up to Fort Worth for a day or two!" and told him of Temple's statement.

That evening Nelson met the senator in the hotel lobby. "I hear we are going to have to fight it out," the cowman said.

Houston asked him to explain. Nelson did, and the genial

orator replied: "Hell, I had to say something. Let's go get a drink."

Subsidization of public officials was common practice. The Panhandle Stock Association had learned as early as its formation that men of integrity and competence could not be expected to serve for the pittance returned in salaries and fees. Browning had resigned as the first district attorney because the office would not support him. Temple Houston had resigned to run for the legislature for the same reason. Arrington of Mobeetie and Sheriff Al Gentry of Clarendon had stood for re-election in 1884 only on assurances of $500 and $1,500 bonuses from the cowmen. Woodman had been induced to run against Dills for district attorney after being assured of a $1,500 bonus, which he received for a year and a half but which was suspended a few months before the Clarendon trials. Willful corruption? Only an attempt to meet the complexities of social order on a cattle frontier.

In the slow, drawling tone so characteristic of him, Willis made his final plea to the jury of state senators:

If I had refused to try the (Goodnight) case, ignoring the law.... I would have been accused of collusion with a large ranch man to liberate him without trial and to defraud the state of a trial of the issue and of the rental value of the school land, and let the criminal go free by my own judgment instead of leaving it to the jury. It is true that Goodnight's men were on the jury; county officers were forced to take them or else have no jury at all. Now when I came to trial, what should I do? I defy this Honorable Body and the law officers of the state to show me some law that would have authorized me to prorogue and dismiss those juries as a dictator, to step off the bench and issue an ukase depriving the county of a term of court which the law said that it should have.... The charge that these land fraud cases should not have been tried in Donley County at all... is a misconception... since there is fundamentally no jurisdiction in any other county other than the one where the charge is preferred.

Now in the presence of God and this Honorable Body I declare that "Thus saith the Law" governed me in every action I took, and the environment under which I worked and sparse population of the country left me no other course.... I ask no pity and seek no mercy, but I do ask... under the principle of cold law and facts... that this stain on my reputation be wiped out by not only an acquittal but a complete vindication.

The *Galveston News* thought the judge's legal argument "very ingenuous and forcible." Clarendon citizens, in a memorial to the legislature, charged that the trial was "instituted through jealousy and spite." Judge F. M. Patton, in a statement through the *Mobeetie Panhandle* picked up by the *Austin Statesman*, claimed Willis's vindication by the people in the last election. Old Bill Koogle, of the Half Circle K, issued a stinging protest against Browning's

great injustice to the Panhandle people—not for what he has said, but for what he has not said.... He could do Judge Willis a great deal of good by breaking down the uncalled for prejudice that exists against him and the cattlemen... but he dare not and cannot say anything that will not favor him (self).

Others demanded that "Senator Houston come out and either uphold or bemean Willis.... Give justice, is all we ask."

Houston, touched at last, told his fellow legislators, "The Judge has no appeal from your decision; I urge the necessity, therefore, for a calm and impartial verdict." On April 2 the senate voted twenty-two to five for acquittal.

Willis happily left Austin for the sunny, dry ranges of the Panhandle, where Mobeetie received him with a brass band and open arms. More than a hundred people paraded the street with banners and placards held high, the most notable of which bore the painting of a stump-tailed longhorn bull with the appropriate legend "Browning's Cow." All the saloons opened their doors extrawide, torches burned all night, and there was truly a hot time in the old town.

The supreme court decided the Templeton-Browning appeal of May, 1885, in Goodnight's favor, and the old cowman zeroed in on Browning and Houston's land bills in the legislature. Browning proposed to abolish leasing, sell school and asylum lands to settlers at two dollars an acre for dry sections and three dollars an acre for watered sections, and give thirty years to pay. His bill was in house committee. Temple proposed throwing the country back into open range and making the maintenance of existing unauthorized enclosures a penal offense subject to fine and imprisonment. His bill, reported out of the senate judiciary committee as "the most perfect free grass measure ever introduced," showed every indication of passage.

Mass meetings denouncing both bills were held throughout western Texas. Already the depreciation in cattle and land values was estimated at $100 million, one-fifth of which was on the tax rolls. Further depreciation would result in ranges where alternate sections were state owned. No lands would be leased that could not be fenced for exclusive use of the lessee. Even the settlers realized that the big cattlemen would continue using the range to the exclusion of others if fences were removed.

The *Austin Statesman* reminded its readers that "Senator Houston is a free-grasser, pledged and elected by a free grass constituency in a free grass district, and it does not require a microscopic view to detect the hidden intent of his bill."

Goodnight knew that the legislature was not interested in hidden intent and that, without fences, the Canadian drifts of thousands of cattle would eat out his ranges every winter. He again appealed to Buck Walton. Walton knew of a man who might stop it, but his services were not cheap. Goodnight told Walton to bring him to Austin posthaste.

The next morning George Clark, a big, heavy-set man, strode into the office. An Alabaman who had risen to the rank of lieutenant colonel in the Civil War, Clark had moved to Texas in 1867, settling first at Weatherford and then at Waco, where he became a prominent member of the state Democratic committee. He served as secretary of state under Governor Richard Coke, became attorney general in 1874, and from 1876 to 1878 served on a commission to revise the Penal Code and Code of Criminal Procedure of Texas. After serving as judge on the Texas Court of Appeals in 1879–80, he had resumed private practice at Waco and was an outstanding railroad attorney.

Clark offered to lobby for five thousand dollars, and Goodnight agreed to pay his price to kill Temple Houston's bill.

Clark left for the capitol. Goodnight hung around Austin for nearly two weeks, hearing nothing of the bill until Clark came back to Walton's office and reported that he had killed it. Asked by Goodnight how it had been accomplished, the big lawyer relaxed in a chair and explained: "First, I got the bill tabled, then went around to them old corn-cob pipe fellows from down in East Texas and asked, 'What are you going to do with Goodnight's enclosure bill?' 'Goodnight's bill?' they would say, 'that's Temple Houston's bill. Why, Houston and Goodnight don't even speak.'

"'Why should they speak?' I would ask. 'Don't you know Houston is working for Goodnight, and that that rascal wants this law passed because he wants free grass?'

"'Oh,' the old corn-cobber would say, 'is that so?'

"'Of course, it's so! Aren't you a hell of a fine feller to be up here trying to serve the state.'"

His suggestion and simulated sarcasm had its effect. "When the bill came to a vote," Clark concluded, "those old East Texas fellers jumped on it and just stomped hell out of it!"

Clark returned to Waco, the legislature went back to rehashing the lease question, and Goodnight went on record with other leading cowmen as favoring a ten-year lease system at a low rent so that lessees might be secure for a term and justify the expense of enclosing lands, destroying prairie dogs, building tanks, digging wells, erecting windmills, and making other necessary improvements.

But Houston pointed out—and most of the legislators agreed—that western Texas would be settled too quickly for a ten-year proposal. Already railroads were stabbing into the Panhandle from two directions; new towns were springing up, more counties were being organized, and the *Tascosa Pioneer*, *Mobeetie Panhandle*, and *Clarendon Texan* all "averred positively" that the lease law "is a blight on all business, a hindrance to settlement, an immovable barrier across the path of further development."

In April, chiefly through Temple's persuasive efforts, the legislature approved the Sales Act Amendment of 1887. This act proved acceptable to both nester and cowman—to the nester because it forced payment for grazing the public domain, to the cowman because it reduced the lease rate to the original four cents and allowed leasing of any land not previously filed on for a period of five years. The press diatribes continued, however, and the troubles of lease and fencing, perennially inspired by ambition and politics, would not work themselves out until the adoption several years later of the Four Sections Act, which allowed a maximum of four sections of school, asylum, and public lands in all Texas counties except El Paso, Pecos, and Presidio to be purchased or leased by settlers for crop planting and stock raising.

10
"Texas Stands Peerless amid the Mighty"

On January 25, 1887, before the investigation into the conduct of Judge Willis began, Temple delivered a stirring endorsement to the state Democratic party executive committee meeting at Austin. No attempt was made to regulate nominating procedures of political parties in Texas until 1895, and not until enactment of the Terrell Election Law in 1905 was a statewide direct-primary system established. All Texas congressmen and every governor since the overthrow of the hated Reconstruction governor Edmund J. Davis by Richard Coke in 1874 had been elected under the banner of the Democratic party. An executive committee, consisting mostly of senators from each senatorial district with a chairman usually named by the governor, handled party affairs between conventions. United States Senator Samuel Bell Maxey was ending his second term in Congress, and the committee was caucused to select a candidate for the upcoming term.

Behind Maxey lay a long and colorful career. Graduating from West Point on July 1, 1846, he was immediately assigned to the Seventh Infantry as second lieutenant in the Mexican War. He was breveted first lieutenant for gallantry at Contreras and Churubusco, and commanded one of the companies composing the City Guard after the capture of Mexico City. Upon returning to the United States, he resigned his commission to enter law practice with his father at Albany, in his native Kentucky. He served as clerk for the circuit and county courts of Clinton County, married in 1853, and in 1857 moved to Paris, Texas, where he established a law practice and served two years as prosecuting attorney of Lamar County. He was elected to the Texas senate in 1861 but declined to serve, raising instead the Ninth Regiment, Texas Infantry, under General Albert Sidney Johnston at the outbreak of the Civil War. He participated in the battle at Port Hudson, the Big Black Campaign, and the siege of Jackson. From 1863 to 1865 he commanded the military district of Indian Territory, organizing three brigades of Creek, Cherokee, and Choctaw Indians; he gained their almost pathetic good will as no other Texan had done since the days of Sam Houston. He was superintendent of Indian Affairs until the surrender of the trans-Mississippi Department on May 26, 1865, having attained the rank of major general.

After the war Maxey returned to his law practice at Paris. In 1873 he was commissioned judge of the Eighth District of Texas, and in 1874, he was elected to the United States Senate. During his twelve years in Congress, Maxey, not unlike other members of the group known as the "Confederate Brigadiers," opposed the prevailing policy of protective tariffs and advocated economy, but he never failed to obtain appropriations for Texas harbors and rivers. He served on the post-office committee and did much toward developing Texas's postal system and establishing the stage route from Fort Worth to Yuma.

His most noteworthy efforts, however, were in the field of Indian relations. He was among the first to favor individual farms as the ultimate solution to the Indian problem, which rankled a great number of his constituents. Others, pointing out that he was sixty-two years old, thought two terms in Congress long enough, which rankled Temple Houston.

The chairman of the caucus declared nominations to be in order, but the senators seemed hesitant to make them, waiting for someone to break the ice. After several minutes had elapsed, Temple took the floor, and amid profound silence addressed the assemblage as follows:

> Mr. Chairman and Senators—For the fifth time since the chains of federal despotism fell from her peerless form Texas has come to claim her loftiest right, to name her choice for the national senate.
>
> For the third time Texas has risen to judge the worth of the great

"TEXAS STANDS PEERLESS AMID THE MIGHTY"

man whose name I have the honor to place before you.

Texas demands a man whose intellect is commensurate with the vast trust imposed upon him, whose name is a stranger to reproach.

To fulfill this high mission the man we send should unite every quality of worth and blend all the essentials of merit—proven by trial.

I will name such a man, great in mind and pure in spirit, whose truth has been tried where spears are tried—christened by the fires of two wars, and true to every trust. He first, as a youth of 21, fought the battles of his country, and at Contreras and Churubusco, beneath the eye of Winfield Scott, and beside Lee and Jackson, he was accounted spotless and brave, and was breveted on the battlefield. The Mexican War over, entering the legal profession, he removed to Texas, and when the clarion warned her to man her warriors he cast aside all civic honors and proved his devotion to Texas in the front of battle—a test the brave alone may bear. Those of his regiment, his brigade, his division, who have seen him stand amid the falling forms of her slain sons, will not here deny his love of Texas or his title to her glories, nor say that, worthy to lead her soldiers in battle, he should not speak her voice in the councils of the nation.

While the black pall of Reconstruction darkened o'er the land, and the shadow of deep grief filled the hearts of her sons, this man did not despair. The great enemies of the South were entrenched in the Capitol, and the while he, almost unaided and alone—for the South had few voices there and then—rising to the full height of a saviour of Texas and speaking for her and Southern sisters, beat back the Xerxes hosts of oppression and sectional hate.

He was among the earliest to raise his protests against all forms of governmental extravagance. When he entered the federal senate there was gathered the brightest constellation of genius and talent within the Republican party, and, although almost the only senator from a disenthralled state, in a hopeless minority and beleaguered by the myrmidons of hate, the man of whom I speak did not quail. He had fought for his country's rights on the greens of Chapultepec and with the same courage he battled for them in the arena of the national senate. At battle's close his sword knew no stain, and now a free South and a united nation answer his trusts.

Ne'er did knightliest crusader on the far sands of the Orient bare his bright blade, or place his good lance in rest with deeper favor or holier faith than has this man fought the battle of Texas.

I mean Sam Bell Maxey!

In weighing him the third time in the balance, why should he be found wanting now, and never before? What reason is given? Is a single vote of his objectionable?
No!
Has he, of all the thousand trusts confided to him, neglected one?
No!
Is he in anywise unworthy?
No!
Reason should hang her head in shame at the suggestion proferred. Because he has had two terms!

The very cause which enhances his fitness is quoted for his disparagement. Whoever before heard of experience impairing, or of success disqualifying, a public servant? What encouragement will you give, then, to the youth for a faithful performance of duty? To heed this objection would be Athenian ingratitude and sacrilege which I hope will never sully the fair name of Texas!

Were such a doctrine correct the victory of Fredericksburg would have removed Lee from Chancellorsville, whose crowning glories would not now beam around his brow, and Lord Nelson, because he won the Nile, would not have known Trafalgar and died amid the deep thunders of his mightiest victory!

After twelve years of toil General Maxey can say, as did the grandest Apostle: "I have kept the faith." No pledge violated, no promise broken, and his plighted troth as pure as when he gave it.

Call this man, the chief of her choice, and from her cities, villages and fields, from the east, where her pines, tall and dark, moan in the breath of the passing breeze, from the south, where snowflake never has fallen and the north wind chills not; from the rushing and radiant rivers of the west, from her long line of coast, where sounds forever the thunder of the sleepless deep, from her vast and silent plains, and from the virgin wilds of my own home, where the violet and wild rose bloom in the depth of her valleys, from yonder eternal mountains that saw the birth of light, whose brow has felt the kiss of every dawn and been bathed in the glories of all sunsets, Texas, with one glad acclaim will say: "Lo, ye have done well, for ye have chosen my worthiest!"

Temple's endorsement, described by the state press as a masterpiece of word painting, did much to move Maxey toward a third senatorial term. But the opposition pitted against him John Henninger Reagan, a native Tennessean and an early political enemy of Sam Houston.

Reagan had come to Texas in 1839, serving briefly in the Union Army in the Cherokee War and as deputy surveyor of public lands between Nacogdoches and Dallas from 1839 to 1843. He studied law, was admitted to the bar in 1846, and practiced at Buffalo and Palestine. He served in the Texas House of Representatives in 1847 and as district judge from 1852 to 1856, when he was elected as a Democrat to the Thirty-fifth Congress (convened on March 4, 1857). He was overwhelmingly reelected to the Thirty-sixth Congress (convened on March 4, 1859), despite the opposition of Sam Houston and leaders of the southern wing of the Democratic party who advocated reopening the African slave trade and acquiring territory in Cuba, Mexico, and Central America.

In 1861, Reagan represented the Secession Convention of Texas in the Provisional Congress of the Confederacy. He was appointed postmaster general of the Confederacy by Jefferson Davis on March 6, 1861, was reappointed in 1862, and served as acting secretary of the treasury of the Confederacy briefly preceding the close of the war, after which he was imprisoned for several months at Fort Warren in Boston harbor.

Returning to Palestine in December, 1865, he and James W. Throckmorton directed the formation and adoption of the short-lived Constitution of 1866. He was chairman of the judiciary committee of the Constitutional Convention of 1875, advocating enlarged jurisdiction of the lower courts, fewer officials, longer terms, and higher salaries. Although he failed in all these policies and lost ground with his Texas constituents, he again was elected to the Forty-fourth Congress (convened March 4, 1875), to five succeeding Congresses, and to the Fiftieth Congress, from which he resigned to become senator in 1887.

Sorely defeated by Reagan, General Maxey continued his law practice at Paris. He died at Eureka Springs, Arkansas, on August 16, 1895, and was buried at Paris in the Evergreen Cemetery.

Although Temple lost a few battles, his performance in the 1887 session of the legislature proved more than satisfactory to the voters of his district. He was considered a cinch for reelection; many encouraged him to run for a higher office. In 1882, Samuel Willis Tucker Lanham, a former school teacher at Clarksville and one of the state's leading attorneys, had been elected to Congress from the Eleventh District (called the "Jumbo" because it was composed of ninety-eight West Texas counties), and it was suggested that Temple "may be induced all in good time" to seek this "congressional prize."

"Should he do so, even a good man like Lanham will need to keep his fences in the finest possible trim," warned the *Tascosa Pioneer* of February 11, 1888. On February 18, it added, "Temple is one of the Panhandle's brainy men, one of Texas' brainy men, and when he enters the lists with armor full and visor closed and good lance in rest there's going to be somebody hurt, and some laurels fade." Browning's performance, on the other hand, had been somewhat less than gratifying. On December 3, 1887, the *Pioneer* asked:

> Mr. Browning, doesn't it begin to look as though you could afford to relent in the matter of the candidacy for a return to the legislature? You have observed the unanimity with which the press of the district calls for your discontinuance in service; and if the press voices the sentiment of the people, as it honestly tries to do and conscientiously believes it does, the constituency are of one mind in all quarters.

Browning, however, did not "relent." He again represented the Forty-third District when the Twenty-first legislature met in the spring of 1889, still opposing the large acreage leasing of school lands to stock raisers, serving as a member of committees on penitentiaries and irrigation and as chairman of the judiciary committee. He was lieutenant governor of Texas from 1898 until 1903, when he was appointed to the University of Texas Board of Regents. For the next sixteen years he practiced law at Amarillo. He died there on November 9, 1921, and was buried in the Llano cemetery.

The *Pioneer* of February 25, 1888, reported that "Temple Houston has announced over his signature that he is not and will not be an aspirant for Lanham's seat in Congress." In another issue the *Pioneer* told its readers why:

> Temple Houston ... has secured the position of attorney for the Santa Fe railroad company in Texas. This is something of a plum, itself.
> The probabilities are that he will not be a candidate for reelection to the position now held by him.

A greater opportunity was in the offing.

The old state capitol at Austin, built shortly after annexation, had been destroyed by fire on the afternoon of November 9, 1881, and Governor Roberts immediately called a special session of the legislature to provide temporary quarters for the state government and take steps toward erecting a new structure. A previous legislature had authorized a capitol board composed of the governor, comptroller, treasurer, attorney general, and land commissioner to dispose of three million acres of western Texas land at no less than fifty cents an acre to finance the building and to sell an additional fifty thousand acres at competitive bidding to meet incidental expenses such as "surveying said lands" and employment of an architect. No further action had been taken, and the fire transformed what had been until now an "expression of desire" into a necessity.

Mattheas Schnell, of Rock Island, Illinois, accepted the contract, receiving the 3,050,000 acres as compensation. He transferred it to Taylor, Babcock & Company of Chicago, which organized the Capitol Syndicate. In addition to Abner Taylor and his father-in-law Amos Babcock (an Illinois representative to Congress), John V. Farwell and his brother, Charles (a U.S. senator from Illinois), were the chief investors.

On the advice of Babcock the syndicate established the XIT Ranch in the double tier of Panhandle counties running from Dallam more than two hundred miles down the border of New Mexico to Cochran and Hockley, to use the land until it could be subdivided for agriculture after farmers moved into the Plains area. In order to secure money for stocking the ranch and meet the tremendous operating expenses, the syndicate formed an English corporation, the Capitol Freehold Land and Investment Company, Ltd., of London. John Farwell became ranch manager, and the capitol contract was turned over to Taylor as syndicate representative.

Elijah Myers, the architect, drew plans for a building modeled on the National Capitol, shaped like a Greek cross with projecting center and flanks and a rotunda at the intersection of the main corridors. The dimensions at greatest measure were 566½ feet long by 288 feet 10 inches wide, by 308 feet 4 inches high, the floor area covering 18 acres. Located on a commanding elevation near the center of Austin in the square originally selected for the capitol of the Republic of Texas, it would be constructed with a copper roof and dome and of red Texas granite throughout quarried and hauled seventy-five miles from Burnet County on a specially built railroad by five hundred convicts contracted to Taylor from the state's prisons.

Work on the building had continued during the two terms of Governor Ireland. Difficulties arose from the use of convicts in competition with free labor and the importation of sixty-five stonecutters from Scotland. Construction was delayed by the Granite Cutters strike and the filing of charges, at the behest of the Knights of Labor, in Federal District Court at Austin against the members of the Capitol Syndicate for violation of the Alien Contract Labor Law, passed in February, 1885. Judgment, finally rendered in August, 1887, made the contractor liable for fines totaling $64,000 and costs of approximately $1,000. He was granted twelve months' stay to seek relief in Washington. Following an inquiry by a committee of the House of Representatives and a plea to the president, his liability was reduced to the costs plus $8,000.

The phenomenal structure, second in size only to the National Capitol at Washington, D.C., and larger and finer than the German Reichstag or English Parliament buildings, was

Texas State Capitol at Austin. Houston gave the dedicatory oration on May 16, 1888. Courtesy of Western History Collections, University of Oklahoma Library, Norman.

completed in April, 1888, at a cost in materials and labor of $3,744,630.60. May 16 was the date set for officially opening it to the public. Temple Houston, "Old Sam's word-slinging son... who has become an important factor in the senate," was chosen to deliver the dedicatory oration.

An immense crowd jammed Austin the week of May 14 to 19 for the Great Military, Musical and Civic Celebration, which featured Gilmore's Famous Concerts, a baby contest, a rodeo, a fireworks display, a great sham battle with cannon and cavalry, and an interstate military-drill contest (won for the sixth consecutive time by the Houston Light Guard, which carried off the five thousand dollars first prize).

The *Houston Post* created a sensation on the drill grounds by distributing thousands of ballots that promised each visitor to its tent a beautiful Cape Jasmine bud and a copy of its imperial twenty-four page edition, besides allowing them to vote for their choice for United States senator. Former Governor Richard Coke of Waco, elected as a Democrat to the United States Senate in 1877 and reelected in 1883, was again a candidate for renomination.

It was an exciting period for otherwise quiet times. A dispatch from London printed in the *Austin Statesman* briefly noted that "the Russian military chiefs who recently assembled in St. Petersburg declared that Russia would not be in a position for a long time to attack European powers." In another item, from Berlin, Bismarck complained that he had been misquoted and believed that there was a chance for peace in Europe.

On the state scene Galveston millionaire William H. Willis "stumbled on some stairs while carrying a cocked pistol which went off and killed him." A dispatch from Gainesville under the headline "A Terrible Revenge" described how a young citizen had shot his wife and her boyfriend with a Winchester rifle and then "returned to his house where he traded his growing crops for a horse and saddle and left for parts unknown." And land agent Frank Lerch bought a full page in the *Statesman* to advertise Tom Green County, "the Garden Spot of Texas."

The dedication ceremonies took place on Wednesday. An estimated twenty thousand proud Texans filed through the new statehouse, peered from the windows, and swarmed over the grounds. The morning was sultry. Threatening black clouds were coming up in the southwest.

Governor Sul Ross and Attorney General Hogg stood on a special platform built in front of the great arched entrance, flanked by other members of the Capitol Board, the Farwells, Abner Taylor, and Senator Houston, with several members of the legislature and the Capitol Building Commission.

Governor Ross lauded the structure in detail, mentioning every fine point from the basement to the Texas Star shining inside the dome and the torch of liberty installed on its top glistering to the sky. There was a round of applause, and another when he introduced Houston.

The low rumble of thunder turned heads to observe the approaching storm. But every eye was on Temple as he stepped to the podium:

The greatest of states commissions me to say that she accepts this building, and... reason ordains a brief reference to the deeds and times that eventuate in this occasion....

Texas has changed the site of her government oftener than any other state in this union, or any nation on this side of the globe.... San Felipe, Washington, Harrisburg, Galveston, Velasco, Columbia, Houston, Austin, Washington a second time, Houston a second time, and Austin again.... The state today stands first in area, sixth in population, and seventh in taxable wealth among the sisterhood of states that comprise the American union. And when the tribes are numbered in 1890, she will stand third in population, fourth in wealth....

She has a history all her own, wild, romantic, heroic. Minstrel's lay never told of deeds more daring than her sons have wrought, nor ever in castle hall hath harp of bard hymned praise of purer faith than that her legends bear. Child of storms, the nursling of revolutions, the twilight of her history made her coil the battlefield of freedom, her children the crusaders of liberty.

Situated at a remote angle of the gulf, midway between the Aztec empire and the valley of the Mississippi, she for a while felt neither that spirit of Spanish conquest which laid in the dust at a blow the throne of Montezuma and the empire of the Incas, nor that gentle spirit of colonization which marked the footsteps of France and Britain upon this continent.

But this repose was brief. In 1522, shortly before the conquest of Mexico, the royal standard of Spain was unfurled upon Texas soil.

Calmly, with his usual "sententious clearness," Temple described the sweep of Pánfilo de Narváez and his glittering cavalry from the Río Grande to Mobile, the fierce quests of

DeSoto and Coronado; how Spanish ascendancy remained inactive until excited by jealousy of French encroachments, the landing of Robert Cavelier Sieur de La Salle upon Matagorda Bay; how fell the last hope of French dominion in Texas with La Salle's death at the hands of his followers in the unknown wilds of the Neches forests:

He, like the cavalier that he was, gave his life to his king and his God... but his efforts were not without their results.

The French attempt at colonization roused the activity of Spain. Grasping and ruthless as she was, Spain ever set religion's seal upon her conquests, and as soon as she had quenched the last spark of French settlement within the borders of Texas, she began the establishment of missions... about twenty... dotting the valleys of the San Antonio, the Nueces and the Guadalupe; also at Nacogdoches and on the San Saba.

The noble order of the church, the Franciscan fathers, reared these missions. Thou father, half priest, half knight, and all courage, lend a mingled air of piety and romance to the annals of Castilian conquest.

In those missions showed both the censor and the sword, the mitre and the helm, for those pious fathers in the spread of their Master's faith, dared the wilderness, but whosoever opposed their path felt the thrust of lance....

They came as conquerors. Nor did their name or deeds belie the martial name of their loveliest mission—San Juan de Espada.

Within the portals of those missions might dwell the saintliest abbot and the holiest men, but from these frowned Hispania's artillery, and at matins and vespers floated the melody of her bugles.

For more than one hundred years from the destruction of La Salle's colony until The Stars and Stripes rose above the Crescent city, upon the Purchase of Louisiana, these missions were the seats of Spanish power around which settlement clustered. Standing desolate yet beautiful, grand even in ruins, these old missions appeal to us with an eloquence beyond all words. They are the landmarks of a vanishing era, boundary stones of a receding empire. They are the monuments of the mistaken zeal of a powerful and pious order.

The extension of the limits of the United States to the Sabine caused the concentration of Spanish military forces upon that stream....

"TEXAS STANDS PEERLESS AMID THE MIGHTY"

The interval of fifteen years between the arrival of Stephen F. Austin and the independence of Texas is filled with events to which such brilliant and exhaustive reference has been made... that any allusion from me would but mar the delightful memory.

But I will advert to one feature of that period.

On March 1, 1836, the convention of the then province of Texas assembled at Washington on the Brazos. On the second day of its existence, that convention formulated a "Declaration of Texas Independence," which, in literary merit, challenges comparison with the finest productions of our language. That same body of men in fourteen days prepared the constitution of the Republic of Texas which remained for nine years, without a suggested amendment, the organic law of Texas.

It should not be forgotten that this constitution was framed amid an overwhelming invasion, that participation in the proceedings of that convention was threatened by death, and that those who drafted that constitution laid down their pens to grasp the sword; that it was indeed born amid clash of arms and rocked in the cradle of war.

The beneficence and perfection of its provisions, the rapidity with which it was prepared and the reverence with which it was obeyed, made the constitution of 1836 one of the evidences that the Anglo-Saxon race is capable of self-government. The men who devised that constitution were the apostles from Runnymede, they were the disciples of Jefferson, they were the evangelists of liberty, for, wherever that race breathes, on land or sea, oppression ceases instantly.

The principles which they proclaimed at Washington on the second of March, 1836, they, fifty days later, at San Jacinto, sealed with their blood.

A roar of applause arose from the capitol grounds. Temple flicked his coattails, as only he could do. His gray eyes snapped, and his flowing auburn hair dragged his shoulders as his head dropped forward like a charging buffalo:

It was the old conflict between Latin and Teuton. It had been fought between the armies of Arminius and Varus. It had been battled when the Armada was dispersed, and at Trafalgar and Waterloo, and fate had decreed that the Anglo-Saxon should triumph. . . .

When the last hour pealed, its sounds rang from a spot where the republic of Texas died and the State of Texas was born.

Another roar of applause.

Temple expressed the Texas people's indebtedness to the Farwells, Babcock, and Taylor:

... not only for the best state house in the United States, but more especially for bringing our public lands into world-wide notice by agreeing to build the house for three million acres set aside for that purpose.... The building has cost nearly three times fifty cents an acre, and is really worth more than five times that amount, if we are to measure its value by the cash cost of similar buildings in other states.

He congratulated the state and the Capitol Syndicate for demonstrating, "whatever may have been thought by critics," the wisdom of a contract that made it possible:

The state—because she has realized for these lands much more than she could have done under her land laws for their sale and got them under tax and ... at the same time secured the use for all time of this noble building, which probably would never have been built in any other way.

The syndicate—because they have obtained three million acres... which in due time will increase the wealth of the state by hundreds of millions of dollars, instead of leaving them for the free use of foreign cattle companies whose earnings would not have remained in Texas.

Temple then referred to the old state capitol, destroyed by fire, in which he had been born:

Let us not pass lightly by that old structure. Its halls knew so much of the grief and glory of Texas, so much of her splendor and her sorrow, and so often saw her destinies alternately flit between triumph and ruin.

Within the walls of that old capitol, whose buried foundations rest yonder, the government of Texas was administered for twenty-eight years. Beneath its roof were assembled thirteen legislatures and four constitutional conventions, and was framed our organic law.... It was there that the fair fruits of annexation withered beneath the simoon breath of war. Here, too, in frantic haste, was consummated the act which shattered the golden links welded by sixteen years of union, and hurled Texas into the vortex of secession.

And after Southern valor had wrecked itself against the might of the union, that same old capitol, on whose ruins many of this multitude stand, saw Reconstruction plait its crown of thorns around the weary brow of Texas and press the sponge of bitterness to her lips.

Yet that same old building saw the departed sceptre return to Judah when the Fourteenth Legislature calmly grasped the reins of power and submitted the constitution under which we live.

In the adoption of that constitution, you, the people, decreed the erection of the building which you today accept and dedicate to your use. It decrees eternal union. . . . Hereafter let no man seek to put asunder that which the fathers united. Let the fiends who wait upon the lost hiss their hate and shriek their curses in the ear of him who would plot the dismemberment of Texas!

His concluding remarks were typically Houston:

Texas stands peerless amid the mighty and her brow is crowned with bewildering magnificence!

This building fires the heart and excites the minds of all. It stands alone the haughtiest type of modern civilization. In other lands, the hand of man hath reared walls as stately as these and pierced the sky in prouder heights. The architecture of a civilization is its most enduring feature, and by this structure shall Texas transmit herself to posterity, for here science has done her utmost.

The quarry has given its granite and marble, the mines have yielded their brass and iron, and an empire has been passed as an equivalent for this house. All that enlightment and art could do has been done. Were I to repress the reflections that occur to me now, I would be untrue to my convictions and to this occasion. It would seem that here glitters a structure that shall stand as a sentinel of eternity, to gaze upon passing ages, and, surviving, shall mourn as each separate star expires.

Were we to feel thus, precedent would justify us. Those who builded the Pyramids thought the Egyptian empire eternal; those who reared the Colliseum boasted that it was a pledge that Rome was everlasting.

More solemn lessons are taught at our own doors. Great races have swept o'er this continent like waves o'er the bosom of the deep, and left traces almost as faint.

Who reared the Pyramids of Uxmal, the palaces of Palenque, the mausoleums of Mitla? The splendors of towered Tuloom? What is the date, the origin, the fate of those mysterious civilizations that have vanished forever in the forests of Mexico and Central America, and flee from the searcher like illusive lights that flash and fade above the silent tomb?

They were our predecessors. Shall oblivion fling her darkening pall over us? Ah! we are but one of that vast procession of races which it was decreed should pass across this hemisphere. We have no right to say that ours is the first or the last of those civilizations whose impress it was ordained this continent should feel.

More than once the world has lost and resumed civilization.

If our civilization possesses the elements of perpetuity, it differs from any of its predecessors. If the lessons of the past have not been taught in vain, they tell us that the future holds in hand an hour when the curious antiquarian shall wander through the roofless chambers amid the shattered arches and fallen columns of all this imperial magnificence, and ask when these walls reared—was this edifice palace or prison, tomb or temple?

Babel's marble columns are as proud as these, yet who chiseled them? Who carved the hieroglyphics that plead for interpretation from the sculptured walls of Palenque?

The past hath a fearful lesson of instability of earthly greatness. Men dwelt upon the earth thousands of years ere they ascertained its shape. They shed seas of blood before they learned that a drop of it circulated.

They proudly claim an existence of 6,000 years, yet their annals do not include half of it. They cannot explain their diversity in language or the secret of their existence. The destruction of public virtue caused the decline of other civilizations, but does our civilization carry with it the means of its perpetuation?

Under certain conditions it may. It possesses characteristics that mark none of its predecessors and particularly can this be said of the state of Texas.

The civilization of Texas, of which this proud capitol is one of the voices that shall speak to after ages, is beneficent. The form of our government is the creation of an expressed wish of the people whom it affects.

The officers are elected and are the servants, not rulers, of the people. We have no obligatory form of worship, our rights of free speech have no limitation; before our laws all men are equal; our government is a subject of criticism, not of hideous dread. Our armies and fleets are for the protection, not oppression, of the people. Our institutions enjoin an education of the masses, and assume that the government is not the heritage of one man....

Texas says to whomsoever casts his home within her benignant realms, she tenders her offspring an education without money and without price.... No matter what race may shame its origin, or what reproach clouds its birth, Texas pledges 35,000,000 fair acres at 12½ per cent of her taxable values, amounting to millions, that every child that asks it at her generous hands shall receive a free education.

The first government on earth to enact the homestead exemption in favor of the family, she stands preeminent in her beneficence to the helpless. Within sight of this structure are the grand charities which Texas bestows upon the blind, the deaf and dumb and the insane; she also has remembered the orphan and her statutes provide for the indigent.

All these would indicate a perpetuity of public virtue.

This noble edifice is a fit seat for such a government. It and the features of our civilization are all we can leave our posterity, and, even should they prove unworthy of our bequest, we can at least pass from life's stage with the proud reflection that we leave behind us a purer civilization and a nobler edifice than has been bequeathed to us by preceding ages.

At that moment a bolt of lightning rent the black clouds hanging above the capitol. A tremendous clap of thunder shook the earth, drowning completely the din of the standing ovation, and for several minutes rain drenched the throng and mingled with tears that rolled down the cheeks of many.

To these rough and sympathetic people Houston was a marvel. Newspapers proclaimed his speech "an able and worthy address from the worthy son of a most distinguished sire." The *Austin Statesman* carried it in full. Afterwards thousands of copies were separately printed and distributed throughout the state.

Temple attended the banquet that evening but was notably absent during the Grand Dedication Ball held in the House and Senate chambers and library of the capitol building that night. In a suite at the Driskell Hotel, he sat with some of Texas's most powerful "kingmakers." Already a move was afoot to place his name in nomination against Richard Coke for the Senate of the United States.

A man of conscience, Temple was not easily understood by political operatives to whom winners and losers were clearly defined. Among his fondest boyhood memories, and a subject much discussed in the Houston household, was the dramatic gubernatorial campaign of 1873, in which Richard Coke, former Confederate Army captain, district judge, and judge of the Texas Supreme Court, had defeated the hated provisional governor Edmund J. Davis to bring a political end to Reconstruction in Texas. More especially he recalled how Davis, even after defeat, had proclaimed the right to serve out his four-year term and the Texas Supreme Court held the election illegal because of alleged fraud and intimidation on both sides. Nevertheless, the Democrats had secured the keys to the capitol and took possession January 15, 1874, Coke and his armed guards on the second floor, Davis and his state troops on the first. The tense situation, near bloodshed, had lasted through January 17, when President Ulysses S. Grant, despite Davis' pleas, refused to declare him reelected and sent a telegram stating that he did not feel warranted in sending federal troops to keep him in office.

Temple quoted verbatim the opening remarks of Governor Coke's inaugural address, begun at midnight: "Let the hearts of the people throb with joy, for the old landmarks of constitutional representative government, so long lost, are this day restored and the ancient liberties of the people of Texas re-established."

He recalled the pride that, as a page in the United States Senate, he had felt upon Coke's arrival in Washington to begin his first senatorial term in 1877, and how Coke had "stood with General Maxey for Texas and her Southern sisters." While district attorney at Mobeetie, he had supported

Coke for reelection in 1883, and he demanded now, as he had of the Democratic caucus little more than a year before in endorsing Maxey for a third term, on what grounds they felt Coke should be retired. To pit him against a man he greatly admired was out of the question.

Perhaps, his proponents suggested, Houston would consider the office of governor. Temple thought this a more likely next step up the political ladder. What would be his platform?

"You already have your platform," they told him. "Just stand on your father's name, and you will win."

Temple, flushing in anger, rose to his full height.

"A man is only what he makes himself," he replied, in clipped tones. "If a lion, he can fight his own battles; if a weakling, no rumor of distinguished lineage can make him strong."

At rare intervals, and to close friends, Temple would talk of his father, whose memory he revered. Many times he had been introduced as "Old Sam's youngest boy" or "the son of the hero of San Jacinto," which he accepted as a matter of fact. But when he rose to speak, he would mildly rebuke the person who had introduced him for mentioning his father's name, and he once declared that he wanted it distinctly understood that he declined always to parade under the wings of the illustrious Raven.

"I care not to stand in the light of reflected glory," Temple said. "Every tub must stand on its own bottom. If my own record isn't good enough, then I'll seek other fields in which to carve my fortune."

And he left the meeting.

That same night Temple lost his taste for politics. Independent and proud, he hated its poisoned atmosphere that bred and nourished what he called timeservers, tide waiters, paid slanderers, fawning sycophants, and spineless parasites. He did not seek a new term in the legislature. Sul Ross was reelected governor in 1888, Richard Coke was returned to a third term in the United States Senate, and Temple retired to his law practice at Mobeetie and legal work for the Santa Fe Railroad.

11

Temple Doffs His White Stetson

In 1881, General Grenville M. Dodge, of Union Pacific fame, who had just built the Texas and Pacific Railroad from Fort Worth to Sierra Blanca near El Paso, was hired to build 110 miles of the Fort Worth and Denver City Railway to Wichita Falls. Seventy-five miles had been completed when construction was delayed by repeal of the land-grant act and the threat of various regulations. Although the Fort Worth and Denver had counted on land grants when construction began, it received only 2,100-plus acres for right-of-way, and construction did not resume until 1886. Meanwhile, a road was built from Denver to Pueblo, and General Dodge organized the Denver, Texas and Gulf to connect the two roads.

Following the Red River up to Childress, the Fort Worth and Denver cut northwest across the Cap Rock through Hall, Donley, and Armstrong counties and reached the construction camp at Ragtown (later Amarillo) late in the spring of 1887. It continued northwest through Potter, Oldham, Hartley, and Dallam counties, reaching Texline on January 26, 1888. On March 14 it finally met the line from Colorado eight miles north of Folsom, New Mexico, where the last spike was driven in great joy and celebration.

During the same period the Atchison and Topeka Railroad, with Santa Fe added to indicate the part of the route that followed the old Santa Fe Trail, extended its line from Kiowa, Kansas, through the Cherokee Outlet. Entering the Texas Panhandle at present Higgins, in southeastern Lipscomb County, it continued southwest through Hemphill, Roberts, Gray, and Carson, finally connecting with the Denver road in Armstrong, southeast of Amarillo, at Washburn.

While the railroads reduced freighting bills and enabled cattlemen to ship their herds instead of trailing them, they also brought hordes of immigrants with their movables and materials for agriculture and industry. The era of the open range and moving masses of cattle was past.

Most of the remaining counties in Temple Houston's old Thirty-fifth District organized as population increased between 1887 and 1891. Boom towns sprang up, and there was nearly a score of newspapers, each proclaiming its town to be the present and prospective metropolis.

To the consternation of their citizens the Panhandle's three oldest cities—Clarendon and Tascosa, which flourished upon freighting and free grass, and Mobeetie, which was chiefly a reflection of the glory of Fort Elliott and the law—were bypassed. Like children abandoned in an hour of need, they found themselves isolated from the lifeline of civilization.

Temple saw Tascosa die, and Clarendon virtually picked up and moved to its new site five miles south of the Salt Fork on the Denver road. Mobeetie citizens with the Santa Fe tracks so tantalizingly close at Canadian and Miami, talked of building a line to Miami themselves, but this prospect never materialized.

Mobeetie suffered another reversal in 1889, when the federal government opened the Unassigned Lands in Indian Territory to white settlement. When the starting guns sounded at noon, Arpil 22, many of its residents were among the estimated sixty thousand eager settlers who made the wild race for choice farms and townsites.

Fort Elliott also had served its purpose in protecting the Panhandle frontier. In October, 1890, the post was abandoned, and Mobeetie lost much of its remaining populace. Many others departed when the Cheyenne-Arapaho Reservation in Oklahoma was opened to settlement on April 19, 1892.

In 1890, Temple moved his family to Canadian, the trading and shipping center of the ranch country and seat of Hemphill County. With the coming of the railroad in 1888, the old settlers had staged a rodeo, one of the first held in Texas, and established an annual custom. Canadian was a railroad division headquarters, with banks and more than a score of other businesses. Here Temple enjoyed an extensive practice in the old courts of the Panhandle region and most of the new ones.

The legends about him grew. At Mangum in Greer County (organized in 1886 and still a part of Texas), he was defending a cattle rustler before Judge F. B. Duke. The prosecuting witness made several conflicting statements, and Houston told the jury, "Gentlemen, I am sure you realize that this man has told a damnable lie."

Judge Duke rapped the bench. "You cannot use such language in my court."

"I got beside myself, forgive me," Temple apologized. "I beseech your most tender mercies."

"All right," agreed the judge, who had known Temple at Baylor University.

However, in reviewing the contradictory points moments later, Houston again used the offensive term.

Judge Duke thundered, "I fine you twenty dollars for contempt!"

Temple searched his pockets. "Your Honor," he said, "you embarrass me. I do not have twenty dollars. May I borrow it from you?"

"Clerk, remit the fine," ordered the judge. "The county can afford to lose that twenty dollars more than I can!"

Whereupon the "unusually pompous" county attorney delivered his summing up to the jury. Capitalizing on Houston's discredit, he asked that they "put no stock in my opponent's remarks" and "send this man to the penitentiary" and then resumed his seat at the table, the very picture of confidence.

Old-timers who remembered the case could name neither the defendant nor his final disposition. But they would chuckle about how "Old Sam's magnificent son" rose in rebuttal and said, "Your Honor, the prosecutor is the first man I've ever seen who can strut sitting down."

Most trials in which Houston participated from 1890 to

1892 were for theft and murder. In a number of these cases he was associated with Amos J. Fires, of Childress. Fires had more "firsts" to his credit than any other man in the Panhandle. He planted the first wheat in Childress County, mailed the first letter from the Childress postoffice, dug the first grave in the Childress cemetery, erected the first brick building, organized the first bank, was leader in the movement that brought Childress the machine shops of the Fort Worth and Denver Railway, was the first judge of the county (having helped organize it in 1887), and laid the cornerstone of the first courthouse.

From the moment Fires took a case he fought through hung juries or continuances until his client was free, and he devoted himself so completely to his work that he seemed a member of the man's family. He and Houston were called the most colorful team of lawyers in Texas. The people of the Plains traveled for miles, and the courtrooms were always full when this pair was defending.

One case of note was a man accused of a murder committed south of Paducah. Cottle County was in the throes of organization, and Fires and Houston assisted in hurrying the process so that the case could be tried there. After organization was completed, they found that the crime had been committed in King County.

Fires went on to become a great lawyer. In private practice he tried one hundred twenty-three murder cases and lost only four. In 1927, Governor Dan Moody appointed him district judge of the One-Hundredth Judicial District, and he was elected for two terms. He died in Wichita Falls in 1941, at age eighty-one.

With his political career in Texas forever ended, Temple cast his lot with the oppressed and the underdog. Josh Young, who had been reared in Washington County and had gone to school with him during the brief period Temple had lived with sister Maggie and West Williams at Labadie Prairie, told how Houston came to the rescue of his son, who got into serious trouble in New Mexico: "Temple went there, cleared the boy, and would not accept a fee nor even reimbursement for his personal expenses—became almost insulted when I insisted in passing any money to him whatever. That illustrates what manner of man he was."

Houston sought the country of the frontier, loved the rough men who occupied it, and found room to lead a solitary life rather than grapple with the vexations and unhappiness of a more burdensome civilization. He gave little thought to his material self, and he never forgot to feed his mind and emotions. When he came into a town to attend court, his first visit was to bookstalls, where he bought many items on Spanish and French history and literature.

He made friends with the peaceful Cheyennes and Arapahoes, traded with them for curios, and fed them in his home at Canadian, whether they were dressed in blankets, or with colored feathers in their hair and paint all over their faces, while Laura and the children watched, expecting to be scalped. He lined his den with pottery, blankets, headdresses, tomahawks, peace pipes, and the beautiful dress of an Indian princess. A number of valuable relics of his father, prehistoric peoples, early explorations, Indian battles of the Southwest, and mementos of Napoleon completed his collection.

Houston also became disenchanted with the Texas Court of Criminal Appeals during these years. Impetuous and outspoken, he let the people and members of the court know what he thought of some hair-splitting decisions they had made in cases where he had represented the losing side. Referrring to an eighteen-month delay in affirming the conviction of one client, he remarked, "If they were to start to hell with a load of ice to sell, the place would freeze over before they got there."

Comparing the court to the great judges of early Texas, he added, "No more mournful contrast is seen along the Nile, where the jackal snarls, sole lord of the desolate temples and deserted palaces of imperial Sesostris." While many Texans agreed, such public assessment lost him the good graces of the appeals court.

Houston looked eastward. He had watched Oklahoma organized as a territory in 1890, with six counties—Logan, Oklahoma, Cleveland, Canadian, Kingfisher, and Payne—and all Indian reservations except the nations of the Five Civilized Tribes and the Quapaw Agency northeast of them. The territory also included No Man's Land as Beaver County and Greer County (in dispute between the United States and Texas) in event the title thereto should be adjudged vested in the United States. The opening of the Iowa, Sac and Fox, and Pottawatomie-Shawnee reservations had added two new counties—Pottawatomie and Lincoln—in 1891, and the opening of the Cheyenne-Arapaho reservations added six more counties—Blaine, Dewey, Day, Roger Mills, Custer, and Washita—in 1892. Now the hordes were clamoring for the greatest land strip of all—the Cherokee Outlet.

Oklahoma was being crisscrossed with railroads. Cities were mushrooming in the heavily settled areas. Temple saw an opportunity to rise in stature *beside* his father, not *because* of him. The circumstances were parallel—a young country fighting for law and order and statehood. The star of Texas doffed his white Stetson. On September 16, 1893, from an open Santa Fe boxcar near the Woodward land office, with his long, tawny hair flying in the hot wind and the boiling clouds of red-gumbo dust, he witnessed the famous run.

Woodward, fifteen miles downstream from Fort Supply where Wolf and Beaver creeks converged to form the North Canadian River, became overnight a mass of settlers, soldiers, railroaders, cattlemen, and gun-toting cowboys. Temple opened a law office at the corner of Main and Eleventh streets. A few months later he moved his family to Oklahoma.

12
"Mercy, Eh! Where Was Mercy Then?"

Seven new counties—Woodward, Woods, Grant, Garfield, Kay, Noble, and Pawnee—were carved from this long-coveted empire stretching fifty miles south of and running parallel to the Kansas border from Texas and No Man's Land approximately 225 miles east to the Osage Nation, bounded on the south by the north boundary lines of the Creek Nation, Old Oklahoma, and the Cheyenne-Arapaho country. Woodward, westernmost of the seven counties and sixty miles square, became the largest county in Oklahoma Territory and was filled with cattle.

More than a dozen big ranchers who had leased from the Cherokees, each worth $50,000 to $150,000, now prepared to build permanent ranch houses. An estimated one hundred thousand people ran for claims in the Outlet. The eastern part was almost completely settled at the opening, but only the more desirable claims in the western part were taken. Fewer than six hundred filings for farms had been made at the Woodward land office by mid-November. Owing to the altitude and the uncertainty of moisture, grain farming had never proved a success in adjoining Texas and Kansas, and presumably there was no exception to these rules laid down by God Almighty in the government of this climate.

Crossed by many fine streams and covered with rich, nutritious grasses between and beyond the purple plateaus from the headwaters of the North Canadian to the wide sandy bend of the Cimarron flowing diagonally across its northeastern quarter, Woodward County would remain pretty much a cattleman's paradise for several years. With statehood in 1907, it was divided into the present Woodward, Harper, western Woods, and northern Ellis counties.

J. D. F. Jennings, first probate judge of Woodward County and father of the Jennings brothers.

Governor William C. Renfrow ordered the population enumerated so that representation in the territorial legislature could be apportioned accordingly. He also appointed county officers to serve until their successors could be chosen in a regular election. The first board of commissioners met the second week in November. The chairman was Robert J. Ray, a bright young lawyer who had the ability and address to get along with the people. The other members were W. D. Judkins and Thomas L. O'Brien, conservative men who used all possible care in doing the county's business. The board divided the country into four townships for election and assessment purposes.

A. O. Kincaid, a young man from Oklahoma City, where he had a reputation for probity and energy, became county clerk and ex officio register of deeds. The first treasurer was Henry F. Emerson, manager of the Exchange Bank, which was already doing a good business.

J. D. J. Jennings, a Democratic patriarch who in his sixty-five years had done much for his party, was appointed probate judge. He was full of business and did it like the loyal veteran that he was.

Another big leader in democracy was Wilson M. Hammock, register of the United States District Land Office. A former circuit judge in Tennessee, he might have become chief justice of the territorial supreme court, except for President Grover Cleveland's home-rule sentiment. He was able, genial, and hospitable—a true southern gentleman.

The most unusual character was Renfrow's choice for sheriff—John E. ("Jack") Love. He was born in San Augustine, Texas, on June 6, 1857, and his boyhood was cast in Reconstruction days. He spent most of his youth on the ranges of West Texas as a cowboy but managed a couple of years as a student at the Sam Houston Normal, in Huntsville, and taught school two terms before coming to Oklahoma City in 1889, where he served as a municipal councilman. Six feet four inches tall, weighing 270 pounds and well proportioned,

John E. ("Jack") Love, first sheriff of Woodward County and close friend of Temple Houston.

he wore an English beard, talked with the polish of a New Englander, and was as brave and quick as a lion, and a thorough westerner. Love had a small horse ranch near Woodward, and was unmarried.

Both native Texans with similar backgrounds, he and Temple Houston became inseparable companions. The affection existing between them might have been likened to that between David and Jonathan.

The county's population was somewhat intractable, and so the position of sheriff was far from being a sinecure. Jack Love's presence and his unvarying kindness and firmness had a very quieting effect and, more than any other single personal influence, helped tame northwestern Oklahoma.

County Attorney B. B. Smith, a lawyer of experience and ability, found plenty of entertainment. Three miles northeast of the Fort Supply Reservation boundary, two men named Hall and McDonald had opened a saloon, brothel, and gambling establishment. The opening of the Outlet ended nearly three years of patrol duty for Fort Supply, and the two hundred troops of the Third Cavalry and Thirteenth Infantry stationed there, bored with the monotony of practice marches and garrison routine, found the Hall-McDonald enterprise all too attractive. The number of men absent without leave rose to such proportions that Colonel Dangerfield Parker, the commanding officer, sought and gained County Attorney Smith's assistance in closing the brothel and gambling house.

The saloon remained open, since the proprietors had obtained the necessary liquor license. Smith tried to close it on grounds that the owners had taken up a claim with a declaration that the land would be used for agricultural and grazing purposes. When this effort failed, Colonel Parker resorted to a general court-martial with a view to dishonorable discharges to stop the absences without leave, there being no privileges at the post of which to deprive the men.

The boys around Woodward also were very lively on occasion as early dockets indicated. The town had a provisional government. Four days after the run city officials were elected.

"MERCY, EH! WHERE WAS MERCY THEN?"

The first ordinance admonished the citizens, "If you must shoot, shoot straight up." Actually two towns in one—a government town and a depot town along the Santa Fe, half a mile apart—it resembled Dodge City on a milder scale.

Here was the Santa Fe's division end with roundhouse and machine shops employing 350 men. There were nearly 500 people, including the military, at Fort Supply with a monthly payroll of seventy-five hundred dollars. In a one-year period six million pounds of merchandise were freighted by wagons from the railroad to Supply, and another million pounds were shipped to the postal exchange.

Woodward also was known as the "emporium" of livestock interests in Oklahoma—an important supply point of stockers and feeders for Kansas, Nebraska, Missouri, and Iowa, and the largest point of original shipments of cattle in the world. Over 250 cars were loaded in a thirty-day period following the opening. These cattle came not only from local ranches but also from the counties carved from the Cheyenne-Arapaho country, still open and free because many settlers, thinking it too far from a railroad and not desirable for agriculture, had refused to waste homestead rights on the area and pressed for entry into the Outlet. Other immense herds were trailed overland from the ranges in the Wichita-Caddo and Kiowa-Comanche-Apache reservations, from Greer County, and from below Red River. Annual shipments at Woodward at one time totaled 4,300 cars. Saddle horses, ranch hacks, wagons, and buggies lined the hitchracks, and the town was full of cowboys.

Woodward was twenty-three hundred feet above sea level—at one of the highest points in Oklahoma. Three miles north was a large lake, a natural waterworks reservoir of pure, clear, inexhaustible water, with a forty-foot fall. The railroad constructed a special waterworks, which it controlled, but until the town developed its own water system, each businessman and householder paid twenty-five cents to have a barrel on his porch filled each day from a horse-drawn tank wagon.

Leading businesses along the winding main street, in mostly false-fronted buildings, were restaurants and short-order houses, dry-goods and general stores, two banks, two lumber yards, three livery stables, an ice factory, a Sing Lee laundry, a bottling works, twenty-three saloons to accommodate all hands, and two lively newspapers. The *Advocate*, established by R. C. ("Daddy") Price on the day of the opening, ran large advertisements for Bull Durham tobacco and Winchester repeating rifles and proclaimed itself the county's "Official Paper," while C. M. Hall's *Woodward Jeffersonian*, first published on September 23, bore as a motto: "We are an old-time, double twisted Thomas Jefferson—Allen G. Thurman—Tom Hendricks—Old 'Rise Up' Bill Allen—Grover Cleveland Democrat." The focus of activity was on the Cattle King Hotel and the Cattle King Saloon.

Buffalo hunts, Indian fights, overland cattle drives and the building of the Santa Fe were typical reminiscences at these gatherings, but the topic that surpassed them all in the fancy of some three hundred Panhandle settlers from Higgins and Canadian was the eloquence of the brilliant son of Texas's liberator and his many courtroom achievements.

The Reverend Alfred Connet, a Congregational minister from Ohio, arrived at Woodward on September 16 and the following day preached on the north side of the first building erected. A hard wind was blowing from the south, and weary-eyed men and women and big-eyed children sat on piles of boards, crates, or nail kegs or just hunkered against the walls. On Sunday night, November 12, in a chair car on the railroad, Bishop Brooke held the first Episcopal services. Churches were going up, and the people, by private subscription, had built a 25-by-40-foot structure in which a school of forty pupils was operating when the Houston family arrived in February, 1894.

By that time Temple had formed a law partnership with Robert Ray. Ray was born on December 7, 1864, at Flatcreek, Bedford County, Tennessee, studied law at Lebanon, and while a boy went to West Texas, later establishing his resi-

Rail Road Eating House, Woodward, Oklahoma Territory, 1896. Courtesy of Western History Collections, University of Oklahoma Library.

Martinson General Merchandise and Woodward Saddle Shop, 1897. Courtesy of Western History Collections, University of Oklahoma Library.

Blacksmith shop, Woodward, in the 1890s. Courtesy of Western History Collections, University of Oklahoma Library.

Woodward in the early 1890s. The Central Hotel is on the left. The streets were always filled with horses and vehicles when Houston was principal actor in a court drama. Courtesy of Western History Collections, University of Oklahoma Library.

Woodward County Courthouse, built in 1901–1902. Courtesy of Western History Collections, University of Oklahoma Library.

Robert J. ("Bob") Ray, Woodward attorney and Houston's first law partner.

dence in Dallas. In 1889 he joined the thousands of settlers who raced for homes in Old Oklahoma and was one of the first lawyers to plead a case in the territorial district courts created by the Organic Act of May 2, 1890. An ardent Democrat, he assisted in the organization of that party in Oklahoma and was a delegate to the first convention held in the territory. When the Cheyenne-Arapaho country opened in 1892, he moved to Roger Mills County, practicing at Cheyenne until the opening of the Outlet.

Like Abou ben Adhem, he loved his fellow men and was a friend to whom one could unbosom his deep sorrows and disappointments of life with the assurance of a sympathetic heart and intelligent understanding. He studied his Bible, followed the meek and lowly Nazarene, and was never known to compromise or swerve from what he considered just and proper in his law practice or private dealings.

He chose not to run for county commissioner in 1894, but was elected to the territorial council from the Woodward district. The legislature consisted of two houses—a council of thirteen members and a house of representatives with twenty-six members. Ray was the only democrat in the Third Legislative Assembly of 1895, but he was so well informed on territorial matters and conscientious in considering every subject that he wielded more influence than any other member of that session.

During Ray's absence at Guthrie, the territorial capital, Temple handled the firm's business. Their partnership continued until August, 1895, when Ray accepted a two-year appointment, replacing Wilson M. Hammock, as register of the United States land district comprising Woodward and Beaver counties.

Excepting the supreme and district courts, the big courts in the territory in the early years were the United States land offices. Title to lands opened to settlement was in the Federal government and could be obtained through application and entries made at these offices presided over by a register and receiver, whose decisions, and those made on appeal to the

Members of the Oklahoma Senate, Third Legislative Assembly, 1895. Number 5, center, back row, is Robert J. Ray.

commissioner of the General Land Office and secretary of the interior in Washington, D.C., were final. Therefore, lawyers having any practice at the time were land-office lawyers, many of whom made fortunes and arose to the foremost rank.

More than a dozen of these attorneys went to Woodward in 1893. The *Advocate* named T. M. Grant, A. G. Cunningham, David P. Marum, A. M. Appleget, Charles Swindall, William A. Briggs, O. C. Wybrant, Clyde H. Wyand, Sherman Smith, A. W. Anderson, L. J. Gaady, L. E. Moyer, Judge Jerry Rowland Dean and Sidney Benton Laune, adding:

At the head of the list stands Col. Temple Houston.... His practice is not limited to this country or even the courts of the Territory as his ability has become known all over the Southwest.... His education and rare forensic powers coupled with extensive reading and a wonderful knowledge of law in all its forms has made him famous while yet in the early prime of life.

Temple fought courtroom skirmishes with most of these attorneys, always respecting their fitness and legal attainments. He, Dean, and Laune became lifelong friends.

Dean, a heavy-bearded, white-haired Kentuckian and former Union cavalry officer, began his law practice at McPherson, Kansas, in 1872. Later he moved to Deaf Smith County, Texas, participated in its organization, was its first county judge, and served one term as representative from that district in the Texas Legislature.

Laune, fresh out of law school at Ann Arbor, Michigan, and yet to see a client, went to Woodward by way of Higgins, Texas, as president of the Cherokee Outlet Colony of homeseekers organized in Denver. He and Judge Dean secured adjoining lots the day of the run and opened their respective offices by simply taking some legal blanks from their suitcases and then sitting on the suitcases and waiting for business. One of them would guard their claims while the other was away on a trip to the land office or to obtain food and other necessities. Eventually they erected a two-roomed, board-and-bat structure centered on the line dividing their lots and put up a

Jerry Rowland Dean, former West Texas county judge and Woodward lawyer.

sign—"Dean & Laune, Lawyers"—to announce their partnership.

There was a decided bend in Main Street at this point where East and West Woodward merged. Dean and Laune represented East Woodward, the part of town in litigation platted near the first railroad station where Laune's colony settled. West Woodward had been platted by the government before the opening. Some residents claimed the lawyers were so crooked that they had actually caused the street to jog at their office. Dean and Laune won their case in the courts, and the Department of the Interior gave them the final victory. The feud between the towns did not die, however, until the Santa Fe moved its station. The *Advocate* thought Woodward's contingent of attorneys "a mighty slender list for a county of over 35,000 people," with scores of new settlers pouring in daily and "more than enough legal work to go around."

There were sharks in every new land opening, and Woodward had its share. Often locators would show a quarter section over and over, and then give the homeseeker the location numbers of a worthless piece of land. Several such instances ended in gunplay. Cowboys and ranchers went fully armed, as did nearly everyone else. Feuds were common, and there were numbers of killings. Community meetings were sometimes broken up by gunplay. Physical encounters between settlers usually resulted in a suit before a justice of the peace. Combatants sought lawyers to represent them, and Houston was the popular choice.

More often he appeared in behalf of the Santa Fe, which suffered considerably from damage to tracks or other property, thefts from shipments, and conspiracy to defraud the company by changing the description or weight of freight stated on waybills. In a six-month period Temple aided in prosecuting over a dozen such violations unearthed by railroad detectives.

He found his life even more hectic than in Texas. He first attracted territory-wide attention in his defense of Tom O'Hara, alias Red Tom. O'Hara had some cattle on the

Sweetwater in Roger Mills County, was of the desperate type, and allegedly had served as a Texas Ranger. On Monday, November 20, 1893, he arrived in Cheyenne to look for stolen horses. Cheyenne was a wide-open trading center. All freight was brought in by team-drawn wagons from railroad points at Canadian, Vernon, and Quanah, Texas, and from a hundred miles east at El Reno. It boasted a weekly newspaper, a drugstore, a barber shop, a whiskey store and saloon, and half a dozen mercantile establishments doing a profitable business with cattlemen and the Indians along the Washita, mostly congregated about the Indian agency at Hammon.

O'Hara made most of his inquiries at the saloon, getting more than comfortably full as the day wore on, at one point badly frightening an inoffensive Negro (the only one in town) and causing some apprehension among other citizens. A Cheyenne named Wolf Hair happened to be in town trading. As he came out of Hazelwood & Moody's store across the street west of the courthouse square, O'Hara reportedly remarked, "I haven't killed an Indian in a long time."

Wolf Hair, apparently wanting no trouble with Red Tom, hurriedly loaded his purchases into his two-horse open hack and drove off. O'Hara quickly mounted his horse, slid his Winchester from his saddle scabbard, and followed him over the hill to the southeast. Shortly afterward two shots came from that direction. Then Red Tom rode back into town and surrendered to Sheriff "Skillety Bill" Johnson, saying, "You will find a dead Indian over the hill, but if he is not shot over the left eye, he is not my Indian."

The body was found "shot over the left eye." Wolf Hair had been unarmed, and O'Hara offered no explanation. He was locked up in the town's little wooden jail, and word was sent to the Indian camp on the Washita.

The *Cheyenne Sunbeam* of November 24 stated that

the body was left where found . . . it being deemed advisable to show he was killed where there were no whites to protect him.

Late in the evening the messenger returned, bringing Chief Red Moon and his brother Iskie and two squaws. They took charge of the body and effects of the dead Indian and said they would return the following day to investigate the matter.

This caused nervous speculation about what action the Indians might take. Fear of a general massacre became so great that during the night women and children were evacuated from the town into Texas or hid out in the country nearby, while a courier rode sixty miles north to Fort Supply with a letter asking for the immediate protection of United States troops.

Colonel Parker dispatched Lieutenant Kirby Walker with Troop D, Third Cavalry, and scout Amos Chapman to the Washita, only to learn that a large band of Indians had escaped the guards at Hammon agency and were making their way to Cheyenne to avenge themselves for the killing of Wolf Hair.

On Tuesday morning, while the coroner's jury was holding its inquest, several shots were heard over the hill where Wolf Hair had been slain. Then about eighty Indians, in warpaint and heavily armed, swept into town, sending everyone scurrying for cover.

The *Sunbeam* report continued:

> The Indians dismounted near the jail and wanted Sheriff Johnson to turn the prisoner over to them. The officer explained that the white men were then making medicine at the log courthouse to hang the prisoner for his crime, and it was impossible to accede to their request.... One Indian chief [White Shield] replied tauntingly that if he (Johnson) thought they could not take the prisoner to bring out his palefaces and let them try to guard him. [The building contained two steel cells, in one of which Red Tom was confined, the other barricaded by three special deputies. At the saloon twenty some cowboys armed with six-shooters and rifles stood ready to assist the sheriff if such an attack occurred.] The situation was certainly critical... but Johnson finally induced the Indians to wait and see what the coroner's jury would do.
>
> As soon as the jury finished its investigation, Red Moon, Spotted Horse and others crowded into the room and wanted to know the result. An Indian named Robert acted as interpreter, and it was

some time before the spokesman, Spotted Horse, understood that the deed was not done in the town. It was explained to him that the citizens were his friends; that they had the murderer and would hold him until next term of court. . . .

The chiefs finally expressed themselves as satisfied, the Indians leaving for their camps. Some of them declared, however, that they would return and take the prisoner. . . if they had to burn down the jail.

Most of the citizens believed that they would surely come back under cover of darkness and probably murder all the white people they found. A score of guards was sworn in to protect the jail, fortifications were built of cordwood, and a vigilant watch was set until Lieutenant Walker arrived with his troops.

Walker stationed his soldiers in Cheyenne and then joined scout Chapman at the Indian village. They spent the night talking with Spotted Horse, Red Moon, and White Shield, and the next day reported that there would be no further trouble—the sheriff could keep Red Tom; the red men had received enough "civilization" to be amenable to the laws of the country. The guards were discharged, and the town returned to normal.

Houston arrived to defend O'Hara and asked for and was granted a change of venue to Canadian County. His client languished without bond in the El Reno jail until the spring term of court.

It was plainly a case of cold-blooded murder for the prosecution. Before Red Tom could be tried, however, events transpired that worked in the defendant's favor. On Sunday afternoon, April 1, William Breeding and T. S. Cotter rode to a Cheyenne camp in Custer County near Hammon to claim a pony belonging to Cotter that had been taken up by an Indian known as Chief Hill. A disagreement arose when Hill insisted on retaining the rope with which the pony was tied. Cotter's version was that the Indian refused to give up the animal, that he grabbed a Winchester from his tent, and that Breeding shot him twice in the breast with his six-shooter.

Breeding and Cotter then put spurs to their mounts to escape with the pony. Two other Indians opened fire with rifles, killing Breeding instantly. One shot struck Cotter in the left arm. Breeding fell from his horse about a hundred yards from the camp. The Indians would not let Cotter return for the body and he rode fast to his home a few miles distant, spreading word on the way that the Indians were on the warpath and that Breeding had been murdered.

His exaggerated story caused considerable excitement, and the whites began to form companies and arm themselves. When they found Breeding's body, the Indians had set fire to the clothing, burning everything except his sleeves below the elbow, and his boots and hair. He had been shot four times—between the shoulders, in the left side, and through the right arm and wrist. The back of his head had been crushed by the butt of a rifle.

This caused a storm of rage among the settlers, and nearly one hundred men surrounded the camp with the intention of wiping out the tribe. Deputy United States Marshal William Banks, Constable Vance, and Indian Farmer Hammon arrived in time to prevent an attack. But the settlers continued so threatening that the Indians left in a body to join White Shield's camp, four miles away.

Banks sent for the coroner. The corpse was examined, wrapped in blankets, and sent home. The rest of the evening was consumed taking Cotter's testimony. Then Banks and the coroner went to White Shield's camp to take the statement of Chief Hill. During the night Chief Hill died of his wounds, and his Indians denied any knowledge of the killings.

The settlers, augmented in numbers by new arrivals, grew impatient. The next morning an Indian runner informed the marshal that they were approaching a mile below the camp. Banks immediately rode out to meet them.

He found about one hundred fifty men from Custer and Washita counties who wanted to take the camp and lynch Breeding's murderers. Banks told them everything must be done according to law. He took Cotter into the camp to see if he could pick out the Indians who had been with Chief Hill when the shooting occurred. Banks told White Shield what was wanted. The chief summoned all the bucks to be looked at; Cotter pretended to identify two of them—Sandy and Mike Buffalo Thigh. The marshal placed the pair under arrest and started with them for Arapaho.

The *Oklahoma State Capital* and *Oklahoma Daily Press-Gazette* of April 12 gave this conclusion of the affair:

The Indians were alarmed at the crowd.... the prisoners had to be stopped repeatedly and the people ordered back, it taking about six hours to move them four miles. They finally were gotten into a dugout, where Marshal Banks turned them over to Sheriff Malone (of Custer County). The crowd was getting worked up and sent a note to Marshal Banks giving him fifteen minutes to give the prisoners up, which he and the sheriff firmly refused to do.... The people by that time had become almost uncontrollable and it looked like a fight between the little handful of officers and the crowd... when Captain A. A. Woodson, Fifth Cavalry [in charge of the Cheyenne-Arapaho agency at Darlington], arrived with Captain Hunter and a detachment of troops detailed to the grounds by Colonel George Purlington [commander at Fort Reno] to investigate the alleged uprising.

They ordered the settlers to disperse and allowed the civil authorities to proceed to Arapaho with the prisoners. An examining trial was held the next day and the two Indians remanded to jail without bond.

The Indians maintained that Chief Hill alone, though badly injured, had seized his Winchester in self-defense, wounded Cotter, and killed Breeding. There being insufficient evidence to the contrary, and Cotter's identification not being positive, Sandy and Mike Buffalo Thigh were discharged *nolle prosequi*.

At Red Tom's trial the prosecution referred to "these recent attempts to get up some excitement" as having "no more foundation than the average 'race war' in the South" and predicted that no general Indian uprising would ever take place again in Oklahoma or Indian Territory. "The Indians of these Territories, both civilized and those who are comparatively savage... have buried the tomahawk too long ago to think of digging it up at this propitious time, and would soon learn their mistake." Newspapers that "persist in publishing exaggerated reports" and the actions of such men as Breeding and O'Hara "work great harm in this country.... We must be merciful with those who have lived among the white men long enough to understand the futility of dashing themselves against the walls of civilization" and "incarcerate this defendant in the territorial prison for life."

Houston offered little in O'Hara's defense. Red Tom testified that he had followed Wolf Hair because his team resembled the horses he had come to Cheyenne to look for and that, when he overtook Wolf Hair and stopped him to examine the animals, the Indian leaped from the hack and wrenched the rifle from his hands. "He turned it to kill me.... I drew my pistol and fired."

Sheriff Johnson testified that the Winchester had been discharged. However, it was shown the bullet that killed the Indian came from Red Tom's leg gun. If Red Tom's statement was not exactly correct, there was no witness to disprove it.

Temple then made the speech of his life. Most of the jurors were former Texans. It was Houston's custom first to get a Texas jury angry. He recapped the atrocities and pillage committed upon the Panhandle plains during the Inidan War of 1874, worked upon their prejudices, and twined his eloquence with garlands of metaphor.

At a moment when their temper was at fever pitch, he shouted: "Not one of you but remembers the time when, with drawn bow and lifted lance, the Indians of the same tribe, by the light of your burning homes, were murdering your wives and children. Mercy, eh! Where was mercy then?"

Within minutes the jury brought in a verdict of acquittal.

13

Silver-Tongued Orator

By act of December 21, 1893, Congress provided two additional judges for the Supreme Court of Oklahoma Territory. President Cleveland appointed John L. McAtee of Maryland and Andrew G. Curtin Bierer, a Pennsylvanian, who had begun his law practice in Kansas and had been a Guthrie attorney since 1889. Thus membership of the original Supreme Court and the number of judicial districts increased from three to five. Judge Frank Dale of Guthrie, formerly prosecuting attorney of Sedgwick County, Kansas, and an associate justice since May, 1893, became chief justice.

On February 3, 1894, the supreme court redistricted the Territory as follows:

First District (Judge Dale presiding), embracing Logan, Payne, Lincoln, and Pawnee counties

Second District (Judge John H. Burford), Canadian, Kingfisher, Blaine, Washita, and Garfield counties

Third District (Judge Henry W. Scott, of Oklahoma City), Oklahoma, Cleveland, and Pottawatomie counties;

Fourth District (Judge Bierer), Noble, Kay, Grant, and Woods counties;

Fifth District (Judge McAtee), Woodward, Dewey, Custer, Day, and Roger Mills counties and Beaver.

All that portion of the Osage Reservation lying south of the township line between Townships 25 and 26 North was attached to Pawnee County (First district); the portion of the reservation lying north of that line, together with the Kaw Indian Reservation, was attached to Kay County; and the Ponca, Oto, and Missouri reservations were attached to Noble County (Fourth District) for judicial purposes.

Section 9 of the May 2, 1890, act organizing Oklahoma provided that the judicial power of the territory "shall be vested in a supreme court, district courts, probate courts, and justices of the peace," the jurisdiction of which and of the probate courts and the justices of the peace "shall be as limited by law"; the chief justice and associate justices "shall hold their offices for four years, and until their successors are appointed and qualified"; each judge "shall reside in the district to which he is assigned," hold terms of court in each county of his district "at such time and place" fixed by the supreme court and serve as members of its appellate function annually at the territorial seat of government, a majority of whom "shall constitute a quorum"; that the supreme and district courts "shall possess chancery as well as common law jurisdiction, and authority for redress of all wrongs committed against the constitution or laws of the United States or of the Territory affecting persons or property."

The supreme court early ruled that, during the absence of the regular presiding judge from his district, one of the other justices could be assigned to try, hear, and determine all matters and business that came before him and during such assignment had the same power and jurisdiction actually possessed by the regular presiding judge of that district.

Section 10 of the act provided that all offenses or crimes in the territory, if committed within any organized county, "shall be prosecuted and tried within said county"; and if committed within territory not so embraced, "shall be prosecuted and tried in the county to which such territory shall be attached for judicial purposes." All civil actions "shall be instituted in the county in which the defendant, or either of them, resides or may be found"; actions arising within any portion of the territory not organized as a county "shall be instituted in the county to which such territory is attached." But any case, civil or criminal, could be removed to another county by change of venue.

Section 12 extended the jurisdiction of the district courts over "all controversies arising between members or citizens of one tribe or nation of Indians and the members or citizens of other tribes or nations" in the territory; "any citizen or member of one tribe or nation who may commit any offense or crime in said Territory against the person or property of a citizen or member of another tribe or nation shall be subject to the same punishment . . . as if both parties were citizens of the United States;" and any person of Indian blood residing in the territory "shall have the right to invoke the aid of courts therein for the protection of his person or property." No jurisdiction lay, however, in "controversies arising between Indians of the same tribe, while sustaining their tribal relation."

In this legal framework Temple Houston appeared in nearly every court of the territory but also became a familiar sight in the far-western counties of the Second and Fifth districts, presided over by Burford and McAtee. He took some part in most of their cases and all the important ones.

Judge Burford was Temple's favorite. In many ways Burford reminded him of Judge Willis in the Panhandle. He was born February 29, 1852, in Parke County, Indiana, the son of the Reverend James Burford, a prominent member of the Baptist clergy and a descendant of Elijah Hastings Burford, of English, Scotch, and Welsh ancestry, who had emigrated from Oxfordshire County, England, and settled in Amherst County, Virginia, in 1713. The family also had given the nation a gallant patriot-soldier in the Revolutionary War. Burford spent his childhood on the farm and acquired his early education in local schools. In 1874 he obtained his bachelor of laws degree at the University of Indiana and thereafter serving as assistant in the law offices of Judge D. V. Burns, of Indianapolis, until moving to Crawfordsville, where he began his independent practice and became an intimate friend of the distinguished General Lew Wallace and of Indiana's brilliant novelist Maurice Thompson. He soon gained professional prestige and success, served two terms as prosecuting attorney of the Twenty-second Judicial Circuit of the state; espoused the Republican party and as a member of its state central committee in 1888 was a vigorous and effective supporter of

The Supreme Court of Oklahoma. Chief Justice John H. Burford and four of the associate justices before whom Houston practiced: John L. McAtee, B. T. Hainer, B. F. Burwell, and C. F. Irwin.

General Benjamin Harrison as candidate for the nomination to the presidency.

In 1890 he went to Oklahoma Territory to accept appointment by Governor George W. Steele as first probate judge of Beaver but resigned shortly and located in Oklahoma City to become register of the United States Land Office. In March, 1892, he was appointed associate justice of the Supreme Court by President Harrison to succeed Abraham J. Seay, who had resigned to become governor of the territory following Steele's resignation and return to Indiana to be elected to the United States House of Representatives. Judge Burford moved to El Reno in order to reside within the Second Judicial District.

A man of high character and fine legal mind, he was loyal to his profession, persistently endeavored to raise its standard of ethics, and openly denounced unwarranted attacks upon the integrity or good faith of the judiciary. An outstanding characteristic was his pronounced interest in the progress and success of young lawyers, many of whom he assisted and specially befriended. Temple admired him most for his broad views and understanding of the real spirit of the law of the frontier.

The people were new to the territory, going through the melting-pot period, and gun-toting was a habit. While they respected the men on the bench, no opportunity was overlooked to put some spice into a court session.

In beginning a term in one western county populated mostly by cowboys, Judge Burford issued his usual disarmament order. Shortly after court convened, a fun-loving cowman strode quickly down the aisle, pulled a cheap toy pistol from his pocket, and placed it on Burford's desk, saying, "Judge, you left your revolver under your pillow at the hotel, and I thought I ought to bring it to you."

The cowman wheeled quickly and walked out, deadpan. The courtroom audience roared, and the judge joined in for a few minutes before rapping for order.

Though determined to administer the law properly and seriously, Burford used discretion and overlooked things now and then to preserve decorum. Sometimes he was the innocent cause of such outbreaks himself. A woman plantiff in a divorce suit swore that she had been married only eighteen months but was the mother of seven children. She forgot to mention that there was a previous marriage and that the children were born of that union.

Burford inquired severely: "Do you mean to state that you've given birth to seven children in eighteen months?"

She gave him a look of withering scorn and asked, "What do you think I am, Judge, a Belgian hare?"

In a case involving a family with little schooling, it developed that the father was an amorous old goat whose escapades had gotten him into court trouble. The wife was on the witness stand, and attorneys were having a difficult time eliciting details of her husband's romances. She could not understand their "big words," so Burford, ever kindly and courteous, took a hand.

"Madam," he asked, "is your husband passionate?"

"No, Judge," she replied, "he's a barber."

When a jury cleared an attorney of taking a shot at another lawyer, Burford, in telling the defendant that he was free, added, "I don't know but that I ought to fine you for being such a poor shot."

Such blunders delighted Houston. Judge Burford liked him and often took him on the circuit to defend anybody who needed counsel. In the courtroom Temple would sit quietly, doodling or sketching pictures of Napoleon, until the opposition made some remark that would give him an opening. Then he would leap to his feet, parading and gesticulating, and drop his rhetorical bomb.

Burford frequently reprimanded him telling him to conduct himself with more dignity, but Temple's use of every art, every trick, every stratagem known to the profession, overlooking no decision ancient, medieval, or modern by which to befuddle judge or jury, was no less fascinating. Hitchracks around territorial courthouses, as in the Texas Panhandle, seldom had room for another saddle horse, buggy, or wagon on days when Houston was the main actor in the drama.

A week was assigned to each county twice a year for the court sessions. The first day or two were spent on federal business, after which territorial cases were tried. The court party consisted of the judge, the clerk, the stenographer, and the chief deputy United States marshal, who kept the payroll and was responsible for jury and witness fees and other court expenses. Often the party was accompanied by other deputy marshals who served summonses and subpoenas and made arrests on warrants issued by the court. Many well-known lawyers also rode the circuit in the western districts, some working on cases and others hoping to get fees as assistants to attorneys practicing in the newly established county seats.

John H. Seger was the "presiding genius" of the model educational and industrial school for Indians at Colony, Washita County, on the Old Trail used by freighters going to and coming from El Reno and other railroad points. The beautiful shady grove, cold springs, and clear, fresh water of Pond Creek (present Cobb Creek) made this place a haven for the weary traveler. The teachers and civil-service clerks lived in the large school dormitory and were served their meals at a common table by the young Indian students. A number of neatly furnished unoccupied rooms were used by the guests. The guests were usually the court party and sometimes a lawyer or two. They contributed to the mess their prorata share of the costs of the meal. After traveling horseback or in a hack, buggy, or chuck wagon for weeks over rough trails from one county seat to the next, they considered it a "vacation" to spend two or three days in this oasis in company of congenial friends and be entertained by a host who knew more Indian history, stories, traditions, rites, ceremonies, and myths than any other man.

Seger saw Houston many times and always asked him to address the teachers and students. Everyone was called upon to make a speech, whether he was the judge, a lawyer, or a deputy marshal. If a visitor did not make a talk, the Indians thought he was slighting them.

Thompson B. Ferguson, who brought a primitive press from Kansas to establish his highly successful and influential *Watonga Republican* in 1892, and for years championed law and order and cultural progress in western Oklahoma, reported many court sessions in Blaine County. He recalled that there was never a more complete assortment of men thrown together to whom position and place meant nothing then—like Jesse James Dunn, dignified, astute philosopher and zealous follower of Samuel N. Wood during Kansas' famed Stevens County War. Dunn settled at Alva at the opening of the Outlet and practiced law with George Lynn Miller, a brother-in-law, riding the circuit after his 1894 defeat as candidate for prosecuting attorney of Woods County at the hands of the Populist party. Ferguson's fondest recollections were of United States Deputy Marshal Chris Madsen, veteran of four wars, fearless, relentless peace officer, and of Temple Houston, with his long tawny hair, high-heeled boots, and tongue touched with fire.

Temple found the open country fascinating. It was a succession of prairies carpeted with buffalo grass, low-lying mesas with red banks, sandhills patched with sagebrush, soapweed, saltgrass, and wild-plum thickets; white gypsum and salt deposits glistening in the sun; small creeks bordered with elm and cottonwood; deep canyons full of fine oak, walnut, and cedar; and here and there a ranch house or settler's shanty with a patch of trees, a "can patch," a windmill, and an occasional barbed-wire fence enclosing a large ranch or pasture. Scattered herds of cattle grazed on the prairies or in the canyons or watered at the springs and shallow streams. Sometimes the court party sighted antelope and deer or flushed large coveys of prairie chicken. Coyotes were numerous, and rattlesnakes a cautious hazard. "We always watched for rattlesnakes," Temple said, describing these trips to Laura.

An extant tale involved two cowpunchers, one of whom had thoughtlessly dismounted within a few feet of a rattler, which bit him on the leg. The day was hot, and the poison would soon bring dire results. The other cowboy quickly tied his neckscarf above the wound, and they made a dash for some timber a mile away. There he securely bound his partner to a tree with his lariat, built a fire and heated his picket iron to a bright red, then placed the point as close to the wound as possible without touching the flesh.

As the heat drew out the poison, the iron, turned a greenish color, whereupon he reheated and applied it again. After a few applications the iron failed to turn green, and the cowboy recovered. Had he not been tied securely, he would have broken loose from the terrible agony.

Judge Burford had his own aversion to snakes, and confided to Houston: "Snakes or anything resembling them gives me the shivers. I wouldn't touch a live one for five hundred dollars!" Later, when Judge Burford was sitting for Judge McAtee in Dewey County at Taloga, Temple appeared for the defense resplendent in satin-striped trousers, a fine silk shirt ruffled at the cuffs, and a neckcloth made from the skin of a mammoth rattler.

The idea of a snake being tied around a man's neck worried the judge. As the trial progressed, he kept peering at it over his glasses, growing more and more nervous.

Finally, he remarked: "If the distinguished counsel will permit, I wish to say that he distracts my attention from the business at hand. The gentleman from Woodward will oblige the court by returning after dinner without his rattlesnake-skin cravat."

Temple cheerfully apologized and came back in the afternoon smiling and wearing a gorgeous green tie that would have cheered an Irishman.

One morning when Burford opened court, Houston appeared nervous and irritable.

"Temple, you promised me you would never drink when I was on the bench," said the judge. "You cannot do justice to your client and had better lay off the rest of the day."

Houston (in black hat and coat) with unidentified friends at the McFadden Saloon, Taloga, Oklahoma Territory. Courtesy of Western History Collections, University of Oklahoma Library.

"I haven't been drinking," Temple declared, "and haven't been for a week. This is an old one wearing off."

"But you have taken a drink today," the judge said.

Temple replied: "Don't you know, your Honor, that you have to do that to get over one that has lasted a long time."

The judge dropped the matter, and Houston was amicable and courteous the rest of the term. During the long years he practiced before Burford, Houston always treated him with respect. With others he was often arrogant, harassing witnesses, and tormenting attorneys for the prosecution. When more or less under the influence, he sometimes became unruly and rash action on his part was usually expected.

Judge McAtee of the Fifth District feared him. After Temple "shot the jury out of the box" at the Enid trial of the friendless cowboy charged with murdering the trigger-fast Day County rancher, McAtee made it a rule that all parties in his cases be unarmed. He was not always successful.

An important suit involving a section of land near Woodward came up in his court. McAtee knew that the case already had engendered some bitter feeling, and he ordered a thirty-minute recess in which lawyers and witnesses were to dispose of their firearms. Heavyset, affable Will E. ("Billy") Bolton, secretary of the Oklahoma Live Stock Association and editor of its monthly publication, the *Live Stock Inspector,* had his printshop nearby. The sheriff and his deputies escorted everybody concerned to the back room of the building, where allegedly they were searched one by one. A bushel basket of weapons was taken from the men, including Houston's Old Betsy, and the trial resumed.

Attorney Tom Ward, who represented the plaintiff, stood before the jurors bending over and showing them a diagram of the tract of land. McAtee noticed a "protuberance" in the vicinity of Ward's hip pocket and stopped the proceedings at once.

"Did you dispose of your gun, Mr. Ward?" he asked.

"Naw-suh, your Honor," replied the lawyer.

"I fine you twenty-five dollars," said McAtee, as Ward laid a six-shooter on the table.

The trial continued, but during the next few minutes two-thirds of the audience left the courtroom. Some of the jurors even looked uneasy. When court adjourned, with Houston the victor, McAtee inquired of him why the exodus. Temple slapped his thigh and remarked, "Lord, Judge, that was a narrow escape; they thought maybe you were going to make the order general."

Afterward Houston stepped into the printshop to retrieve Old Betsy. Bolton remembered that he picked up the weapon, twirled it on his finger and suddenly brought it to a shooting position, full-cocked.

W. E. ("Billy") Bolton, publisher of the *Live Stock Inspector*, Woodward.

David P. Marum, Woodward attorney and Houston's second law partner, later state senator.

After dissolving the firm of Ray & Houston at Woodward, Temple associated himself with David P. Marum. Marum, formerly a member of the New York bar at Brooklyn and a descendant of Dutch ancestors that settled in New York when it was a province of Holland, had come west in the early 1880s and at the opening of the Outlet was United States commissioner at Fort Supply. When the fort was abandoned in 1895, Marum set up a law practice in Woodward.

Temple's strength was in criminal law; he handled comparatively little civil litigation. Marum took care of that class of business and did most of the paperwork. But in the courtroom Temple would take the forefront to play upon the emotions and minds of men as a master artist. On circuit, like his old Panhandle friend "Yellow House Canyon" Woodman, he tried his cases without a partner. He seldom lodged at a hotel but seemed to delight in being with the early-day cowpunchers and in loitering around cow camps. If a cow camp or ranch dwelling was within reasonable distance along his route, he would ride to it, probably for supper, and often sleep the night away on his saddle and slicker. Cowboys called him the "Lone Wolf of the Canadian."

When he dropped into a saloon for a drink, it was his custom to insist that every man in the house have one at his expense regardless of the number. Money had no special value to him; consequently, he never possessed an abundance of it, though he was skillful in securing large fees. He also retained a large clientele, for once his client, always his client. His characteristic greeting to officials when they came to court was, "Have you come out to the hangin'?"

William W. Cullar, who lived on a claim with his family near the Persimmon Creek tributary of the North Canadian between Woodward and Taloga and operated a part-dugout and cedar-log trading post, recalled:

> We were prepared to feed and care for people hauling freight between the two places. Officers coming through with criminals would stay overnight; the officer would shackle the criminal to himself so he couldn't get away. Temple Houston often stayed with us,

and every time ... he would come carrying a chicken to the house, saying his horse had killed it. He would ask us to cook the chicken, which we did, and he would pay for the chicken as well as his meal and night's lodging.

Another of Houston's eating habits was described by Fred Barde, a territorial journalist, who knew him well:

> His early days in Brazoria County, Texas, had made him fond of condiments and highly seasoned foods. He carried with him in following the court circuits of Western Oklahoma, where hotel service was often poor, a "magic bottle" whose contents, he said, would make any dish palatable. It was filled with tabasco sauce, the hottest imaginable.... I was among a party of friends whom he invited to a restaurant to eat fried oysters. Reaching into his vest pocket, he took out the mysterious bottle, from which he dashed a liberal supply of sauce over his oysters. Handing me the bottle, he begged me to use it. I shuddered when I felt its human warmth, and wept the moment I tasted an oyster. It nearly burned me alive.

However eccentric, hard, and unyielding he seemed on circuit and in local courtrooms, Temple was a devoted husband and father. He loved jokes and was forever performing antics that kept his children laughing. He had four now—Temple, Jr., Sam, Mary Lea, and Richard.

Richard, in later years, described his father as

> sort of a genius, which amply compensated, it seems, for his one great failing—the intemperate use of strong drink.... All the classics of literature Father had in his library, and he would sometimes read intently, in spite of my mother's remonstrances, throughout the night....
>
> His brain was like a dynamo, ever active and restless in search of more knowledge ... and most retentive; once he read or was told anything it continued with him. He never marked a book, being able to turn at will to any section or part of it he wished, so keen was his power of recollection.
>
> He never inflicted corporal punishment on any of us children, but had any of us spoken or acted disrespectfully toward any woman, our penalty certainly would have been summary and severe. In manner he could have been likened to Lord Chesterfield—courtly, gallant

and chivalrous. . . . His regard for women was actually reverent.

To Laura Houston, he was

one of the gentlest men I have ever known. When he was reading a paper or book, and I spoke of something, no matter how busy he was, he would lay his book or paper aside and become interested in what I had to say. When I would fly up and lose control of myself, he would call me his "handful of powder on a red hot stove."

He loved clothes. He would dress up in a yellow-beaded vest, Spanish caballero style trousers and sombrero with a great silver eagle on it, and go to Kansas City on railroad business. Of course, he attraced a lot of attention. When people asked why I let him dress that way, I would say "That's why I married him—because he was different." He never bothered me about things I did, and I never interfered with things he wanted to do.

Ever attentive to her needs, Temple would bring her perfume, delicate apparel, and other gifts from the shops he visited on his trips to help her bridge Oklahoma's harshness and the Louisiana gentleness she had left behind. He never seemed so happy, or eager as when a court term had ended and he was heading home.

Once he and lawyer Swindall had been attending court for a week at Cheyenne. Starting back to Woodward in the afternoon in a buggy, they found the South Canadian out of its banks because of heavy rains and were forced to spend the night with a rancher named Crawford. Next morning Crawford sent his son to test the river on horseback. The water was still high, and young Crawford advised against going into it. Temple, however, grew impatient and insisted that they venture across.

They soon reached deep water. The team had to swim, and the buggy capsized, throwing the men into the torrent. Both went under. Swindall became entangled in the buggy, but managed to free himself and swim to safety. Temple came up a short distance from Swindall, found his footing, and, shaking the murky red water from his flowing hair, ejaculated, "Talk about the Ol' Mississippi being the Father of Waters; why it wouldn't make a ramrod for this damned Canadian!"

A short time afterward he and Sidney Laune were returning from a court term at Beaver in Laune's buggy pulled by a bronco team. As they plodded along, Temple kept telling Laune that it was necessary that he reach Woodward as soon as possible, but Laune refused to hurry the horses. Noon came; Laune stopped the team and began to unhitch. Temple remonstrated in fervid eloquence, to no avail. Laune hung on the nosebags, and never did two animals take more time to munch their grain. Then Laune picketed them to graze. The horses, he said, were too tired to continue the journey and needed rest and grass. Finally he lay down in the shade of the buggy to nap.

Temple always declared his innocence of what happened next. Telling friends about it, he said:

After expending my breath in futile argument, I stretched out on the prairie myself. . . . Suddenly I was awakened by the most frightful ripping and snorting, and looked up to see those broncos tearing across the prairie like the furies of Hades were driving them. Laune was standing there with a hurt, baffled look on his face, watching them high-tail with harness and picket pins flying into the far blue distance.

I said, "I hope to God those poor weary beasts get some rest and grass!" then closed my eyes and went back to sleep while Laune trudged over the prairie through the blistering heat after those damned horses. He caught them somewhere, cornered in a pasture, or they'd be running yet.

Though Temple was often criticized by his contemporaries, they generally agreed on his genius as a lawyer. Veteran western Oklahoma attorney L. E. Moyer found him a very dangerous man to oppose in a lawsuit. Charles Alexander, a Woodward attorney for over forty years, never saw his equal in the courtroom. C. W. Herod, Woodward land-office attorney and later county judge, considered Houston one of the most skillful trial lawyers of his day and time anywhere in the United States. El Reno attorney Colonel R. B. Forrest was the most specific:

He was not a law student, never studied law hard. It was his feelings of the moment giving vent to themselves through a magnetic nature, incapable of control when wrought to excitement. No man had a finer control of the English language. His thoughts were expressed in the most exquisite and often infrequently used terms. His voice, while not strong, was chimey and musical, and when raised in strains of invective, penetrating and thrilling. He never spoke long. From forty minutes to an hour would cover the space of time. In sympathetic appeals he developed remarkable force. The heart stricken wife, the weeping and aged mother, the fatherless child, the disappointed and unconsolable sweetheart—whatever the object of distress, he could touch a heart of stone in painting its sorrows. He seemed to feel the agonies of others and portrayed them with electric power. His arguments were Socratic. He would make his point by propounding an unanswerable question. His comparisons were uproariously absurd or pathetically tender, on occasion beautifully epigrammatical.

In commenting on the testimony of one witness, Houston declared: "He sat there manufacturing perjury as gaily as a mocking bird ever sang its lay."

The *Guthrie Daily Leader* of August 21, 1894, called him "the silver tongued orator of Oklahoma."

14

Guns and Death

The *State Capital* of January 25, 1895, noted that "Temple Houston, son of General Sam Houston of Texas fame, has been viewing the work of the legislature for the past week." The *Oklahoma Times-Journal* noted that he was still in Guthrie on February 1: "A conspicuous figure about the legislature is Temple Houston ... the attorney at Woodward." He was in Guthrie ostensibly consulting with Robert Ray on some cases he was handling during Ray's attendance at the Third Legislative Assembly. While he was there, Temple offered suggestions and expressed great interest in an act approved February 18 amending several sections of Chapter 6, 1893 Oklahoma Statutes, governing the duties of attorneys, causes for suspension or revocation of license to practice, proceedings and appeal in such suspension or revocation, claim to lien on money or property of a client held for an attorney fee, and the client's release of lien by giving bond with sufficient sureties. Many said that he represented the powerful lobby of the Oklahoma Live Stock Association.

The association had been organized in Woodward County for the destruction of wolves and the protection of members against thieves by employing inspectors at all principal markets and shipping points on the range and offering rewards. Hundreds of strayed and stolen animals had been recovered for their owners, and its *Live Stock Inspector*, the only range newspaper devoted exclusively to livestock in America, had become a journal of national importance. Its annual conventions, attended by many shippers and representatives from all markets east and west, as well as nearly two thousand members spending thousands of dollars, was sought by several cities.

The association also was concerned with the leasing of public lands and had been instrumental in securing the first modification of the federal quarantine line intersecting Oklahoma Territory. This line—commencing on the Arkansas River at the Kansas border and running south along the western borders of the Osage, Creek, and Seminole nations to the South Canadian, thence up the Canadian, down the western boundary of the Wichita reservation to the Washita, west along the northern border of the Kiowa-Comanche-Apache Reservation to the North Fork of Red River, and up the Red to the one hundredth meridian—gave ranchers on the west and north the privilege of shipping cattle on the open market at an estimated increase of two to five dollars a head. In the Third Legislative Assembly the association again proved its usefulness by influencing passage of an act favoring maintenance of the federal line and another act requiring all parties butchering stock or purchasing hides or pelts to keep a record of the marks, brands, color, person from whom purchased, sex, and age. The Cattle act also ordered purchasers to

keep all hides together, with horns and ears complete, for at least five days from time of butchering during the months of May, June, July, August, September and October, and during the remaining months of the year, ten days, said hides are to be free for inspection to anyone wishing to see the same.

Violation of any provision of the act was punishable by a fine of not less than twenty-five dollars or more than two hundred dollars, imprisonment in the county jail from ten days to six months, or by both such fine and imprisonment.

Thus the big cattlemen of northwestern Oklahoma retained their grip on all land that had not been preempted, often dictated territorial policies, and extended their influence to the Indian reservations and Washington. Nesters seldom owned more than fifty to 150 head of cattle. Governor Renfrow made a special trip to Woodward in 1893. At a meeting with the association details were worked out whereby the cattlemen were leasing every acre of school land in approximately the western one-third of the Outlet, and Renfrow allegedly promised to do all in his power to protect them against the encroachment of the settlers. In 1895 Territorial Attorney General C. A. Galbraith went to Woodward and prosecuted several school-lease cases in district court. The cattlemen thought that by fencing unoccupied domain with the school lands they would not have to pay lease for the school land enclosed. Chief Justice Dale ruled otherwise, and the attorney general got judgment against several cowmen amounting to over ten thousand dollars for the territory. Their "fixers," however, continued diligently on the job at the territorial capital and indirectly controlled local courts and peace officers.

A case in point involved a Woodward deputy sheriff, a close friend of the big cowmen, who was charged with stealing nesters' cattle. A jail delivery under guise of a jail break was carefully planned, but not as carefully executed. In a sharp skirmish with a posse in the Beaver Creek bottoms, one of the deputy's arms was shot off at the elbow. He was forced to stand trial and found guilty. Before sentence could be passed, the cattlemen fixed local officials and the prisoner was allowed to depart for regions unknown. Old-timers repeatedly declared that Houston received attractive retainer fees from the big cowmen to keep them out of the penitentiary.

Another tale handed down the years was that Temple incurred the ire of the Jennings brothers over a lease lawsuit involving Jack Love. There were four Jennings boys—Edward, John, Frank E., and Alphonso ("Al") J., the youngest—the sons of Judge J. D. F. Jennings and all lawyers. Born in Tazewell County, Virginia, educated at Emory and Henry College in religion and medicine, the father served as a surgeon with the Forty-first Virginia Infantry during the Civil War. After the war he moved his family to Marion, Illinois, where he was a circuit-riding minister and studied law. He served as county attorney of Williamson County from 1872 to 1874, when his wife died. He then located at Manchester, Ohio, practicing law there until 1880, then at Appleton City,

Missouri, until 1884, when he moved to Comanche County, Kansas, serving two terms as probate judge at Coldwater. In 1888 he moved to Baca County, Colorado, practicing law at Trinidad until April 1889, when he joined the Oklahoma land rush and secured a claim southeast of Kingfisher. Ed and John accompanied him. They had learned enough law in their father's office to pass the bar examinations, and they set up practice at El Reno. Al, graduating from the law school at the West Virginia State University and Military Academy, soon joined Ed and John, and from 1892 to 1894 served as prosecuting attorney of Canadian County.

All the Jenningses were active in Democratic politics. Judge Jennings had been awarded the Woodward judgeship for his work in early territorial conventions and for his staunch support of President Cleveland. Ed and John moved to Woodward with their father, and Al, failing of renomination as county attorney, joined them the fall of 1895. Frank remained in Colorado as a deputy clerk in the district court at Denver.

Al, in his biography, *Beating Back* (written with Will Irwin and published in 1913), and his novelized autobiography, *Through the Shadows with O. Henry* (1921), claimed that Ed and John represented a man named Frank Garst, who was pasturing eighteen hundred head of cattle on a range fenced by Love. Love held no title to the pasturage, and when the rental fee of three thousand dollars came due, Garst moved his herd and refused to pay. Love gained an attachment through attorney Houston, but the Jenningses proved that Love had "appropriated" government land and therefore was himself a trespasser. Garst and Love and their attorneys locked horns in court. Garst does not exist in contemporary reports.

There was a lawsuit involving Love's cattle interests. Not wishing to succeed himself as sheriff, Love had accepted the Democratic nomination for representative in the territorial legislature at the November, 1894, election. But he had made no personal canvass, his friends having placed his name on the ballot, and he had been defeated by the Republican nominee by two votes. Love then devoted his full time to ranching.

Cabinet Saloon, Woodward, scene of the Houston-Jennings gunfight. Leaning on the porch post is John Garvey, the proprietor. The man on horseback is Al Jennings.

With cattlemen P. L. Herring, Wilson & Short, Pryor & Hume, and Grimes & Murphy he had contracted from the territorial leasing board the grazing rights on fifty-seven sections of school land lying in different townships west of Range 13 of the Indian Meridian, to be paid for, $470.25 cash from January 1, 1895; $1,410.75, December 15, 1896; $1,881.00, Decemember 15, 1897; $1,881.00, December 15, 1898; and $1,881.00, December 15, 1899, each party standing good for "one-fifth of above." Upon learning that reserved school land in the Outlet, by congressional act of 1891 and rules prescribed by the secretary of interior, could not be leased for a period exceeding three years and that one section was the maximum quantity allowed one person, Love and his fellow cowmen refused to perform, and the attorney general of the territory sued for $3,291.75 damages and breach of contract.

Houston, Marum, and Ray represented the defendants. The Woodward district court held that the leasing board could not recover damages for breach of a contract it had no legal authority to make, and the judgment, removed to the state supreme court by petition in error, was affirmed. No Jennings was involved.

C. W. Herod traced the Houston-Jennings controversy to the time when

Temple brought suit in the county court at Woodward for recovery of a horse which had been sold to John Jennings. The horse, at the time sold, was covered by a valid and unsatisfied chattel mortgage. The case was heard by Judge Jennings, who ruled in favor of Houston's client, but John still had the horse. . . . The father would not make an order restoring the horse to its rightful owner, nor take the animal away from his son John. This irritating experience caused Temple to litigate no more cases in the county court of Woodward County so long as Jennings was the presiding officer.

On October 8, 1895, several young men were arraigned in Justice of the Peace Williams' court charged with the theft of a keg of beer from a Santa Fe freight car. Temple appeared with County Attorney Smith for the prosecution; Ed and John

Jennings appeared for the defense. During examination of a company witness Ed questioned the admissibility of his testimony. An argument over a number of other minor points followed, and Temple suggested that his opponent "must be grossly ignorant of the law." Ed's temper flared. Slamming his fist on the table, he shouted, "You're a damned liar!" and lurched at Houston to slap his face.

Herod continued: "Temple's cases often had been tempestuous, but he had never allowed another man to lay a hand on him in anger. Guns were drawn, but others present in the court room interfered, and a bloody shooting affray was avoided.˙... Court immediately adjourned to reconvene the next day."

That evening at Ed's office Judge Jennings allegedly reproached his sons for their hot tempers and for putting him in a ticklish position. Ed and John agreed to apologize to Houston. Meanwhile, with "feeling high" and "everybody in Woodward expecting a shooting before morning,.... home was the only place for a Jennings." Ed and John remained to wind up affairs at the office. The Judge and Al went home to wait for them. It was a warm night, and Al and his father fell asleep. They were awakened by someone called from outside: "Judge! Get up quick! Your boys are killed!"

Al stated: "No one can imagine the sick feeling that came over me. I dressed hastily and ran out of the gate past father, where I met John, who was sorely wounded. He told me to go to Garvey's saloon, that Ed was dead."

A Woodward dispatch to the territorial press on October 9 gave this account of what happened:

> Last night about 10 o'clock, this town was aroused by a fusillade of shots in one of the principal saloons here, known as the "Cabinet," and owned by Jack Garvey. Hastening there the spectators beheld lawyer Ed Jennings weltering in blood, his brain oozing from a bullet hole in the left side of his head, his hand still clinging to a smoking revolver, half concealed by his prostrate form.
>
> Lawyer John Jennings was fleeing up the street with one arm limp and dangling by his side from which the blood poured in streams.

Lawyer Temple Houston and ex-Sheriff Jack Love were on their way to the sheriff's office to surrender their persons to his custody. Neither Love nor Houston were wounded, although several bullets passed through their clothes and hats.

Here is Judge Herod's version:

I saw the Jennings boys milling about during the evening, going from saloon to saloon drinking and beyond a doubt preparing for serious trouble.... Toward 10 o'clock Love and Temple Houston stepped into Jack Garvey's saloon on the north side of Main Street, ... drank, loitered about the bar a few minutes, then retired to the gambling room in the rear. Presently Ed and John Jennings came into the saloon and drank at the bar. I was lounging in the lobby of the nearby Cattle King Hotel....

The Jenningses loitered about the bar for a short time, observing Houston and Love in the back room. Each drew a revolver from concealment on their persons and swung them from their waistlines in plain view. Houston and Love saw the boys thus juggle their guns by their reflections in the bar mirror. Finally the Jennings boys stepped into the back room.

Garvey's saloon faced south. The gambling room was in its north end. Love and Houston sat at a card table in the northeast corner. In the north wall and near the table was a door to the outside. Along the east wall stood a long table used for dice games and a large stove. Ed stepped between the table and east wall and John stopped behind the stove. There was a piano in the room too, and the man who played it....

Houston and Love continued sitting at the table. Houston, however, so he claimed, got so nervous in the midst of such an untoward situation that he ... got up ... stepped toward the outside door and addressed Ed Jennings thus: "Ed, I want to see you a minute." Ed replied, "See me here and now, you son-of-a-bitch!" ... drew his gun quick as a flash, and Houston drew and fired at Ed Jennings.

The concussion of the first shots put out the lights. More shooting followed by Ed Jennings and by John from behind the stove. Love opened fire on John Jennings.... Houston emptied his gun, then threw it in the direction of the Jennings boys, and ejaculated, "Shoot—shoot!" Darkness, of course, enveloped everything....

Love shot John Jennings once, the bullet striking John in the chest at such an angle that it inflicted only a flesh wound but shattered the bones in his left arm between the shoulder and elbow. He ran from the saloon and Love pursued him, shooting at him once more as he dashed south across the street. The bullet missed John and lodged in a frame store building.

Another man and I dashed from the hotel for the saloon. We met John Jennings stumbling up the street with his left arm limp and profusely bleeding. He told us... Houston had shot his brother Ed and that Jack Love had shot his arm off. We rushed on into the saloon... the bartender had gotten a light or two on again... he and the dying Ed Jennings were the only people in the house. Ed Jennings lay near the center of the room face down in a pool of blood, still clenching his gun and more blood oozing from his nose and mouth. Houston's first shot had struck him above the right ear and took away a piece of the skull. Its effect apparently only addled Ed.... he had continued shooting at Houston, but because the room was dark none of his shots took effect. It appeared that he tried to work out from behind the dice table and collapsed facing his antagonist....

I turned him over on his back, wiped the blood from his face with my handkerchief, and the man with me took off his own hat and placed it under Ed Jennings' head as he breathed his last. Soon Judge Jennings arrived, and kneeling over the body, exclaimed, "I murdered my own boy."

The only interpretation I can give this remark was that Judge Jennings felt he indirectly had contributed to the killing because of the wrong treatment Temple Houston had received in his court.

Upon examination it was found that Ed Jennings also had been shot in the back of the head, the bullet entering from the left and lodging just behind his forehead.

Temple Houston had emptied his gun and Ed Jennings likewise. All shots from Houston's gun were found and so were Ed Jennings'. Jack Love had shot only twice, one bullet shattering John Jennings' arm, the other going wild into the store building. John Jennings had discharged all the cartridges in his gun, too, but only four were accounted for. I verily believe to this day that it was the shot from John Jennings' pistol that killed Ed, his brother.

Coroner J. M. Workman conducted the inquest. The jury, composed of well-known citizens H. C. Thompson, R. B. Clark, James Hunter, James Haybaugh, Paul McCloud and Joe Hedrick, rendered a verdict that "deceased came to his

Alphonso J. ("Al") Jennings.

death as a result of a shooting affair engaged in by Temple Houston, J. E. Love and John Jennings."

Though Temple took full responsibility for the killing, both he and Love were charged with first degree manslaughter and released under $5,000 bonds. The love, amounting almost to veneration, with which Houston was held in Texas, was again shown by a constant stream of letters and telegrams received, solicitous of his acquittal, from citizens of the Lone Star state.

After much bickering and delay the case of *Territory of Oklahoma v. Temple Houston and Jack Love* began in the Woodward district court in May, 1896. County Attorney Smith disqualified himself, being connected with the principals in the affair. Attorney General Galbraith, assisted by County Attorney Shannon McCray of Day County, prosecuted; and Henry E. Asp, general counsel for the Santa Fe, with Marum and Ray, appeared for the defense.

A Woodward dispatch of May 15 reported that

> some difficulty was experienced in getting a jury, the regular panel having been exhausted. The taking of testimony was begun this morning and concluded except for the testimony of Houston. The prosecution made a weak case being hampered by the general feeling that the killing was justified and the further fact that none of the Jennings' appeared to urge the prosecution, not even the (wounded) brother of the deceased.
>
> A peculiar feature developed by the evidence shows that Ed Jennings was shot twice through the head and from the range, it appeared that his brother John who was behind him, must have fired the fatal shot.

Attorney Asp said, after the trial:

> Houston was the calmest man in the courtroom. He was not placed on the stand and didn't speak a word during the proceedings. He apparently did not pay any attention to the testimony, but sat at the table all the time drawing pictures of Napoleon, which were beautiful. He drew them and tore them up, one after the other. Then he drew pictures of cowboys, with guns in their hands, shooting.

Most of the twenty-some witnesses to the battle testified that Temple had "fired clearly" in self-defense. He and Love were acquitted.

Al Jennings blamed it on the perfidy of the county attorney (Smith did not participate), and swore he would kill Houston. He stated, in *Beating Back:*

> The day we buried Ed, Frank came from Denver.... [He] felt exactly as I did [and] told me so.... Father asked us whether, with

Henry E. Asp, attorney and general counselor for the Santa Fe Railroad, who defended Houston in the killing of Ed Jennings.

one of his boys dead and another... delirious and in danger of his life... we wanted to pile a new tragedy on him.... We did not trust ourselves in Woodward, where Love and Houston would offer continual temptation. The night when the doctors pronounced John out of danger, Frank and I saddled our horses, took what money we had, and rode away toward Southern Oklahoma, intending to establish among the outlaws some base from which... we could make a raid and kill those two men. We were outlaws in spirit. The rest came as gradually and easily as sliding down hill.

Because of his traumatic experience at Woodward, Judge Jennings moved to Shawnee, where he continued to practice law, was elected probate judge of Pottawatomie County in the Populist victory of 1896, and moved to Tecumseh. John, recovered from his wounds, served as probate clerk. Judge Jennings was reelected to a four-year term in 1898. In 1901 he retired, moving to Slater, Missouri, where he died in 1903. Meanwhile, Al and Frank drifted about the territory, hunting Houston but somehow never finding him. Generally they would put in an appearance in towns where Temple was not attending court.

Various tales have been told how friends managed to keep them apart and avoid trouble. But in his book *Oklahombres* (1929), former United States Marshal of the Territory E. D. Nix, who was familiar with the situation, stated: "Houston would not have made the least effort to avoid [Al and Frank], or any set of men that ever lived." As one old Panhandle lawyer said, "Temple would have charged hell with only a bucket of water."

James Griggs, who worked as night clerk at the Cattle King Hotel, told of the time Al Jennings sent word that he was returning to Woodward to "fight it out." Temple was attending court at Canadian, Texas. Friends wired him of Al's purported coming, and he returned to Woodward immediately. Griggs went with the hotel bus to meet the train:

> Temple rode the bus up town with several passengers who were to spend the night. Jennings was thought to be in Woodward.... Temple drew Old Betsy from under his coat and sat composed in the rig

with gun in hand and eyes flashing. The bus was to stop first at the Central Hotel, where some of the passengers were staying, then take Houston home and return to the Cattle King. When the rig reached the Central, every passenger was more than ready to get out regardless. . . . Temple was taken on to his residence safely, and nothing was seen of his enemy.

Al Jennings told how, later that night, while Temple sat by a lamp reading, he leveled his Winchester upon him and, but for the passage of Mrs. Houston between the window and Temple, would have killed him. It is doubtful, however, that Al ever returned to Woodward after he and Frank left together, for, while visiting Colonel Forrest one day at El Reno, he declared:

"I will not assassinate Houston. I will kill him when he has equal show for his life." Colonel Forrest

endeavored to persuade Al to drop the matter and settle down again, but to no avail. . . . My relations with both parties were such that Judge Jennings, in '97, while probate judge of Pottawatomie County, requested me to use my offices of conciliation to get both Temple and Al to agree that they pass each other as entire strangers, should accident ever throw them on the same street. I had correspondence with Temple and personally saw Al, and showed him Temple's letter, which was not entirely clear. It rather indicated that he was fearful of such an arrangement. And so the matter dropped. It was an affair of such a delicate nature that I confess I was not so courageous in pressing it.

The killing of Houston or Jennings, one by the other, or both, would probably have occurred had not Jennings started train robbing. On the night of August 16, 1897, Al and Frank, self-styled leaders of a gang composed of a couple of Tecumseh "hardcases," Morris and Pat O'Malley, and the remnants of the Doolin-Dalton band of outlaws, Dynamite Dick Clifton and Little Dick West, held up the southbound Santa Fe at Edmond, failed in their efforts to dynamite the Wells Fargo safe, and fled into Indian Territory. Two weeks later they made an abortive attempt on the Katy express at Bond Switch, southwest of Muskogee. With posses hot on their trail, they returned southwest across the Seminole and Pottawatomie lands into the Chickasaw Nation, where they were thwarted in burglarizing the Santa Fe station at Purcell. Down to their last penny, their clothing tattered, and eating only such meals as they could obtain from scattered farm houses, the gang members grew desperate.

Shortly after eleven o'clock on the morning of October 1 they stopped the southbound Rock Island passenger train eight miles south of Minco. Dynamiting the express safe again proved a failure. An oversupply of explosives shook the entire train and shattered the express car. After rifling the mail coach, they lined up more than one hundred passengers alongside the track; secured about four hundred dollars in cash, diamond studs, pins, and other valuables; and escaped northwest into the Wichita Reservation.

Houston and Colonel Forrest were attending district court at Arapaho. Forrest recalled:

Late that night, a messenger came riding into the little village in hot haste. He had started from Woodward at 4 P.M. and had covered the distance in about twelve hours to bear the tiding to Houston that the Jennings gang had taken a western course and were heading toward Arapaho where they knew Temple to be. . . . The news had reached Woodward by telegram over the Santa Fe. Bill Fossett [William D., formerly a Rock Island detective and now chief deputy United States marshal] was at court and immediately organized a couple of squads, going himself with one of them, to intercept the robbers. There was much excitement generally, but Houston was as quiet as a grave. He showed not the slightest apparent interest in the affair.

The second day after he was due to start home. Nothing had been heard of the robbers. There was no means of communication to Arapaho west of Geary except by stage mail. The country for miles between was open prairie and timbered streams. You could travel all day and meet no one. Al Jennings knew every cow path and every brush patch, every river and creek crossing, and if he had entertained the design to catch Houston at a disadvantage, he had his opportunity. It was believed the robbers would rendezvous some place between Arapaho and Woodward and intercept Temple'on his road home.

I told him it would be well to remain at Arapaho until some word arrived as to where the gang was located. He said he had an engagement somewhere in the Panhandle the first of the week and had no time to lose. He did not express a word of alarm nor breathe a sign of fright. He got into his buggy with the faithful cowboy friend who had brought the message, and with a Winchester and a couple of six-shooters, was off as if not the slightest danger had made its appearance.

The Jennings' made but a short detour westward from the railroad and turned back to Indian Territory. No danger, in fact, existed, but nothing could prove the absolute fearless nature of the man more than his going under such conditions.

The gang divided the loot and rested at a friend's home near El Reno. In mid-October, when the pursuit had died, they drifted down the Cimarron toward the Creek Nation. About two o'clock on the morning of October 29 they entered the Crozier & Nutter store at Cushing, in Payne County, took fifteen dollars from the till, and outfitted themselves with the best hats, gloves, and overcoats the mercantile establishment had to offer.

Disenchanted by the outfit's failures, Dynamite Dick and Little Dick West left the Jenningses and O'Malleys, each riding to his separate fate. On November 7, Dynamite Dick fell to the gunfire of Deputy Marshals George Lawson and Hess Bussy as he fled from a cabin hideout west of Checotah. A few months later Little Dick West was found working as a hired hand on the Harmon Arnett farm on Cottonwood Creek southwest of Guthrie, and was killed by a posse under Chief Deputy Fossett and Sheriff Frank Rinehart of Logan County.

Deputy Marshal James F. ("Bud") Ledbetter of Muskogee struck the trail of the Jenningses and the O'Malleys as soon as they entered the Creek Nation. He and his posse found them at the Spike S Ranch near the junction of Snake and Duck creeks, where a gun battle took place the morning of November 30. Morris O'Malley was captured. Al, Frank, and Pat O'Malley were wounded but escaped in the Duck Creek bottoms. On December 5, Ledbetter learned that they were heading out of the country, their wounds dressed, concealed under straw and blankets in a wagon. He intercepted the wagon at a rock crossing on Carr Creek, captured the trio without firing a shot, and lodged them in the federal jail at Muskogee.

When the news reached Woodward, Temple Houston wired Muskogee that he would defend the Jennings boys if it was a "sure thing" that they had been captured. "This is generosity with vengeance," commented the December 8 *Oklahoma State Capital*. Of course, Al and Frank refused the offer.

Al was convicted of assault with intent to kill Deputy Ledbetter in the fight at the Spike S Ranch and was sentenced to five years at hard labor in the Fort Leavenworth Penitentiary. He was held in jail at Ardmore until February, 1899, when he was tried for train robbery and looting of the United States mails on the Rock Island south of Minco. He was found guilty and sentenced to federal prison at Columbus, Ohio, for life. Frank Jennings and the O'Malleys received five-year sentences in Leavenworth.

15

Chicago "Alkali"

Temple's problems with the Jennings brothers ended, but he had not allowed Old Betsy to become rusty. Though he had abandoned a political career in his native state for a principle, he continued to support the Democratic party and was quick to make cutting remarks when he observed a stale performance. Upon hearing that the state Democratic convention at Dallas had adjourned at four o'clock one morning after days of disagreement over a platform and candidates, he dispatched the following to Texas newspapers:

> Out on the marge of a moonlit strand
> The whing-whang sits with his tongue in the sand,
> And writes his name with his tail on the land
> And rubs it out with his ogreish hand.
>
> Is it the voice of guns or geeks,
> Or what is the voice the whing-whang seeks
> As he prowls around midst winding creeks,
> And holds his breath for weeks and weeks?

Since coming to Oklahoma he had resisted efforts of party wheelhorses to nominate him for one public office or another. As with civil cases, he preferred handling political matters through his law partner David Marum, the 1896 nominee to succeed Robert Ray as senator from the Woodward district in the Fourth Legislative Assembly. Still Temple's services and opinions were much sought after.

The inflationary ideas of Populism, the direct descendant of the Greenback movement and inheritor of most of its liberal characteristics, was appealing to more and more people during the early 1890s because of the nation's severe economic conditions. In the presidential election of 1892, Populists drew so heavily from normally Republican states that Cleveland won over Benjamin Harrison. The Populists also won ten seats in the United States House and five in the United States Senate and gained control of the state governments of Colorado, Kansas, Idaho, and Nevada. Over fifty thousand votes were cast for the party in Texas.

Most of the people who took claims in the openings of 1891-93 and the Kickapoo Reservation in 1895 had been sojourners in Kansas and Texas before their migration to Oklahoma Territory, and the poor crops and extremely low prices after settlement influenced them to espouse Populist doctrines. In 1894 the Populists captured a number of county governments and held the balance of power in the territorial legislature. Thus encouraged, they began girding themselves for an all-out battle in the election of 1896. An intensive campaign of organizing at county level prevailed, and more than a score of territorial newspapers supported the Populist cause. In Woods and Pottawatomie counties there were Populist organizations in practically every township.

The chief office within the electoral gift of the people was that of territorial delegate to the United States House of Representatives, held since 1893 by Republican Dennis T. Flynn. While that official had no vote in the House, he did have every other privilege and was the recognized spokesman of the territory. The Populists were exceedingly eager to nominate some man for the office whose character, campaigning ability, and personal popularity would help carry the party to victory in November. Rumor swept the territory—and the *Enid Daily Eagle* (with wide circulation in northwestern Oklahoma) printed the suggestion—that Temple Houston was that man.

Temple denied it categorically in a letter to the *Eagle* on May 31, 1896:

> Your article . . . . while doubtless written by some person friendly to me. . . . was without my consent. On all sides I have constantly said that I was in no sense a candidate, that I did not want the position—that my time and money were the property of my

conditions—hence I trust that my attitude certainly would take me out of the list of aspirants. Nothing except the most emphatic command from my own party could induce me to overcome my aversion to political ambitions. Believe me,

Sincerely yours,
TEMPLE HOUSTON.

The Populist party, outraged by President Cleveland's repeal of the Sherman Silver Purchase Act of 1893, propagandized on the virtues of increasing the amount of money in circulation, accepting the formula proposed by one of its most effective spokesmen, W. H. ("Coin") Harvey, that farmers and workers would benefit greatly by adopting the free coinage of silver at the ratio of sixteen to one of gold. They also believed that the cure for the nation's economic distress lay in a program of graduated income tax, government ownership of railroads and telegraph, and a public-works program for unemployed laborers. The popularity of these proposals brought dismay to the Democrats, although they had accepted most of them as elements in their programs and platform. Many felt that placing the country on a silver basis independently of the action of other great nations would "impair contracts, disturb business, diminish the purchasing power of the wages of labor, and inflict irreparable evils upon commerce and industry."

There also was an ever-increasing national trend to form a separate silver organization and of integration and fusion of the two parties. The *Eagle* editor's wish to know how Houston stood on these matters drew this response on June 25:

I have delayed answering your favor of the 19th inst. on account of absence and a desire to investigate fully the questions contained in your letter.

I beg leave to most earnestly dissent in the idea of a separate silver organization unless it is within the lines of the Democratic party— and especially do I believe that such a course would be premature unless we were assured that the gold element was oppressive to the democracy.

My ideals on this subject can be briefly stated—I have never sanctioned the vituperative attacks made upon the Populist party—have always felt that some of their demands were entitled to recognition and that their party embraced many good men who really had at heart the betterment of our condition—and while many of their demands were visionary and impracticable, and some of their leaders were unscrupulous and almost revolutionary—still that furnished no reason for condemning the entire party and ignoring their just demands. I believe too—especially in my native Texas—that the Populist party has been more heavily recruited from the Democratic than from the Republican party. I therefore think that these people largely can be won over to democracy—many of their demands are democratic—and I think that our convention at Chicago and our Territory Convention should bestow all proper recognition upon whatever just and righteous demands they make—as to any understanding to be effective with their leaders, etc. I have no suggestions and have never sanctioned fusion. The history of men and measures founded in fusion is not of a kind to encourage such. Believe me.

Sincerely yours,
TEMPLE HOUSTON.

The Republican national convention, meeting at St. Louis on June 16, nominated William McKinley of Ohio on the first ballot and nominated Garrett A. Hobart of New Jersey for vice-president. The platform characterized Cleveland's administration as one of "unparalleled incapacity, dishonor, and disaster," eulogized protection and reciprocity as the "twin measures of Republican policy," and opposed free coinage of silver "except by international agreement with the leading commercial nations of the world" and said that "until such agreement can be obtained, the existing gold standard must be preserved." This stand on gold brought a determined effort by the silver delegates, led by Senator Henry M. Teller of Colorado, to secure adoption of a free-silver plank as a substitute. Overwhelmingly defeated, Teller and thirty-four delegates from the West and South, including four United States senators and two representatives in Congress, withdrew from the convention. This action strengthened the silver wing of the Democratic party.

The Democratic national convention met at Chicago on July 7. The money question already had been fought out in state conventions, thirty of which had declared for unlimited coinage in emphatic terms. The silver forces were in control from the start, and increased representation of Oklahoma, Arizona, and New Mexico territories bent on unseating "gold" delegations gave silver men a two-thirds majority. The platform adopted was unusually long and full of denunciation. It criticized the Republican party as a "prolific breeder of trusts and monopolies," railroad "mergers," government by injunction, and "arbitrary interference by Federal authorities in local affairs as a violation of the Constitution and a crime against free institutions." It also severely criticized the United States Supreme Court for having reversed its former decisions concerning the constitutionality of the income tax and attacked Cleveland's whole financial policy, his issuance of bonds in time of peace, his "trafficking with banking syndicates," and his efforts to maintain the gold reserve, as though these were the crimes and blunders of the Republicans. Cleveland's friends, led by Senator David B. Hill of New York, who favored the gold standard and were opposed to radicalism in the party, exerted themselves to secure the adoption of the customary minority report "commending the honesty, economy, courage and fidelity of the present Democratic National Administration." They were voted down almost without respectful consideration.

The convention then turned to nominating its candidates. Party sentiment had not fixed on any one man. Congressman Richard P. Bland of Missouri, leader of the "Silverites" in the House; Robert E. Pattison, twice Democratic governor of Pennsylvania when his party was in the minority; and Governor Horace Boies of Iowa were the recognized candidates. But in the course of debate on the silver plank a new leader emerged. William Jennings Bryan, a Nebraska attorney and editor of the *Omaha World-Herald,* defended the Democratic platform in an impassioned speech on the floor in which he charged the opposition with wishing to "press down upon the brow of labor a crown of thorns," and "crucify mankind upon a cross of gold." This eloquent outburst brought the convention, or rather the silver portion of it, to its feet and won him the party's presidential nomination. As a concession to eastern money power, the convention chose Arthur Sewall, a wealthy shipbuilder of Maine, for vice-president. The "National" Democrats took no part in the balloting, convinced that control of the party had fallen into the hands of men who were not really Democrats but Populists and that the principles of the Chicago platform were such as no good Democrat could support.

It was indeed a strange spectacle. Temple Houston would add his own. Despite his aversion to political ambitions he was one of seventy-five delegates to the convention from Oklahoma. The Democrats among them were a unit for the nomination of "Silver Dick" Bland. They held their first meeting at ten o'clock on the morning of July 6 and selected A. J. Beale of Oklahoma City as chairman, Mort L. Bixler of Norman as chairman on resolutions, W. S. Denton of Enid on credentials, W. C. Brunt of Chandler on permanent organization, E. P. Mitchell of El Reno on order of business, and Houston on notification.

Governor Renfrow headed the contingent, wearing Bland and free-silver badges. William C. Whitney, Cleveland's secretary of the navy from 1885 to 1889, manager of the Democratic campaign in 1892, and leader of the gold men, noticed the badges when the governor called at his headquarters. Renfrow informed him that Oklahoma and the West generally had sent silver delegates, however he might regret it personally. Whitney expressed great surprise that terrritorial officials had not been able to send up administration support and then, working up gradually to the sour point, demanded why Oklahoma, Arizona, and New Mexico had quietly allowed the administration to be defeated. Renfrow announced simply that the silver fellows had "run off with the bandwagon." In due time he escaped and reported to Senator James Kimbrough

Jones of Arkansas. Jones, who had been potent in securing Renfrow's appointment, assured him that, should the ticket to be nominated be elected, he and his coterie of friends would remain in charge in Oklahoma. Governor Renfrow thereafter gave this matter his utmost attention.

E. F. Mitchell of El Reno tried to make a new deal. He had been promised the position of treasurer of the territory by Renfrow, but there had been "a slip," as Mitchell explained it. He had come to Chicago to turn the kicking machine against Cleveland and the Oklahoma officeholders but found the very man he wanted to lift off the earth (the governor) serenely shielded by those who might control the next administration. Mitchell was not in the best of political spirits.

His idea was to nominate a silver man for territorial delegate to Congress and have Democrats and Populists support him. If he could unite both factions on himself, he would at once announce as a great-friend-of-the-people candidate. That now being an unlikely arrangement, he insisted that Houston have the nomination. The delegate, not having a vote in the House, could do nothing for silver by way of legislation, but Temple, coming from far-western Oklahoma, had not been connected with the factional squabble and would be the man to spring on an unoffending public. Temple suggested his old law partner Robert Ray, but Ray was holding down the Woodward land office and would have to surrender that job in order to make the race. So by way of keeping it in the family, it seemed the better plan to bring out Houston.

Houston and Mitchell tried to persuade the committee on resolutions to denounce the party's record on public land laws and ask for a "free-homes" plank for Oklahoma. All Oklahoma land, except platted city lots, had to be proved up to obtain a patent. That required paying a registration fee, making improvements, and maintaining a residence of six months out of the year for five years or living on the land fourteen months and paying for it at $1.25 per acre, or $200 for a quarter section. Delegate Flynn had been working on a free-homes measure for nearly a year without success, and Oklahoma Democrats were not adverse to taking the issue away from Republicans.

In additon, Houston wanted a plank denouncing Hoke Smith, Cleveland's secretary of the interior, for not opening the Wichita Reservation to settlement according to legislation enacted by the Fifty-second Congress, and a resolution favoring opening of the Kiowa-Comanche-Apache Reservation. This was all in the way of getting the party in line with the wishes of the people of Oklahoma and regaining their confidence by showing more interest in territorial affairs than in free silver.

Whit M. Grant of Iklahoma City and J. H. King of Perry got in a scrap for Oklahoma national committeeman. The committee selected Grant but met on the morning of July 8 and rescinded its action. They were pounded very hard for having chosen an administration man. Senator Jones of Arkansas suggested that they furnish someone who would not at once be placed under a ban by the national committee. Some prominent Silverites also took a hand. If they wanted their member to have any influence, they had better select a silver man.

It was presented to Houston that he had made trouble for himself in his scheme for nomination as delegate to Congress by supporting an administration man. He concluded that it would be better to back down and abandon his deal with the officeholder and arranged with Bixler, also a Grant supporter, to be absent when the committee reconvened. Temple made the motion to reconsider. He, Mitchell, and Denton voted in the affirmative; Beale and Brunt voted in the negative. That left the committee hanging in air and the contest on again. On the final ballot, however, Bixler appeared, and Grant was again chosen.

Then came the fight over who should go on resolutions. Temple wanted to be on resolutions in order to secure credit for the free-homes plank. So did Bixler, who also was expected to run for delegate to Congress and wanted credit for the free-homes scheme. Meanwhile, a dozen other delegates who were around "peddling wind on the subject" held a conference with Governor Renfrow and Attorney General Galbraith, explaining that the free-homes issue was the main thing Oklahoma had on hand at the convention to make a show and that it was time to get to work.

Lon Wharton of Perry offered the following:

Resolved,
That all public lands, together with all purchased or ceded Indian reservations, should revert to the public domain, and be subject to homestead entry free to actual settlers, except the usual land office fees for such entry; that we favor a complete restoration of the original homestead law made applicable to all homesteads in the United States as to original Oklahoma and other public lands, and that we favor more liberty and privilege in reference to Indians holding allotments in their respective reservations, and demand such legislation as will permit the Indians to conduct their business without interference on the part of the Indian department or its agents, and that the Indians having one-half or more white blood be permitted to sell or dispose of their lands without interference by law.

While the resolution was being read, Renfrow colored slightly. He considered it a smash at the secretary of the interior and determined that it should not be adopted. It was wordy, he said. The platform would be a precious document, and space valuable. A long resolution would be blue-penciled or destroyed in full.

A committee consisting of Renfrow, Galbraith, Wharton, Denton, and Roy V. Hoffman of Guthrie was named to condense a literary production that could be presented to the conference. Again the argument arose that Oklahoma had no electoral vote, and there was a decided disposition in the national committee to pay no attention to it.

Robert L. Owen, the delegate from Indian Territory, explained that it was the burning issue in other western states as well as Oklahoma and should be given some attention. Owen did not like the redraft submitted by the committee and proceeded to cover the matter as follows: "We are in hearty sympathy with the wishes of the people of the territories in seeking statehood, home rule and free homes." This was accepted and reported. The result constituted only three lines in the platform:: "The Democratic party believes in home rule and that all public lands of the United States be appropriated to the establishment of free homes for American citizens." Thus the Oklahoma delegation was not entitled to credit for the free-homes plank. The credit went to Owen, and Houston and Bixler, finding themselves in their rivalry left out of the calculations, caused the whole group to "take on terribly."

Temple did not wait for the presidential nominations to begin but boarded a train for Oklahoma. Having also some railroad business in Kansas City, he registered at the Midland Hotel. The Chicago "alkali" was so thick in his craw that a trip to a nearby saloon only heightened his disgust at the turn of events. After a heated discussion of free silver and politics in general with several luminaries who chanced to be present, he retired to the Midland's Turkish-bath parlors.

Facilities there did not suit him either. He announced that he was from the rockiest forty acres on Bitter Creek, and then he declared war." The sight of several attendants in Abyssinian costume inspired Houston. He whipped Old Betsy from under his coat and waved the muzzle in the attendants' faces, commanding that a war dance would be the proper thing. The attendants almost fainted and fled for their lives. Temple brandished Old Betsy again, as they disappeared in all directions.

When he found himself alone, Houston gave a series of war whoops that almost shook the glassware in the barbershop above. Finally he laid his weapon aside. As he was preparing to bathe, a policeman nabbed him. Manager Stockham would not allow his patron to be taken to the station, so he was sent to his room under guard. The next morning Temple conducted his business and continued to Woodward.

The *Beaver Herald,* a Republican weekly, in its July 16 issue exaggerated the incident: "While in Kansas City . . . Temple Houston got hilarious and proceeded to paint the town red.

He made a few artistic strokes, in which his big six-shooter and a war whoop played a part, but in the midst of the show a policeman stopped the fun." Lon Wharton's *Noble County Sentinel* of the same date reported: "Houston was on the notification committee, but so much of his time was spent 'notifying' that he missed part of the convention.... The gold bugs of Oklahoma stole the national committeeman through the treachery of four of the delegates, Brunt, Bixler, Beale and Houston." Commented the *Norman Transcript:* "Temple Houston was the fair flower of the Oklahoma delegation at Chicago. It may be that he is the 'Fair God' of the land."

The Populist and National Silver parties met in convention at Saint Louis on July 22. Both endorsed the candidacy of Bryan, but instead of Sewall, the Populists nominated Thomas E. Watson of Georgia for vice-president. The Democrats who refused to support Bryan on a free-silver platform met in Indianapolis on September 2 and organized the National Democratic party. John M. Palmer of Illinois was nominated for president; Simon B. Buckner of Kentucky, for vice-president.

Oklahoma Populists met in convention at Guthrie on August 4, reiterated the statements of the national Populist platform, and, following the national trend of fusion with Democrats, endorsed Bryan, but held out for their vice-presidential nominee, Watson of Georgia. They were nip and tuck on selecting from more than half a dozen favorites a nominee for territorial delegate. Finally, on the twenty-sixth roll call, they broke the stalemate with a big swing to James Yancey Callahan, a Methodist minister who resided on his claim in the Cheyenne country northwest of Kingfisher. A native of Missouri, Callahan had moved to Kansas in 1886, had once been elected register of deeds of Stanton County on the Republican ticket, but had become "indoctrinated and enamored with Populist theories" since coming to Oklahoma.

Aware that the combined votes for the Populist and Democratic nominees for delegate in 1894 had greatly exceeded the vote for Flynn, the leaders of both parties considered integra-

Members of the Oklahoma Senate, Fourth Legislative Assembly, 1897. Number 13, standing, second from left, is David P. Marum.

tion, especially since the populists had endorsed Bryan. Delegates to the territorial Democratic convention at El Reno on September 3 were split into fusionists and nonfusionists. Speeches and arguments were heard. Callahan and his chief advisers were present, and Callahan was invited to address the convention.

The moment he stepped to the platform, the convention went into a "perfect storm of applause." Hoffman, Denton, Bixler, and other would-be nominees needled him on his stand on many issues, but the temper of the majority was for fusion. Minority efforts failed to block his endorsement. Dan Peery of El Reno jumped on a chair, secured the recognition of Chairman A. A. Byers, and moved that Callahan be nominated Democratic candidate for congressional delegate. Bedlam broke loose. Callahan was chosen the standard bearer not only of the Populists but also of the Democrats by a tremendous roar of voice votes and amid "wildest enthusiasm." In the November election Flynn ran an exceedingly strong race considering that the composite forces made Callahan congressional delegate by a vote of 27,435 to 26,267.

Nationally the campaign aroused deep feelings. It was warmly contested in the central states, the Democratic ticket carried the western and southern states, and the Republican ticket swept the East. The total vote was nearly two million more than the total in 1892. The Republican party secured a popular plurality of 601,854. The Electoral College vote stood: McKinley and Hobart, 271; Bryan and Sewall, 186.

Unenthusiastic about Democratic fusion Houston took little part in the national or territorial elections other than to help send David Marum to the Fourth Legislative Assembly. Other problems, legal and personal, consumed his attention.

16

Astronomy and Antiquities

Temple loved his family, and he idolized his son Sam—a quiet child and the opposite of his father. For his tenth birthday Temple gave Sam a pony with instructions to rent some pasture from J. B. Jenkins, a farmer living a mile east of Woodward. The boy could not find Jenkins, but a neighbor assured him that it would be all right to leave the pony on the farm.

About four o'clock on the afternoon of October 8, Sam saw Jenkins in the meat market and approached him about the rental. The farmer had been drinking. In his stupor he took an adverse view of the matter, which he emphasized by spitting in the boy's face.

Sam ran crying to his father's office. Moments later the enraged Houston came striding down the street, long hair and coat tail flying. Jenkins, realizing what he had done, hurried to his horse. Temple intercepted him just opposite the Cattle King Hotel.

Frightened, Jenkins went for his gun, and Old Betsy jumped from nowhere, roaring and blazing. Temple's first shot entered the farmer's left breast just above the nipple, ranging up and out below the shoulder blade; the other went through the fleshy part of his right arm. The Woodward News concluded its dispatch of October 9: "The wound while critical in the extreme is not necessary [sic] fatal, and at this writing, Jenkins still lives and gives promise of recovery. Houston at once gave himself up and is awaiting action of the authorities."

Temple was charged with assault with a firearm with intent to injure the person of said Jenkins, a felony punishable by five years in the territorial prison, or imprisonment in the county jail not exceeding one year. Judge Scott had resigned during the waning months of Cleveland's administration to form a law partnership in New York City and had been succeeded in the Third District by Oklahoma City attorney James R. Keaton, formerly of Kentucky. Judge Keaton was assigned to the Woodward court in the Fifth District during Judge McAtee's absence in December, when the case was tried. Temple defended himself on grounds of justifiable and excusable cause, and the evidence supported him. He agreed to plead guilty to unlawful shooting, a misdemeanor, which Keaton accepted.

Judge Burford's term had expired in May, 1896. He was succeeded in the Second District by John C. Tarsney, a Kansas City lawyer and former Missouri congressman, and opened a law practice in Guthrie. On February 16, 1898, he was appointed judge of the First District and chief justice of the Oklahoma Supreme Court by President McKinley, succeeding Judge Dale, a position he held until after statehood. During a reminiscent mood in 1905, he mentioned the Houston-Jenkins altercation: "Temple was assessed a $300 fine by Judge Keaton, but afterward dared any man to try to collect it. To my knowledge, it was never paid."

There were, however, many pleasant moments for Temple during the years closing the century. For some time Sidney Laune had been courting Seigniora ("Nonnie") Russell, a pretty schoolteacher who lived on the Diamond Tail Ranch on the Salt Fork in the Texas Panhandle. Laune had met Miss Russell through a young friend named Fred Mason, who taught at the nearby Clifford school and had married a Woodward girl. The romance culminated in marriage on July 20, 1896, and, after several days spent in a buggy crossing the plains in the hot wind and swirling sand and fording streams swollen by heavy summer rains, they arrived at the Central Hotel in Woodward and registered as man and wife.

In her beautiful autobiography, *Sand in My Eyes* (1956), Mrs. Laune described the commotion they caused in the lobby after the clerk's excited exclamation. No one in Woodward except Laune's partner, Judge Dean, had heard about her or known of Laune's intention. As the word spread, men from a nearby bar, including Houston, crowded around them to be introduced, shake hands, and extend their congratulations and good wishes.

During their courtship Laune had told her many "fascinating accounts" of events in Woodward—his and Judge Dean's townsite victory, house parties at Fort Supply, plays by the Dramatic Club, other club meetings of the young people, and Houston's killing of Ed Jennings, which had set Al Jennings on the outlaw path. Mrs. Laune had heard so much about the exploits of this "handsome, tall and straight... idol of Texas... with searching eyes" that she thought she would fear him. On the contrary, the moment she placed her hand in his she "felt an instant liking." His "quick step, bell-bottomed trousers whipping about small, high-heeled boots, ... the slow deliberate drawl of his voice"—his "every word and movement represented drama."

As he stood with her hand in his, Temple teased her about her husband, "whom he often opposed in legal battles." The crowd drew closer, providing an added incentive, and he recounted with relish the time Laune's bronco team ran away from him while he was returning from court at Beaver. That Mrs. Laune was tired did not seem to occur to him or to the delighted group around them, and the jibing continued until Mrs. L. B. Collins, who with her husband kept the hotel, showed them to their room.

Nonnie and Laura Houston became close friends. In the later 1890s, Temple was in demand as a speaker at churches, schools, and public celebrations, and Nonnie looked after the Houston children when Laura accompanied him on his engagements about the Territory. Temple reveled in history but also talked well on all subjects that interested him. His lecture on the oldest science, "Astronomy," delivered before a teachers convention in September, 1897, was declared a classic in every way.

The people of western Oklahoma were proud of the broad, generous, and able speech Governor Cassius M. Barnes gave

Houston, lawyer at Woodward, Oklahoma Territory.

at the cornerstone laying of the Northwestern Normal School at Alva in July, 1898, and viewed the remarks of territorial education board members as "the liberal and just position that all should take" toward the institution. But Houston's address, which followed, was "marked for zeal of delivery, eloquence of thought, and beauty of application":

We have assembled here to consecrate a structure to the noblest, the most beneficent of all purposes—the elevation of mankind. The edifice whose corner stone we today lay is more than a mere educational institution, it is one designed for the special instruction of those who have dedicated their lives to the science of education itself.

No superstitious rites, such as the ancients observed, mark these ceremonies. All that takes place here is upon a soil trodden only by the feet of freemen and is accompanied by the invocation of the ministers of a religion that preaches the universal brotherhood of mankind, the immortality of the soul, purity of life and penalties and rewards hereafter, for deeds done in the flesh. . . . The very stone is placed by the hand and under the auspices of that ancient and illustrious order that more than all other earthly institutions has preserved throughout the world the precepts of the Holy Scripture and righteousness among men. . . .

It might be expected that in response to the invitation with which I have been distinguished that I would bestow much of the space accorded me to the question of education. . . but after what has been beautifully said by the learned and distinguished educators who grace this occasion and the profound and entertaining references to that subject by the distinguished officials, whose presence honors us, it would seem surrogation on my part to make more than a passing allusion. . . . I shall discuss those questions which are almost born of this hour, and which affect deeply the destinies of those who teach and shall be taught when this magnificent building shall tower in its completed glory.

The ground on which these stones rest, within historic times, has been owned by England, France, Spain, France again, the United States and under extinguishable title by the Cherokee Indians and again in full sovereignty of the soil by the United States. . . . It has been the hunting ground of the Indians, the grazing land of these true sons of Ishmael—our western cowmen. Even as Old Eden was guarded by fiery sworded Cherabein, waving all away who came near, so federal soldiery with presented steel kept back the pressure of the advancing settlers who sought this garden of promise. The land was in a state of nature, solitude reigned, the bald eagle built his aerie high among the young dizzy crags and watched his nestlings fledge with no dread of man's approach, and the timid deer sipped the crystal waters in the cool depths of its dells with never a fear of the hunter's stealthy tread. Here fearful storms spent their wrath, but save when they burst above the lonely line rider or roaming Indian, their restless lightning flashed and faded unseen of earthly eye and the deep roll of their thunder died unheard of mortal ear. . . . On September 16, 1893, it became in all that such implies an integral part of Oklahoma Territory.

Houston's reference to the opening of the Outlet reads like poetry:

The wand of presidential power waved and as if by enchantment a wilderness became an empire. On every side at the same instant, the envisioning lines broke over the border. And who were these settlers? and whence came their lineage and institutions?

Look at them carefully. Every state in the union is represented and the child of Cavalier stands beside the descendant of the Puritan. They speak the tongue of Milton and bring with them the laws of Alfred, the philosophy of Francis Bacon and the religion of Jesus Christ. They are empire builders.

As far back as the mystic scroll of history reaches, their ancestors were free and they are the real evangelists of liberty, for wherever they abide they rear temples of their God and by their side spring up houses for the education of their children. . . . These are the children of the men who established this government, who in their sublime march pierced the Alleghenys, crossed the Mississippi, penetrated the Rockies and only for a moment paused on the golden shores of the Pacific. Every nation on earth has felt the impress of their might and genius, and this occasion, arising as it does on a spot that less than five years ago was a wilderness, these thronging thousands, with the patriotic pride which they seem to feel in all that transpires here, shows that our heritage of enlightened liberty and of all that secures it is still unimpaired.

Houston took deserving raps at the wail of anguish that rent the air over the legislative action providing for completion of the structure, despite the incalculable benefit certain to accrue to the entire territory, and in conclusion proved himself both a masterful orator and a prophet:

Let no blow now meditated be struck at this institute. Whosoever purpose such should pause. Her educational institutions and their marvelous success are the glory and the pride of this territory. They should be increased, not reduced. With a logic that must convince they show to all the world what we are and what we offer to those who will abide with us for the purpose of rearing their offspring and enjoying the delights of a refined and intellectual society.

Let no selfish or misguided hand mutilate even the humblest of our school houses. The people of this territory love their schools and view with no friendly eye an assault on any of them. You might as well try to take from this territory the groves that crown her hills or the streams that gem her vales as to injure one of them—even the lowest.

Our young territory, not yet adorned with the coronet of statehood, can say of her institutions as did Cornelia, the mother of Gracchi, "Silver and gold and precious stones wear I not," but pointing to her noble children, "these are my jewels."

Blessed with all heaven's bounties, facing a future rich with immeasurable possibilities, if we are true to ourselves, what a noble destiny awaits this fair and young territory. Her history, though short, is replete with progress, courage, goodness and wisdom. Even now her broad fields are mantled in the golden glories of her mighty harvest, her rivers radiantly are rolling down toward the silvery sapphire sea, her valleys all are glad and her countless hills rejoice. Her sons are so brave, her daughters so fair, who shall tell the splendors of her future? You might as well seek to loose the bonds of Orion or solve the sweet influences of the Pleiades.

At the McKennon Opera House in Guthrie, in November, Houston spoke for the benefit of the Woman's Home Missionary Society on the subject "Antiquities of America." The *El Reno Globe* noted: "The house was filled, the audience delighted, and the receipts were all the society could desire." The *State Capital* said: "His lecture is spoken of by competent judges as a masterpiece and a gem of the English literature."

Temple was almost as well versed in antiquities as in law. In

December, 1896, he presented David D. Leahy of the *Wichita Eagle* a

relic of more than ordinary interest... taken from a spot immortalized by Irish valor and consecrated by Irish heroism. [It] is a Colt's revolver dug up recently from the soil in that historic spot in Oklahoma where the brave Pat Hennessey was massacred [and his three drivers killed, scalped, bodies mutilated] by Indians under the leadership of that famous warrior-butcher "Dull Knife" of the Cheyenne tribe. The revolver laid in the battlefield for twenty-two years, and was only recently discovered. It belonged to one of the Indians who attacked Pat Hennessey, and who probably bit the dust in that memorable engagement with the sturdy hearted Irishman. The supposition that the Indian was killed is based on the fact that the revolver was struck twice by bullets from Hennessey's rifle. The dents are yet visible. It still contains two loads, but the caps have long since disappeared, being eaten away by rust....

A hero fell when Pat Hennessey bit the dust. After he was clubbed and stabbed he was tied to the hind wheel of one of his wagons and a fire kindled around him. It was also said that pieces of bacon were thrown in the fire to add to [its] intensity. A day or two afterwards his charred remains were found and buried. The grave is a few hundred yards north of the town of Hennessey on the right of way of the Rock Island railroad. The railroad company erected a monument over the grave.

The revolver was dug up about 150 feet from the grave. Hennessey was a government freighter and when he was killed he was on his way from Caldwell to El Reno [Wichita to Fort Sill] with military supplies.

The relic is much appreciated.

While he was in the Texas legislature, Temple had presented the sword surrendered by General Santa Anna at San Jacinto to the city of Cincinnati, Ohio, because that city had sent two pieces of artillery to the Texans to aid in their struggle for liberty. In March, 1898, the Daughters of the Republic of Texas, who were collecting relics of the war, asked for the sword to place in their museum.

Temple scoured the country for relics from New Mexico to Louisiana, where he and Laura visited her relatives and old friends during the summer or at Christmastime, until his den became a veritable museum and his house of seven gables on Texas Street in Woodward looked like a curiosity shop. Some of his finds were in Nebraska, where he accompanied hunting parties along the Republican River. His choice items were mementos of the days when Spanish smugglers loaded their schooners in Cuba and Mexico with wines, silks, tobacco, liquors, and other delightful luxuries, disguising their traffic with lumber, and set sail for the Texas shores, where enterprising citizens of Houston sold the contraband at a handsome profit.

Temple was not superstitious, but in an interview with Fred Barde in 1902, he related an experience on the Texas coast that he had never been able to explain:

Two wandering fiddlers had been murdered at the mouth of the Brazos, and the story grew that at night when the tide came in the faint sounds of a violin could be heard in the darkness. In company with a friend, I was fishing at the mouth of the river, when he said: "Well, we will hear the music of the dead fiddlers tonight." I laughed at him and ridiculed the story. "You may scoff all you please," he replied, "but I have heard the music."

We had just turned in and were lying listening intently when my disbelief in the supernatural was shaken. The notes of a violin, unmistakable as the stars in the sky or hoarse voice of the tide, came softly on the night air, rising and falling like the faint strains heard when one approaches a lonely cabin where there is dancing, but so remote that the lights shine dimly from the windows. At times there would be a bar or two in succession, which fancy fashioned into a fragment of some familiar air. This uncanny melody continued for more than an hour, and I confess even now that the effect was so startling that I was unable to sleep for several hours. I never found a satisfactory explanation of this phenomenon.

Once Temple witnessed the discovery of a magnificent relic at Galveston:

I was standing on the wharf watching the departure of a Mallory steamer for New Orleans. A gale had been blowing and two sheet anchors had been thrown out. The aft anchor was raised easily, but the forward anchor held fast. In spite of the heavy cable, the vessel

Houston residence at Woodward.

moved forward. The water boiled and seethed near the anchor, and suddenly a great mass of debris covered with oyster shells came to the surface and was lifted on deck. A fluke of the anchor was fastened in the mouth of a cannon. A steam hose was turned onto the mass and the shells broken off, revealing a beautiful brass cannon—a six-pounder. It bore the crest of the Spanish arms, and was undoubtedly centuries old. The touchhole was as large as a saucer. Silver had been used in its composition, and small nuggets were plainly discernible where they had not fluxed with the brass. The captain presented the gun to the Galveston artillery company. It was mounted, and when fired, rang like a bell, the silver giving a charming resonance.

Houston's collection of frontier memorabilia and artifacts in his home at Woodward.

Houston, standing, third from left, with a hunting party on the Republican River in Nebraska.

He had enjoyed rare luck in finding Napoleonic items:

In Galveston one day, a druggist told me that he had a collection of letters and documents and a belt which had been given him by a French soldier who had wandered to this country and died in poverty and claimed to have been a staff officer of Napoleon. I examined the papers and was rewarded with an autograph letter of Napoleon, dated Pamplona, Spain, during the Peninsular war, and was an order for the release of two officers in confinement for breach of discipline. The letter bore the imperial eagle.... it was given to me and I in turn presented it to a cousin, who was a collector.... The belt, worn and broken, was a sabre-tache in which was a small zinc receptacle which locked with a key. Inside were engraved his name and rank. I called attention of the French consul at Galveston to the relics for the purpose of learning the history of the officer, but never learned the result.

While riding along the Brazos river one day my attention was drawn to a lonely grave on the bank, which was crumbling into the waters and would soon disappear. On the headstone was the name, R. P. Jones. I asked a settler nearby if he knew who Jones had been. He replied that Jones was an Englishman who had been compelled to flee his country to escape punishment for participating in an attempt to liberate Napoleon from St. Helena. "I remember," continued the settler, "that he had several mementoes of Napoleon, among them a lock of Napoleon's hair." I became intensely interested. He said that Jones had given his possessions to a merchant named Crawford at Galveston. I lost no time in calling upon Crawford. "Yes," said he, "I have the relics." In a gold locket was a lock of light brown hair, tied with a purple ribbon; another relic was a hardwood casket, beautifully carved and embellished in lacquer of the Japanese style of art. A small settee which Jones had carried with him in his wanderings, he claimed to be a gift from Napoleon at Longwood. Crawford retained all but the last, which came into possession of my cousin.

While defending Josh Young's son in New Mexico, Temple learned that

a negro had in his possession a heavy metal stirrup of peculiar pattern which he had found. I went to his home and was shown a stirrup many pounds in weight, fashioned in the shape of a cross. "This," I said to myself, "is a relic of some conquistador, possibly on a journey to the Seven Cities of Cibola." I was impatient to purchase it, but the owner would not sell. "Seeing that you prize it," said he, "I will tell you how you may get others. In the penitentiary is a Mexican who told me that a cave in the Mogollon mountains he found several big muzzled guns, a number of stirrups like this one, gold balls for the guns, metal hats and metal plates." I knew that the "gold balls" were probably brass bullets for arquebuses and that the "metal plates" and "metal hats" were armor, all perhaps the remains of unlucky Spanish explorers. The convict was sentenced for two years and I did not see him. I delayed my return to New Mexico. Several months ago I read that similar articles had been found in a cave in the Mogollons. I am curious to know whether the story was true.

In Ochiltree County, Texas, he found the remains of what he believed to be prehistoric Pueblo villages and the eastern extension of Pueblo civilization:

I traced the ruins of thirteen houses. The debris may still be plainly seen. I found arrowheads and fragments of crude pottery in the ruins. The foundations were built of stone. I believe that a burial place could be found somewhere in the neighborhood, but my search failed to reveal it. An old frontiersman told me, however, that he had found skeletons two miles away. I visited the spot on the banks of Wolf Creek. It was undoubtedly a burial place.... the water had exposed several skeletons of women and children, but no weapons. Warriors were buried separate. I have long wished to organize an expedition and explore the ruins.

Temple never seemed able to carry out many such expeditions that he planned. "His legal work is piling up," a prominent Woodward County rancher told a *Kansas City Times* reporter while attending a meeting at the Midland Hotel in October, 1897:

You ask me the kind of lawyer he is? In my opinion few men are as little comprehended and understood as Temple Houston. He has been presented to the public as a rowdy, a roisterer, and a genuine remnant of the frontier desperado. He has been embroiled in several quarrels, but it was never of his making. He simply protected himself after the manner of the man of the border, who knew and could maintain his rights. I do not believe that he ever sought a quarrel, but has proved himself a dangerous man to quarrel with.

In fact, he is a kindly mannered, thoroughly educated man. Some time ago my company employed Houston at a salary as general counsel, and I do not believe a better, more painstaking or reliable lawyer ever gave advice or advanced an opinion. A judge of the Supreme Court of the Territory told me a few days ago that he regarded Temple as one of the best read and competent criminal lawyers in the entire country.

What kind of a lawyer is he? There are some twenty murder cases now pending in the courts of the Territory, and Houston is defending counsel in most of them!

17

Go Thy Way, Sin No More

One murder the rancher referred to had been committed in Dewey County and involved a young Texas cowboy named Alfred Son. It was not, as some claimed, Houston's "greatest case;" however, it was tried three times and certainly gave him his greatest problem.

On the morning of January 22, 1895, Fred Hoffman, treasurer of Dewey County and district United States commissioner, left his home, some distance southwest of Taloga, on horseback but never arrived at his office. Four days later a search party found his body in a blowhole in the sandhills three and a half miles west of town and a hundred feet off the roadway, near the South Canadian River. He had been brought down by a bullet through the body near the heart. After he had fallen to the ground, a second shot had been fired into his mouth at such close range as to powder-burn the face. Twenty feet away lay his horse, killed by a bullet through the neck from a rifle or revolver. The tracks of a team and buggy had left the road near the point and stopped at the rim of the hole, and two persons, one wearing extrasmall, sharp-heeled boots, had walked near the body, returned to the buggy and driven back to the roadway. A homesteader and his wife working on a pasture fence half a mile away had seen Hoffman cross the ford on the river and a buggy coming from the opposite direction. They saw only one man in the buggy. About the time the buggy reached the point where Hoffman was killed, they heard shots. They did not see the man and buggy again but shortly afterward saw "a party on a gray horse, not close enough to identify, riding away from the vicinity" toward the river.

In the fall of 1894 a package purporting to contain twenty-five thousand dollars had been expressed from Kansas City to George Isaacs, a wealthy cattleman of Canadian, Texas. When the train pulled into the Canadian station on the evening of November 24, a bandit gang from Oklahoma Territory opened a fusillade on the express car. Sheriff Tom McGee of Hemphill County, who was standing nearby took a hand in trying to defend the express company and was riddled with lead. Several persons were wounded, and the bandits were chased into the butte lands of the Kiowa-Comanche-Apache Reservation. The express package, when opened, contained blank paper the size of bills with two hundred dollars in money on top. The obvious scheme to swindle the express company of thousands of dollars had miscarried and left Isaacs and his associates in the soup. Isaacs was charged with the McGee murder, convicted on a change of venue to Hardeman County, and sentenced to life imprisonment at Huntsville. Two of the bandits, Jim Harbold and Jake McKenzie, had been captured by Deputy Marshals William Banks and Chris Madsen and returned for trial in Hemphill County. Other members of the gang were believed hiding in Hoffman's district, and it developed that the commissioner had been secretly aiding express company detectives and United States marshals in ferreting out the gang members. Just before his death Hoffman had revealed to Wells Fargo officials T. M. Cook and Thomas Smith that his efforts were "being directed" toward Alfred Son.

Son was not an outlaw. He worked for his half-brother Lee Moore, a rancher in the Cheyenne country and a relative of Amos Chapman, the famed army scout. But Son was a friend of McKenzie and Harbold, and in and about Taloga for a few days before Hoffman's murder there appeared a person styled as "Buck" or "Red Buck." Some witnesses gave his name as "Bert Collins." He was a notorious outlaw, according to rumor, seen frequently in the company of Alfred Son and apparently on intimate terms with him.

Further testimony showed that

on the morning Hoffman was killed, Son... procured a box of cartridges for his revolver, and was in a saloon with Collins drinking, in fact became considerably intoxicated, shot his revolver in the air, and so conducted himself that the stable man where he procured two horses and a single seated buggy was about to take same away from him, when Collins interposed and induced him to permit Son to use the rig, upon Collins' statement that he would see the team was properly cared for.... Son and Collins... the latter armed with a revolver and a Winchester rifle, riding in the buggy and leading a gray horse,... left Taloga driving in a southwesternly direction along the same road which Hoffman was traveling in coming into town. Hoffman was slain about the time Son and Collins, the outlaw, would have, by traveling at an ordinary gait, met him.

Collins had disappeared. The homesteader and his wife identified the rig in which Son was riding, and Deputy Marshal Madsen arrested the cowboy who wore the extrasmall, sharp-heeled boots.

The Dewey County Grand Jury indicted Son on April 25. Houston obtained a change of venue to Canadian County. He showed that the cowboy had no occasion to kill anyone and was the victim of circumstances by simply going the same route Collins was taking, that the buggy had not been close enough to identify, and that Son had obtained the rig to return his girl friend, Minnie Shanholster, to Taloga from Lenora, where she had been visiting school. A note from the young lady to her suitor was introduced in proof that he was only complying with her request. The prosecution hinged its case on the sharp-heeled boot prints found at the scene, but the jury disagreed, standing for conviction eleven to one.

Son confided to Houston that if he testified against Collins he would be killed; that Collins actually was Red Buck Waightman, the most vicious member of the Bill Doolin gang, then raiding through the territory; and that it would be better to "take the rap than to be six feet under."

If Temple had doubts about his client's veracity, they were dispelled a few days later. He received a message from the notorious outlaw to meet him alone and unarmed at night at a spot near present Seiling. Temple kept the tryst. Standing in the moonlight, Winchester leveled, the auburn-haired, mustached, cold-eyed gray-horse bandit told him, "I killed Hoffman and don't want another man taking credit for my crime."

Temple assured him that his responsibility in the case was only to defend an innocent boy, not to point a finger at someone else. He kept the outlaw's confidence, saying nothing about the meeting to anyone until after Red Buck had been shot down the following March in a gun battle with officers at a dugout in Custer County.

Judge Tarsney presided at Alfred Son's second trial at El Reno in December, 1896. The evidence was still circumstantial, but more convincing:

T. M. Cook, over the objection of counsel for the defendant, was permitted to testify to the fact that Hoffman was employed to ferret our the parties who had committed the express robbery.... Thomas Smith also testified, over the objection of counsel for defendant, that Hoffman, just prior to his death, was charging defendant with the express robbery, ... that Hoffman showed him letters he wrote, and also received, relative to that matter. The witness Cook testified that it was not generally known that Hoffman was engaged in such work. Other questions were asked and answers given relative to the same matter, to which objections were not properly taken and the court, upon his own motion, withdrew from consideration of the jury all the evidence touching the letters.

When counsel for the Territory first began interrogating the witness for the purpose of showing that Hoffman was, just prior to his death, at work trying to implicate the defendant and his associates in the express robbery, and upon objection being made to such testimony, the court very frankly stated that he thought that the testimony showing that Hoffman was employed by the express company to apprehend the parties... [was] competent, if such efforts were directed towards the defendant. But after the witness had answered that Hoffman was so engaged, and upon motion of counsel for defendant to strike out, for the reason that the statements of Hoffman as to his employment were declarations made in the absence of the defendant, the court said that "unless the knowledge that he, Hoffman, was working for that purpose was brought home to the defendant... it was not competent," and the court then asked the witness this question: "Do you know anything... of his having knowledge of the business in which Mr. Hoffman was engaged, that particular business?" To which the witness answered, "I do not." After this question and answer the witness was permitted, over the objection of counsel for defendant, to testify that Hoffman was engaged in working up the evidence concerning the express robbery against... the defendant.

For some reason (inadvertance of the court) the testimony of this and other witnesses touching this matter was not withdrawn from consideration of the jury, although no attempt was made to show that the defendant... ever knew or had any cause to believe that Hoffman was engaged in an attempt to connect [him] with an express robbery.

The jury found Alfred Son guilty and fixed his punishment at life imprisonment. Houston's motion for a new trial was overruled, the court pronounced sentence in accordance with the verdict, and in the eyes of the prosecution the murder of Fred Hoffman had been legally and satisfactorily avenged.

Houston appealed to the Oklahoma Supreme Court:

> Where the prosecution rely for conviction upon circumstantial evidence alone, and it is sought by the testimony of witnesses as to the conduct and acts of the deceased to show a motive upon the part of the accused for the killing, and it does not appear that such acts and conduct of the deceased were brought to the knowledge of the accused, [there was prejudicial error].

"In order to establish a motive for the commission of a crime," Houston contended, "it is essential that the facts upon which the motive is assigned shall be within knowledge of the party accused." In considering *Alfred Son v. Territory of Oklahoma* at its June, 1897, sitting, the Oklahoma Supreme Court agreed, ordered the judgment of the lower court vacated, and remanded the case for a new trial.

Son was returned from the Kansas prison in August, his bond of twenty thousand dollars was declared good, and he breathed the air of freedom until the United States Federal

Court for the Second District convened for the November term. Six murder cases were on the docket, but it was Son's retrial that jammed El Reno's street with saddle horses and every kind of conveyance and packed the courthouse to overflowing. Colonel Forrest, Major Quigsby, and John Pitzer did heroic service for the young defendant; Houston and the jury did the rest.

After briefly reviewing the evidence that had been introduced, Temple addressed his remarks entirely to the jury, without any brass-band accompaniment, and the twelve men who listened drank in every word that fell from his lips:

Gentlemen, as I told you in the beginning, the Territory has shown no motive for the commission of such a crime, and we have given you a reasonable—a true—explanation of every act and utterance of the defendant—even for his trip that fatal direction. He went only to woo—and win—one of the daughters of the land, tender-eyed, fair to look upon; and how like a boy, to make the shortest route to see his sweetheart, and, seeing her, take her back by the longest. The life of this boy, up to the instant of his accusation, has been faultless; and do you believe that he took this sudden and awful plunge from innocence into fathomless depths of crime—from child-like purity into hideous murder?

When asked to believe such a supposition, refer to your duties, as given you in His Honor's charge: apply the law as there laid down to the proof, and then follow the dictates of your conscience, and I do not fear the result.

This brave boy asked me to say to you that, to him, honor is dearer than life, and as the old exemplar of purest patriotism thundered in the ears of his country's oppressors, he says in this, his hour of trial, "give me liberty or give me death." He demands that you free him or inflict the death penalty. Rather than that you should fix upon his boyish brow the brand of felon, he would prefer to walk from your presence with his body polluted with the scales of whitest leprosy. He appeals to no sentiment of pity; only to the justice of his country's laws, which you are so solemnly charged to administer.

You came into that box with light hearts and consciences clear. Oh, may you leave there thus! untortured with the curse of having wrecked the life of him whose life you hold in the hollow of your hands. And he is so young, too. Boyhood's down still softens upon his childlike face. You will not be here long now. Your homes where loved ones are even now watching, waiting, to greet you, and when you clasp them to your manly breasts may the rapture at that moment be not embittered by the memory of having wrecked the life of yonder boy, whom all law and righteousness plead with you to save.

Gentlemen, be just; heed not the perjured fiends who thirst for this boy's blood, and in the years yet to come, when the pale messenger summons you before the court where you shall be tried alongside the kings of the earth, each memoried hour of life shall come back to you with awful distinctness, then happily can you recall that when you judged here, you judged with justice, and in the very spirit of Him who said: "Even as you did it unto the least of these, so you did it unto me." So that in the perfection of righteousness you tried the stranger within your gates—for he never saw one of you until he fearlessly placed his fate in your hands—even as you would be tried yourselves.

He has a Texas home far across the southern prairies, where the skies are a deeper purple, where the dawn has a brighter glow and the sunset wears a softer gold; where midnight stars look down upon us in a more unspeakable splendor. His loved ones, like yours, are waiting—no! no! not like yours—for his life is darkened even now by the awful shadow of death; and who shall tell what he feels?

Gentlemen, break that suspense; dry those tears; bind up these almost broken hearts, for now no power but you can do so. This noble duty done, each hour of life thereafter will grow proud with this recollection!

The jury returned a verdict for acquittal at two o'clock on the afternoon of November 17. When it was announced that Alfred Son was a free man, but for the interference of the court, his friends would have carried the jury and attorneys in the case boldly out into the street.

Three days later Houston went to Guthrie to institute habeas corpus proceedings in behalf of M. R. Lee, a prominent Tecumseh citizen and hotel proprietor. A Meridian, Texas, deputy sheriff had arrested Lee on a charge of murder committed in Bosque County twenty-four years earlier. In 1873 a youth named Galbraith was arrested for assaulting a Norwegian girl, but broke jail. He was later apprehended in Brown County by Rangers and jailed at Comanche. While being transferred by Deputy Sheriff Pearson from Comanche to Meridian for trial, he complained of being very ill and was placed in the bed of the deputy's wagon. Under some straw in the wagon bed, Galbraith found an iron brake rod and struck Pearson on the head, killing him. "It was cold-blooded murder," said the Texas deputy, "and had he been captured then he would have been strung up to the nearest live oak tree."

A constant search had been conducted, but no clue to his whereabouts was obtained until a relative identified Lee as Galbraith. Lee was a well-to-do married man with two children. He denied any knowledge of killing, said that he had never been south of Red River, and claimed that Missouri had been his home until he went to Tecumseh at the Pottawatomie-Shawnee opening. His Missouri ties, however, did not antedate the mid-1870s, and his identification seemed so positive that Chief Justice Dale honored the Texas writ in December.

On February 14, 1898, after he and Laura had exchanged valentines and other tokens of affection, Temple left Woodward for the low hill ranges of Bosque County that he had first visited while he was a student in Bryan. The Galbraith case was hard fought as usual. Houston charged that the identification of Lee as Galbraith by a distant cousin came nearly a quarter century later, and then only when the cousin was paid fifty dollars to provide officers the defendant's name. Further, the weapon had been one not likely to produce death, and it could not be presumed that death was designed from the manner of its use, nor by circumstances did such intention appear. Failing in both efforts, Temple still managed to save Galbraith's neck, on the grounds that the provisions of the Texas constitution of 1869 on imprisonment for life in lieu of the death penalty in capital cases was not abrogated by the provisions of the constitution of 1876 on crimes committed while the former was in force.

Again, in Oklahoma, Temple saved the neck of boy desperado Clyde Mattox, who was in jail in Newkirk on a charge of murder committed in Kay County. Mattox had been convicted in federal court in Wichita in 1891 for the 1889 slaying in Oklahoma City of John Mullen, a Negro, who refused to gratify a whim of his. At that time Mattox was a smooth-faced boy of twenty-one who had lived in Texas, where he had gained a reputation as a shooter before making the run into Oklahoma. He had been one of the first settlers in Oklahoma City on April 22, 1889. The town was scarcely an hour old when the Texas boy made a gunplay that attracted attention for its nerve. Trouble arose among several rival political factions, each of which tried to organize a city government and appoint city marshals. Mattox was appointed city marshal of South Oklahoma City when its temporary government was organized.

It was not long before he and a rival city marshal clashed. Both fired. Mattox killed his man but fell with a bullet in a lung. He was charged with murder, but nothing was done, and when his lung healed, he went on a spree and killed John Mullen. He was then arrested for both murders and taken to Wichita. A verdict of self-defense was returned in the first case. There was little sympathy, however, for the killing of the Negro, and he was sentenced to the gallows. He won a new trial on appeal to the United States Supreme Court, but before his second trial began, he crawled through the bars of an upstairs window of the Wichita jail, coolly boarded a Missouri Pacific train at El Dorado, and was reading an account of his latest exploit when he was recaptured at Yates Center, Kansas.

His second trial ended in a hung jury. The third trial resulted in conviction, and he was resentenced to death on March 23, 1894. Another appeal was taken to the United States Supreme Court, but this time the judgment was affirmed. Mattox was sentenced to be hanged on October 11, 1895, and was removed to Leavenworth Penitentiary to await execution.

As a last resort Mrs. Sadie W. Hatch, Clyde's mother and the widow of a New York merchant, invoked the sympathy of mothers across America with a plea for assistance that was printed in many leading newspapers. When President Cleveland was inaugurated for his second term in the White House, she appealed to every prominent Democrat for aid. With ten thousand names on a petition she went to Washington, D.C., and prevailed upon Cleveland to commute her son's death sentence to life imprisonment.

Mrs. Hatch did not stop here. When William McKinley took office as president, she found an excuse to enlist prominent Republicans in her cause. On January 17, 1898, she left Washington for Leavenworth with an unconditional pardon for her son signed by the president.

Mattox disappeared briefly following his release. Some thought that he was living with his mother in Kansas City, others that he had joined Roosevelt's Rough Riders and was in Cuba. Still others reported that he was in Mexico. Actually he had found employment as general manager of the extensive Soladini pasturage interests in the Osage Nation, and he soon began appearing in Ponca City, where he always associated with the drinking and saloon element.

One companion was Lincoln Swinney, a cattle raiser and a lessee of a portion of the Soladini pastures. In a drunken quarrel at the White House Club saloon one evening, Mattox stabbed Swinney to death. A two-month manhunt across the Southwest reached a climax when Sheriff Frank Pierce of Kay County learned that Mrs. Hatch had expressed a valise to a "Frank Jones" in Los Angeles. Mattox was arrested soon afterward.

Mrs. Hatch employed Houston to assist E. Bee Guthrey and Will Barnum, Clyde's defense lawyers, in the trial, which began at Newkirk on December 2. She told Houston: "From all I have been able to learn, I think my boy was justified in killing the man. Of course it crushed me, and I must ask God's help to bear me up."

On February 16, the date President McKinley returned John Burford to the bench to succeed Chief Justice Dale, he appointed Bayard T. Hainer, of Guthrie, formerly of Missouri, to succeed Judge Bierer in the Fourth District, embracing Kay

County. Five days later he appointed Clinton F. Irwin of Elgin, Illinois, associate justice of the Second District to succeed Judge Tarsney, and on March 22 he appointed B. F. Burwell, of Oklahoma City, formerly of Kansas, to succeed Judge Keaton. It was decided that Mattox should come before one of the new judges to be designated by the chief justice. On the eve of the trial there was a change of judges at different places. Burford went to Oklahoma City to occupy Burwell's chair, Hainer went to Guthrie to sit on Burford's bench, and Judge Burwell went to Newkirk to hear the Mattox case.

The trouble between Mattox and Swinney supposedly arose over a matter concerning the latter's leasing. During a drinking bout at the White House Club they tried to settle their differences. Public sentiment was divided. Swinney had professed to be a dangerous man himself, had clashed often with local police, and had boasted that he could not be arrested. His brother was serving a term at Lansing Penitentiary for killing a man in a fracas in the Osage country. Many felt that Mattox had been sufficiently provoked.

The prosecution developed its case carefully: The trouble had been brewing for some time, the defendant carried a dirk constantly, and on this occasion he had appeared at the White House Club in a drunken, quarrelsome mood and with felonious intent. The victim had already engaged in a previous encounter, had thrown his coat on the floor, and was daring anyone to walk on it as Mattox entered. Mattox, without being addressed personally, replied that he could walk on it and on Swinney's carcass too, whereupon Swinney knocked him against the bar. Mattox flew into the large, powerful Swinney like a cat; witnesses testified that his fury was terrible. He pulled his knife and slashed Swinney on the hand, face, and neck and as a parting stroke struck him in the back, inflicting a wound just above the hipbone, cutting a gash four inches long and about as deep, through which Swinney's entrails protruded. Surgery could do nothing for the wounded man, and he died a few hours afterward.

Not entirely true, claimed Guthrey and Barnum. The killing was simply the result of a saloon row. Swinney stated that he could whip any man in the house, and Mattox took him up, whereupon Swinney made a broad-handed blow and knocked his hat off. Somehow in the melee Mattox obtained a knife and began slashing. He finally got behind Swinney and stabbed him in the back, and Swinney fell on the floor.

The prosecution alluded, over defense's objection, to the defendant's record and his escape to California as his usual bold policy in doing his utmost to get away. The chief witness examined was Deputy Sheriff Ward, who traced Mattox's flight and assisted in returning him to the territory. The prosecution examined the deputy for some time without bringing out a fact of consequence except that he had been to the Golden State, and then turned him over to the defense for cross-examination.

Houston arose and questioned:
"Your name is Ward?"
"Yes."
"You are duly sworn, and understand the nature of an oath?"
"Yes."
"Now, Mr. Ward, will you state to the jury whether or not you had a pleasant trip to California?"
"Yes, sir," Ward replied.
"That's all," said Houston. "You may step down."

The jury reached a verdict at 7:00 P. M. on December 7: "Guilty of manslaughter in the second degree." Judge Burwell sentenced Mattox to twelve years in the Lansing penitentiary.

Temple's most memorable performance was in 1899 on behalf of Minnie Stacey, a famous madam brought before Judge Burford in the May term of district court at Woodward. For more than a year there had been complaints across the territory about the large number of girls who had adopted a life of shame, bringing distraction to parents and to themselves expulsion from all respectable associations. In the previous August, the *Oklahoma Times-Journal* had lamented: "Within the past three months at least twelve girls ranging in age from fourteen to eighteen have fallen in this city," and charged parents with being "too indulgent and too neglectful" in seeing that their daughters had only virtuous companions or no companions at all. "Girls have been allowed to walk the streets day and night, and to be companions of women notoriously lewd." Other communities blamed the "cataclysm of the openings.... all kinds of society were mixed up and made it difficult for parents to tell what was wholesome and what was not, ... and the result is what might have been expected."

Nearly every town had some bawdiness or a red-light district, and Woodward was no exception, though it was a thoroughgoing city, where the people went to church, contributed willingly to the collection plate, paid their lodge dues regularly, attended local celebrations in force, and entertained at political rallies and cattlemen's conventions. Minnie Stacey was being prosecuted for plying her vocation and operating a brothel. The citizens also wanted her run out of the territory.

Something about the woman's plight aroused the indignation of Temple Houston. He was visibly disturbed as he came down the street the morning of May 26. All sorts of cases—wrangles over land titles, damage suits, and crimes ranging from thievery to disturbing the peace and vagrancy—were to be aired and decided during this court term, and unusual numbers of people were in town to give testimony or just to listen.

Logan Coffee, of Miami, Texas, who had known Temple in his Panhandle days, was there as a witness in a horse-stealing case:

> Houston met me [in front of a saloon], and said: "Let's go in and get a drink." We went in and had one. I said:"Temple, how about another," so we drank again. We talked a while and I decided I had better be getting up to the courthouse. I did not know but what they would fine me if I was a little late. Temple said: "Well, I am going up there too." He told me they had Minnie Stacey up in court. She had bought a lot and a house, and they had taken her money, and then were about to take her place from her and drive her out. Temple

said: "She doesn't have any money to hire a lawyer, but I am going to defend her, and I'm going to raise the roof." We went up and the Judge called her case and asked if she had a lawyer. She said no. Then the Judge said he would have to appoint counsel for her. Temple arose with his long hair falling down his back, and said: "Please, your Honor, and I'll defend the lady, if she will allow me," and she did.

Houston responded with a gallant bow, and the courtroom became expectantly quiet. Everyone in the room sensed that something extraordinary was about to happen. A reporter from the *Kansas City Star* grabbed his note pad.

Judge Burford, benign as a bishop, declared a ten-minute recess to allow Houston to counsel privately with his client. Temple talked to the woman only a few minutes and then announced himself ready for trial.

The prosecution adduced its evidence. The woman offered no defense. The prosecuting attorney made his argument for conviction. Then Temple rose to his feet. After reviewing the legal aspects involved and briefly discussing the evidence, he bent toward the jury so that he could almost touch each man on the shoulder and in a clear, low voice laid his argument on their conscience:

Gentlemen: You heard with what cold cruelty the prosecution referred to the sins of this woman, as if her condition were of her own preference. The evidence has painted you a picture of her life and surroundings. Do you think that they were of her own choosing? Do you think that she willingly embraced a life so revolting and horrible? Ah, no! Gentlemen, one of our sex was the author of her ruin, more to blame than she.

Then let us judge her gently. What could be more pathetic than the spectacle she presents? An immortal soul in ruin! Where the star of purity once glittered on her girlish brow, burning shame has set its seal and forever! And only a moment ago they reproached her for the depths to which she had sunk, the company she kept, the life she led. Now, what else is left her? Where can she go and her sin not pursue her? Gentlemen, the very promises of God are denied her. He said: "Come unto me all ye that labor and are heavy laden and I will give you rest?" She has indeed labored, and is heavily laden, but if, at this instant she were to kneel

Houston defending the "fallen woman" at Woodward, 1899. An artist's conception that appeared in the *Daily Oklahoman*, July 5, 1936.

down before us all and confess her Redeemer and beseech His tender mercies, where is the church that would receive her? And even if they accepted her, when she passed the portals to worship and to claim her rest, scorn and mockery would greet her; those she met would gather around them their spirits the more closely to avoid the pollution of her touch. And would you tell me a single employment where she can realize "Give us our daily bread"?

Our sex wrecked her once pure life. Her own sex shrink from her as they would the pestilence. Society has reared its relentless walls against her, and only in the friendly shelter of the grave can her betrayed and broken heart ever find the Redeemer's promised rest.

They told you of her assumed names, as fleeting as the shadows on the walls, of her sins, her habits, but they never told you of her sorrows, and who shall tell what her heart, sinful though it may be, now feels? When the remembered voices of mother and sisters, whom she must see no more on this earth, fall again like music on her erring soul, and she prays God that she could only return, and must not—no—not in this life, for the seducer has destroyed the soul.

You know the story of the prodigal son, but he was a son. He was one of us, like her destroyers; but for the prodigal daughter, there is no return. Were she with her wasted form and bleeding feet to drag herself back to home, she, the fallen and the lost, what would be her welcome? Oh, consider this when you come to decide her guilt, for she is before us, and we must judge her. They sneer and scoff at her. One should respect her grief, and I tell you that there reigns over her penitent and chastened spirit a desolation now that none, no, none but the Searcher of all hearts can ever know.

None of us are utterly evil, and I remember that when the Saffron Scourge swept over the city of Memphis in 1878, a courtesan there opened wide the doors of her gilded palace of sin to admit the sufferers; and when the scythe of the Reaper swung fast and pitiless, she was angelic in her ministering. Death called her in the midst of her mercies, and she went to join those she tried to save. She, like those the Lord forgave, was a sinner, and yet I believe that in the day of reckoning her judgment will be lighter than those who would prosecute and seek to drive off the earth such poor unfortunates as her whom you are to judge.

They wish to fine this woman and make her leave. They wish to wring from the wages of her shame the price of this meditated injustice; to take from her the little money she might have—and

God knows, gentlemen, it came hard enough. The old Jewish law told you that the price of a dog, nor the hire of such as she, should come not within the house of the Lord, and I say unto you that our justice, fitly symbolized by woman's form, does not ask that you add ought to the woes of this unhappy one, one only asks at your hands the pitiful privilege of being left alone.

The Master, while on earth, while He spake in wrath and rebuke to the kings and rulers, never reproached one of these. One he forgave, another he acquitted. You remember both—and now looking upon this friendless outcast, if any of us can say unto her "I am holier than thou" in the respect which she is charged with sinning, who is he? The Jews who brought the woman before the Savior have been held up to execration of the world for two thousand years. I always respected them. A man who will yield to the reproaches of his conscience as they did has the element of good in him, but the modern hypocrite has no such compunctions. If the prosecutors of this woman whom you are trying had brought her before the Savior, they would have accepted his challenge and each one gathered a rock and stoned her in the twinkling of an eye.

No, gentlemen, do as your Master did twice under the very circumstances that surround you. Tell her to go in peace.

The jury acquitted the woman as soon as they reached the jury room.

Tears ran down the cheeks of Judge Burford and the woman herself, and, according to Logan Coffee, Houston's speech was instrumental in influencing Minnie Stacey to move to Canadian, Texas, where she joined the Methodist church, took in washing for a living, and remained a Christian until her death.

Temple's plea, though entirely extemporaneous, gained him everlasting fame, and it was regarded by the legal profession as a masterpiece. The court stenographer was besieged for copies, and thousands were printed and circulated. A framed copy was placed on a pedestal in the Library of Congress. A card above it reads: "One of the finest examples of American oratory ever uttered."

18

Old Fight Over Again

Despite himself, Houston was back in the political limelight in 1900. Congress, in creating territorial government for Oklahoma and in including Greer County in its boundaries, had also provided for bringing an original action in the United States Supreme Court against Texas to determine title to the tract. On March 16, 1896, the Supreme Court upheld the Organic Act, and Texas lost the section between the North and South forks of Red River (now Harmon, Jackson, Greer, and part of Beckham counties).

Greer was in the Texas judicial district presided over by Temple's old Panhandle friend, Judge G. A. Brown of Vernon. Temple often attended the Greer County District Court, and he was defending a case at Mangum on the afternoon of March 17, when Judge Brown received a telegram from Quanah that the county was now a part of Oklahoma. Upon receiving the news, Judge Brown immediately adjourned court without completing the trial. As a Texas judge he no longer had jurisdiction.

The word quickly spread over town. That night a mass meeting was held at the courthouse, and Judge Brown was selected as a delegate to Washington to ask for legislation protecting the settlers. On May 4, Congress passed an act establishing Greer County in the Territory of Oklahoma, with Mangum as county seat, continuing the Texas officials in office, subject to election on the first Tuesday in November, and providing that "all proceedings and actions of every kind in or before the several courts and officers of Greer county, Texas, shall have the same force and effect as if said courts and officers of Greer County, Texas, had been legally authorized courts and officers of the United States or of the Territory of Oklahoma."

The territorial supreme court added Greer County to the Third Judicial District, presided over by Judge Keaton. Judge Keaton held his first term of court at Mangum the first Tuesday in December.

For legislative purposes Greer was added to the Woodward district represented by David Marum. In April, 1898, before the primaries of the fall elections, the *Wichita Eagle* made much of a rumor that Houston would be a candidate for Marum's seat in the territorial assembly. While in Wichita on a legal matter a few days later, Temple personally delivered this biting response:

> Your correspondent does an injustice in attributing to myself such aspirations. I assure you that I have no such ambitions, and never by word or deed have indicated the purpose imputed to me in your special; in fact, I have never expressed any political wish other than to have him [Marum] retain his present position in the council. . . . You will do me justice to publish this communication.
>
> Yours most respectfully,
TEMPLE HOUSTON.

Victor Murdock, the "red-headed" managing editor of the *Eagle*, not only complied but detailed the visit:

> Temple Houston last week wandered upstairs to the *Eagle* aerie. . . . He is totally unlike any other visitor who comes to Wichita. He is a very large man with a strong Roman face and large head covered with loosely curled hair and goes smooth shaven. His feet are as small as a woman's. . . . his teeth as white and even as a belle's. Part of the time his mental attitude and expression is that of a southerner, with all the southern suavity and grace, the next moment it is the rough and ready, strenuous western sledge hammer way. He is extraordinarily well informed on subjects that the average westerner knows nothing about—the politics of continental Europe, Egyptology, geology. He is always a welcome visitor because you can drag a good story from him, a story that no one else from Oklahoma has thought to tell, and told in Houston's own way. Houston, in southern fashion, takes his hat off when he enters a room and no one

ever saw him put his feet on a desk, an universal habit in this part of the country. He never talks shop, although he is one of the most brilliant lawyers in the West. He is the son of the famous Sam Houston, and is as reticent as his forbear in personal matters. He never talks of his father or his notable history.

In the spring of 1900 territory Democrats, Populists and Republicans prepared for the national conventions and fall presidential campaign. As many predicted, delegate Callahan had wielded little influence in Republican-controlled Washington. Dennis Flynn continued to work with the national administration. In May his free-homes bill was passed by Congress and signed by President McKinley.

Flynn returned to Oklahoma to a series of ovations such as few politicians had been accorded, having saved settlers an estimated seventeen million dollars. Republicans met in convention at Schiller Hall, Enid's handsomest building on May 10. Three brass bands tooted a lively accompaniment to the violent gestures and vigorous language of the faithful who came to save the country and incidentally to thank McKinley for having already saved it. They endorsed expansion and holding onto all the new possessions that had come to the nation through the natural march of civilization. They earnestly requested their delegates to the upcoming Philadelphia convention (June 19 to 21) to use every effort to bring statehood for Oklahoma under such conditions as Congress saw fit. They exulted not only over the fulfillment of all the Republican pledges made to the nation in 1896 and their happy fruition but also over the free-homes pledge made by the Oklahoma Republican party. Thompson B. Ferguson of Watonga, the only nominee for temporary chairman, was elected without a dissenting vote. He made a stirring acceptance speech, and when he mentioned Dennis Flynn, the convention went wild. Flynn was named delegate-at-large to the national convention and was unanimously renominated delegate to Congress.

Between 1896 and 1900 there had been a series of wars throughout the world—particularly the 1898 clash between the United States and Spain, which resulted in Cuban independence, acquisition of Puerto Rico and a naval victory in the Philippines that also put the United States in possession of those islands as an idemnity for expenses incurred in behalf of the Cubans. Sentiment was divided. Democrats favored an immediate promise that independence would be granted to the islands as soon as a stable government was established, with protection from outside interference. Some Republicans desired a colonial system. Others thought that the islands should be given a territorial form of government with a view to ultimate statehood. The Democratic party also opposed McKinley's 1899 invitation to certain European powers to adopt an open-door policy in Chinese waters, labeled his attitude toward international issues "imperialism," and, despite a marked improvement in industrial conditions and an increase in volume of money, reaffirmed the platform of 1896 with its declaration of free silver.

Houston incurred the ire of fellow Oklahoma delegates by stating in a *Kansas City Times* interview that he was opposed to "everlasting tinkering and unwise political disturbances." Accused of being a "gold standard expansionist" who had "impeached" the Democratic party, he replied from Woodward on April 27:

I have always been an expansionist and so declared before the largest audience ever assembled in the territory at the dedication of the Alva Normal Institute in 1898. While I regarded the demonetization of silver and the repeal of the Sherman law providing for its coinage as very unfortunate, still the country had emphatically pronounced in favor of a gold standard and a republican majority seemed secure in the senate the next six years. The gold standard had been deliberately chosen by the people, and I thought it entitled to a full, fair trial and test and if it brought about the blessing promised by its advocates, the nation would be the beneficiary, and if fraught with the evils foretold by silver apostles, it would work its own swift repeal. Industrial and financial conditions have adjusted themselves to the status incident to a gold standard, therefore I think a disturbance of the present state of affairs unwise... just to gratify the whims of ideologists and the ambition of politicians. If the country will now wait and patiently investigate we will soon know who was right, the silver or gold men.

All those who elected me delegate to the territorial convention knew my views and nearly all differed with me.... Mr. Bryan's name was never mentioned except I stated that his friends were in such overwhelming majority that our delegation to Kansas City will be solid for him.

Territory Populists had met in convention on April 9 at Enid, where a long-expected split in the party occurred. The Populists denounced Republicans for placing the money of the country in the hands of banking corporations. There was no talk of fusion, except for a resolution to favor a union of all elements opposed to trusts, imperialism, and militarism—to the end that their combined vote might be cast in favor of the presidential candidates who represented reform.

The row and subsequent bolt came when the chair invoked the gag rule on obstructionists demanding that "Sioux Falls, South Dakota," be stricken from the call of the national committee chairman and "Cincinnati" be substituted as the place for the national convention. The bolters, claiming to represent no less than fifteen hundred true-blue Populists who would stand by straight Populist principles, walked out, marched to the courthouse, organized a separate convention, elected a chairman and secretary, and selected seven delegates to a national convention to be held in Cincinnati on May 6. Upon their departure, the regular convention resumed business, adopted unanimously the report of the committee on resolutions, including the fundamental principles of the party as enunciated in the Saint Louis platform in 1896, and selected ten delegates instructed and pledged to cast their votes for the great champion of the rights of common people, William J. Bryan, at the Sioux Falls convention on May 9.

If there was turbulence in the Populist party, the territorial Democratic convention at El Reno on June 5 was a riot. The *State Capital* attributed it to

> the result of a new alignment of old foes. Joe Wisby of Guthrie (a congressional candidate in 1894), Col. J. W. Johnson (Sixth district

Scenes from the Territorial Democratic Convention at El Reno, June 5, 1900.

representative in the Territorial Assembly), Dan W. Perry and Jasper Sipes [Oklahoma City school equipment dealer, central committee chairman, and candidate for national committeeman] have always stood for fusion—and against the democrats who happened to be at the pie counter. They were bitter opponents of Governor Renfrow. They wanted much and got nothing—and rebelled.

When Wisby appeared on the scene, he found strong forces against him. At the head of these was Col. Roy Hoffman [of Chandler], one of the shrewdest politicians in the territory; J. W. McClelland, "wah hoss" of Grant county; Temple Houston, the mesmeric meteor of Woodward county; James Diggs, the "Mexic" soarer of Noble county; W. S. Denton, the Lydite explosive of Garfield county; Leslie P. Ross, the Texas "straight" of Cleveland county; C. J. Wrightsman, the Calhunic warbler of Pawnee county; James R. Jacobs, the democratic tenor of Shawnee, and a lot of other fighters of the true democratic variety. They declared Wisby and his cohorts populists—and said all populists should have no quarter in a democratic convention.

The fight was one of brains and determination. The like of the rivalry was never before seen, and never will be again, in Oklahoma. Every giant of the party was on his mettle. The sparks flew. Old knives, such as Hoffman's against Wisby, were unsheathed anew; and not a turn or vantage was lost.

The first gladiators, the Hoffman-Houston-McClelland crowd, signally won. They made a combine which shut Wisby, Sipes and Peery out.... Col. Johnson and his followers were sent to the hole and the hole closed over them. This combine had a majority.... a compact unshakable. But they grew too arbitrary; they gloated too much.... gave excuse—lame though it was—to bolt; and the "snowed under" crowd only wanted a chance to bolt. The combine should have been magnanimous. It should have let everybody of the opposition "spout," then voted its slate in. Thus their victory would not have had any tinge of doubt.

Every point of order leading up to the bolt was unfounded. The point that the body was unorganized and a roll call therefore out of order, was senseless, for national and state conventions everywhere submit to and have called a temporary roll made up by the central committee.... So the combine chairman rightly overruled these points of order. But he was over-zealous in pushing the roll call. He should have given the ... "underdog" a chance to explode....

But to bolt was the only chance the anti-combine had to get their names in even as quasi-delegates. However, the combine gave them a legitimate cause.... The motion to lay Johnson's amendment on the table was an unnecessary and unfortunate one. Followed by the chairman's foolish arbitrariness, it produced a row Oklahoma democracy will not get over for ten years....

But the "regular" will be seated. Saying nothing of the bad example of the chairman of a great party central committee heading a bolt, because of self-interest.... Sipes, when he called the convention to order and turned the body over to a temporary chairman and secretary, became defunct so far as his official duties related to this convention. He had done all that the central committee had authorized him to do.... he had not legal or moral right to organize another convention, for which there was no call, in the same hall and for the same purpose.

Wilder scenes were never witnessed.... Men were crazy. Parlimentary law, decency of demeanor toward each other—all the amenities of public bodies were cast to the winds and a free-for-all indulged in.

Houston, McClelland and Ross of the combine, O. H. Travers of Lincoln County, L. P. Apperson of Kay, Lon Wharton of Noble, and J. F. Palmer of the Osage Reservation won seats on the resolutions committee, with Travers as chairman. While the convention of delegates who had protested the rulings of the chair organized in the rear of the hall, the committee retired and drafted its report:

We hereby reaffirm our faith in the party of Jefferson, Jackson, Tilden and Bryan, and declare our conviction that the nomination of Bryan to be made at Kansas City, on the Nation's natal day (July 4), will be ratified by his triumphant election in next November, and... instruct the delegates to be selected by this convention to support him.

We declare our adherence to the Chicago platform of 1896 which is the second declaration of American Independence; the principles therein enunciated... are as vital today as ever before....

We favor perpetrating forever independent forms of government.... look forward to the time when these governments shall dominate the earth.... believe the Constitution follows the flag, and the flag can never rightfully float over any territory not a part of our Union, nor over any people not a part of our citizenship.

Much of the remaining content was Houston's:

That governments derive their just powers from the consent of the governed is as true today as when Jefferson wrote it, and we declare that neither this, nor any other country has a right to force a government on a people against that people's will; and... more emphatically to express our zeal in this direction, we pledge the sympathy and support of the democracy of Oklahoma Territory to all people, in all climes, at all times, where there is sufficient intelligence to... adopt a Constitution in consonance with ours.... hereby extend our sympathy to the Republic of the Transvaal in their heroic struggle for existence against the tyranny of England, and denounce the action of the McKinley administration in its dealings with the unfortunate people of the Philippines....

We condemn the McKinley administration for its duplicity and dishonesty in dealing with Porto Rico whose people gladly transferred their allegiance from Spain to our country; this allegiance entitles them to every guarantee of our Bill of Rights and our Constitution; these guarantees have been wrongfully withheld, and we condemn, as a cowardly subterfuge, the pretense of the republican party that the tariff between the United States and the Island of Porto Rico is for the purpose of creating a revenue for Porto Rico, and declare that the pernicious legislation of this congress in relation to this matter is solely to prevent the American people from having an object lesson in Free Trade.

The grasping greed of plutocracy which actuates the unjust and un-Constitutional course of the McKinley administration toward Porto Rico controls its inhuman and bloody policy in the Philippine Isles, resulting in the sacrifice of thousands of the best and bravest of our loyal and patriotic boys in blue.... this inhuman policy we denounce and condemn.

We favor legislation that will emphatically annihilate those vicious combinations denominated as Trusts and believe that one of the most effective methods of their destruction is the passing of laws placing on the free list every article manufactured or produced by trusts.

We believe in the most rigid economy of public affairs and in holding to strict accountability the public servants of the people, whether at home or abroad, and so believing, impeach the present administration of high crimes and misdemeanors in its dealings with the Cuban people. . . . declare its policy wrong in principle and most vicious in practice, a disgrace to the American people and a blight on civilization.

The report—the most damning document drafted by a state or territorial convention—was adopted in full. Afterwards, celebrating the defeat of the anticombine—but mostly for entertainment of party well-wishers—Temple Houston shot the feathers off three hats on display in Callie Reams' Millinery Store. He paid for the hats the next day.

Bryan was again nominated for president in Kansas City. Adlai E. Stevenson of Illinois, vice-president during Cleveland's second term, was nominated for the same office. Both were endorsed by Silver Republicans and the Anti-Imperialist League, which numbered among its members many prominent Republicans disenchanted with the government's imperialistic policy. Most of the Populists supported Bryan and Stevenson; the middle-of-the-road bolters nominated Wharton Baker of Pennsylvania.

The Republicans renominated President McKinley at Philadelphia. Theodore Roosevelt, governor of New York and Rough Rider hero, was nominated for vice-president by acclamation.

In nearly every large city in Oklahoma the Democrats and Populists held Bryan-Stevenson ratification meetings, paraded in the principal business streets in the wake of marching clubs and bands, carrying banners unique in their phraseology, and set the heavens ablaze with rockets and Roman candles.

Congressional timber in both parties was slow in maturing. The democrats listed Colonel Forrest, who had his own and most of the short-grass counties lined up and showed the greatest numerical strength; William Cross of Oklahoma City, who was asking support of no one but making many friends; W. T. Willis of Chandler, backed by the entire Lincoln County delegation; Leslie P. Ross, with an instructed Cleveland County delegation pushing his claims; and Roy Hoffman, whose friends were legion.

The Populists offered Judge Robert Neff of Newkirk, who had Kay County solid and claimed other strength; R. E. Bray and W. O. Cromwell of Garfield County, with a divided delegation, the former getting the lion's share; Dr. Delos Walker of Oklahoma City and W. H. French of Chandler, in the race merely because friends were pushing them; and former delegate Callahan, whose entrance in the contest was hardly expected.

On July 30 the executive committees of the Populist and Democratic central committees met at the Lee Hotel in Oklahoma City and decided on a joint convention as the solution. It would consist of 191 delegates from each party—the number of delegates composing each convention under call. No caucus nominations would be made by either party; nominations would require a two-thirds vote of the joint convention and be closed only after some candidate won that majority. Both conventions would then reconvene separately and ratify the joint nominee.

Again Houston expressed disgust at this return to fusion, with his usual scoring of Populist efforts in the territory. A young man named Harry Hamilton had been sentenced to life imprisonment the previous winter by Judge Irwin on a change of venue at Enid for killing a fellow cattle raiser in Day County. Hamilton's mother, arriving from Ohio in mid-July, engaged Houston and Marum to try to obtain a pardon for her son. The youth had become very ill in the Lansing Penitentiary and had been moved from the coal mines to employment above ground. Temple and Marum went to Guthrie to present and argue the case before Governor Barnes, and Robert Ray led the Woodward delegation to the Oklahoma City congressional convention on July 31.

But Hoffman was there, with Denton, Diggs, Ross, Jacobs, and other fighters of the original combine. Hoffman's endorsement of Jacobs for national committeeman brought forth vigorous cheers and yells, and Jacobs knocked the persimmon with a resounding roll-call majority over Captain Taylor, the Wisby candidate from Guthrie. The name of Jasper Sipes was not presented. For the sake of harmony Taylor moved that Jacobs's selection be made unanimous, and the motion was adopted. Jacobs then thanked the convention, saying that he harbored malice toward none.

The convention reconvened on the morning of August 1. The report of the conference committee was reread. Colonel Johnson moved to amend by giving the Populists 207 votes in the joint convention inasmuch as the Democrats had seated delegates from the reservations and had that number. Denton of Garfield offered a substitute providing for appointment of a committee composed of one member from each delegation better to determine what action the party desired to pursue in cooperating with anti-Republican forces. Robert Ray opposed the substitute, maintaining that the convention first should determine whether it was desirable to cooperate with the populists, and if so, along what lines. Colonel Forrest took the floor and vigorously assailed the conference committee's report, insisting that the Populists owed it to the Democrats to endorse their nominee inasmuch as the Democrats had endorsed the Populist nominee in 1896 and refused to allow his name to go before a joint convention. Senator J. R. Clarke of Oklahoma County strongly favored the conference report as the best means of welding the reform forces under the Democratic banner. Judge Bierer of Logan agreed and begged Democrats living in counties where Populist support to elect was unnecessary to consider the condition of Democrats living in counties where such support was absolutely necessary to success. Travers of Lincoln County made an eloquent appeal for a joint convention and harmonious union. Some of the Washita and Roger Mills delegates sided with Forrest in favor of a Democratic nominee and Populist endorsement of him.

Denton's amendment failed, Johnson's was accepted, and the conference report was adopted without division by a large majority. A committee consisting of Clarke, Taylor, and John Clark of Payne County was appointed to confer with a like committee from the Populist convention and arrange for the joint session.

Meanwhile, the Populists held an interesting and somewhat bitter meeting in the district courtroom. There was considerable wrangling as committee reports were presented and amended, rejected, or tabled before the house, but a war of words came over the conference committee report providing for merger of the two conventions and two-thirds vote requirement to nominate a congressional delegate. For fifteen minutes Edward Clark of Pawnee spoke on why Populists were entitled to the candidate this year and proposed that they should have him. This was warmly seconded by W. H. Redwine of Pawnee, delegates from Logan and Kingfisher, and others, some going so far to say that they would not support a Democrat for Congress that fall. French of Lincoln, Thomas Kearse of Kay, and T. J. Griffith of Oklahoma opposed the motion. Judge Neff was present but took no stand.

Redwine broke the deadlock with probably the best speech of the meeting. He agreed that he would not be too hasty and that he would support the meanest Democrat in the territory in preference to the best Republican, and he closed with an impassioned appeal to all anti-Republicans to band together against the common enemy. A motion was made and carried to appoint a committee of three to inform the Democratic convention of their action. The chair appointed French, Griffith, and J. S. Soule of Logan County.

The Democrats reconvened for the joint convention at 1:30 P.M. The *Daily Oklahoman* said:

> It was nearly two o'clock when the populists filed into the opera house and they were given a shout of welcome that might have been heard by Mr. Flynn at Guthrie had his ear been placed to the ground. The populist delegates marched around the hall and each delegation took its place with the democratic delegation from its county.... The house was packed.... many ladies occupied the gallery. Chairman A. C. Huston, after obtaining order, introduced Chairman J. F. Todd of the populist convention. Mr. Todd was given an ovation which lasted several minutes, and in a short

speech, characterized by a wonderful amount of applause, . . . paid glowing tribute to the reform forces of the territory . . . now merged into a harmonious whole for the present campaign. Chairman Huston also made a short speech, punctuated by much applause.

The first business was the selection of a chairman. . . . and it was moved that, inasmuch as a populist had presided over the joint convention before, that honor be accorded to the democrats this time. This motion was vigorously seconded by a number of populist delegates . . . carried with a whoop, and Mr. Huston was chairman of the convention.

On motion the two committees on resolutions, appointed while the conventions were in separate sessions, were named as a committee on platform. . . . and the two great reform parties of Oklahoma proceeded with a roll call of counties for nominations of a candidate for delegate to congress.

The selection was not as harmonious as predicted. Every county offered a favorite son, and nominating speeches were interrupted so frequently by raucous shouting and explosions of cheers that it became increasingly difficult to restore order and proceed with the balloting. Finally, on the thirtieth ballot and after much heated exchange between backers of leading candidates Neff, Cross, Ross, and Callahan, enough Callahan and Ross supporters suddenly changed their votes to Neff that he was declared the convention nominee.

Neff was one of the most entertaining candidates that ever addressed an Oklahoma audience. Throughout the campaign he stressed the union of anti-Republican factions, interspersed his remarks with anecdotes, set large crowds in an uproar of laughter, and was cheered repeatedly. But the voters apparently were more concerned with questions arising from the war with Spain than entertainment and fusion. Flynn carried sixteen of Oklahoma's twenty-three counties, defeating Neff 38,252 votes to 33,539.

Many Democrats, including Temple Houston, won wagers. The usual bet on the congressional race was that Flynn would, or would not, carry the territory by 5,000.

On the national level Democrats expounded free silver but declared Republican "militarism" and "imperialism" the paramount issue. Republicans declared that the nation's policy had been one of territorial expansion from Jefferson to Cleveland, that the Philippines had been forced upon the country as the result of a war waged in the interest of humanity and liberty. They could not be abandoned as prey to other foreign nations but must be held and protected by the United States until they were capable of governing themselves and finally became independent.

In time imperialism and militarism came to be regarded as bogeys rather than real dangers, and Bryan turned to trusts and tariffs. President McKinley made no speeches, but Roosevelt toured the northern and western states, rivaling Bryan in democratic manners and aggressive discussion that contributed greatly to a sweeping Republican victory. Nebraska, Kansas, Wyoming, Utah, South Dakota, and Washington—states that Bryan had carried by substantial majorities in 1896—even deserted the free-silver ranks for McKinley and imperialism. The Republicans also retained control in both houses of Congress.

Temple received the Associated Press results at the *News* office in Woodward early Wednesday morning, November 7, and remarked: "The only thing good that has happened to the country is Teddy Roosevelt."

19

Fire-Eaters Cross Swords

Flynn carried Woodward County by a comfortable majority, but Democrats had won territorial legislative seats and most county offices. Sidney Laune was elected county attorney, and he soon clashed with Houston in the prosecution of Sol Dreiling, a recalcitrant homesteader.

Dreiling became enraged when a neighbor encroached on his pasture. Laune refused to file a trespass charge and tried to soothe the farmer: "All you need to do, Sol, is put up a fence according to the surveyor's marks. You stay on your side; your neighbor will stay on his. No need for further trouble."

A few days later the neighbor complained that Dreiling was building a fence on his property. Laune asked the county surveyor to go out and, with both men present, run the lines again. Neither farmer was satisfied, and Dreiling grew so belligerent that he had to be put under a peace bond.

Within a week the neighbor reported that Dreiling had removed the surveyor's stones to points that "better pleased him." Laune issued a warrant, the sheriff arrested Dreiling, and the justice of the peace jailed him for thirty days "to cool his temper."

Dreiling took his punishment in stride. He suggested certain changes to beautify the courthouse grounds, and was allowed to carry out his plans as a trusty. One weekend he asked permission to go to his farm. It was growing season with much work to be done, and he wanted to see his wife and children. A parole was granted, and he began his long walk home.

Laune was at breakfast Sunday morning when the sheriff rode up to his door and announced that he had Dreiling back in jail. Shortly after dawn on Saturday, the farmer had shot and killed another neighbor he had caught with his wife in the field, where they had gone, they claimed, to drive the hogs out of the crops.

The territory charged murder in the first degree and demanded the death penalty. Dreiling employed Temple Houston. Houston maintained that the defendant had acted in defense of the honor of his home.

The prosecution presented its case and rested; Houston became increasingly argumentative. Darting one way and another, like a cutting horse heading a steer, he quoted the Bible and history—anything to keep the line of thought as far from his client as possible. The evidence was against Dreiling; Temple sensed no sympathy from the jurors. His only chance was to brand the prosecutor a vengeful, heartless hounder of the innocent, and he launched into a story:

Gentlemen, last night after pondering the insidious machinations of men and their relentless vengeance and vindictiveness aimed at the poor unfortunates that have momentarily strayed, I fell finally into a troubled sleep.... I dreamed that I died, and it may not cause you astonishment to learn that in the dream I went to hell.

Houston drew heavily upon Dante in describing his meeting with the devil himself as he continued:

He was writhing on his throne, his forked tail curling and entwining itself about his legs. I came close and asked, "What possibly can have brought you, your Satanic Majesty, to such a state of despair?"

The glowing eyes of the devil gave me a searing glance. "Temple," he said, "I have lost my job. All through the vaults of hell the rumor is flying that I am to be displaced."

"But who," I asked, "could possibly replace you?"

"Rumor has it," replied Satan—his voice came rumbling with all the fetid breaths of Hades—"that I am to be replaced by that arch fiend, Sidney Laune."

Paul Laune still remembers how his father, recounting this story in later years, would become so swept away by fond memories of his days in court with Houston that he always forgot to tell which of them won the case.

Dreiling was found guilty and sentenced to life at Lansing. He escaped and came to Laune's home one night to kill him, but was recaptured. He was not returned to prison but was given a mental hearing and was committed to the territorial asylum, where he remained until his death.

One day after Dreiling's conviction, Temple was sitting in Judge Burford's court, unoccupied and watching Laune arraign a horse thief. The man had no money to hire a lawyer, so Burford appointed Houston to defend him. Temple discussed the case with the judge, the sheriff, and the county attorney. He then asked to take his client into an adjoining office for private counseling. Burford agreed, and Laune quipped: "Give him the best advice possible."

After a reasonable time had lapsed with no word from lawyer or client, Laune and the sheriff entered the room. Houston sat, composed and alone, before an open window.

"Where is the defendant?" demanded Laune.

"Well," Temple said, "after hearing his story, I did as you told me—gave him my best advice."

Despite such antics, he and Laune remained warm friends.

Possessed of a military spirit, Temple was disappointed in 1898 that no opportunity presented itself by which he could obtain a colonelcy to enter the Spanish-American War. He respected Roosevelt for his military leadership, but mostly because the vice-president understood the wants and necessities of the people. Both Roosevelt and President McKinley favored admission of Oklahoma and Indian territories as a single state. When Governor Barnes' term expired in April, 1901, and he chose to retire to private business, McKinley elevated Secretary of the Territory William M. Jenkins to the governorship. On August 6, during Jenkins' brief tenure, the surplus lands of Kiowa, Comanche, Apache, Wichita and Caddo Indians were opened to settlement. The 2,080,000-acre region was divided into three new counties—Comanche, Kiowa, and Caddo—with seats at Lawton, Hobart, and Anadarko, respectively, and Oklahoma took another step toward becoming the Forty-sixth Star. One month later, while holding a public reception in the Temple of Music at the Pan-American exposition in Buffalo, President McKinley was shot by anarchist Leon Czolgosz. He died September 14, and Roosevelt succeeded to the presidency, pledged to carry out the McKinley policies and retaining all members of his cabinet. In Oklahoma, Thompson B. Ferguson replaced Jenkins as governor.

The territory now had twenty-six counties. The rapid increase of population and property right brought such growth of business in the courts that Congress, by act of May 2, 1902, added two judges to the territorial supreme court. On May 20, President Roosevelt appointed J. L. Pancoast, of Perry, formerly of Kansas, and Frank E. Gillette, of El Reno, formerly of Kansas, to these positions, and appointed J. K. Beauchamp, of Enid, to succeed Judge McAtee.

On June 4 the territory was divided into seven judicial districts:

First District (Chief Justice Burford presiding), embracing Logan, Lincoln, and Payne counties

Second District (Judge Irwin), Canadian, Cleveland, Kingfisher, Washita, and Custer counties

Third District (Judge Burwell), Oklahoma and Pottawatomie counties

Fourth District (Judge Hainer), Noble, Kay, and Pawnee counties, including the district court at Pawhuska, Osage Nation

Fifth District (Judge Beauchamp), Garfield, Grant, Blaine, and Roger Mills counties

Sixth District (Judge Pancoast), Woods, Woodward, Beaver, Day, and Dewey counties

Seventh District (Judge Gillette), Comanche, Kiowa, Caddo, and Greer counties.

It had been rumored that Houston might be appointed to one of the new judgeships. Though a place on the supreme bench might have satisfied his aspirations, Temple nurtured no such expectation under a Republican administration and publicly said so, repeating a remark he had made at Mangum when Greer County became a part of the territory: "Some day we shall have statehood, and I only hope to be able to go to the constitutional convention for the proposed new state."

Governor Ferguson was already proving himself a wise and capable administrator, placing honest, sober, economical government before personal gain. Under President Roosevelt federal laws were being strictly enforced, the army reorganized, and a strong foreign policy so successfully maintained that the popular demand for his renomination in 1904 was imperative.

Temple expressed little hope for the Democratic party in Oklahoma until statehood could be achieved, and he agreed with the *El Reno Democrat* of August 5, 1902 that

the voices of all the old-time Democratic sages and warriors of the territory are hushed.... Nothing is heard but the quacking of a lot of political goslings who have not been here long enough to find the town pump. Every man who fought and won the early battles of Democracy in this territory has been insulted, snubbed or turned down by a lot of pinworms shipped in from abroad....

The committees have been filled up with Pops and nonenities, under whom no self-respecting Democrat of intelligence will work.

"Houston was not party hidebound," Colonel Forrest said. "Neither was he a Mr. Callahan.... He was relentless in his opposition to populism."

A Woodward delegate to the Populist congressional convention at Oklahoma City in 1900 informed Houston that God created the Populist party. Temple retorted, "God also created a jackass, but there is an old tradition that says He laughed when He saw what he had done."

Judge Beauchamp, of the Fifth District, opened his first term of court at Enid in December, 1902, and heading the docket was a murder case defended by Houston. It was the old story of homesteader versus rancher, a controversy now white-hot in northwestern Oklahoma. Frank Sears, of Macon County, Missouri, ran a herd of cattle in Roger Mills County, which had invaded Robert Riggins' unfenced fields and done considerable damage. The two men met on the road, and after a heated exchange Riggins shot Sears dead. Sears had been armed with a pitchfork. His brother in Missouri looked upon it as cold-blooded murder, demanded the most serious penalty, and employed Macon lawyer Ben Franklin to assist in the prosecution.

Franklin recounted this experience:

Long before I reached Oklahoma I began to hear startling tales about the dexterous gentleman Riggins had employed to save his neck, and wondered if I had observed proper caution in leaving my revolver at home....

I arrived in Cheyenne and sat down in the little office of the only hotel in the place. It was a very hot day in August. Before long a rather remarkable looking man arrived on horseback, threw the bridle reins across the hitchrack and stalked inside. His silver spurs glittered in the sunshine. I noticed that almost immediately the citizens began to gather around and shake the newcomer warmly by the hand. He wore a white cowboy hat, long dark hair rolling down his back, and had his pants tucked in his boots. A strong smooth face, a swarthy complexion, and dark piercing eyes fairly completed his description as I remember. After having acknowledged the salutation from all his friends, the gentleman approached me, and bowing courteously, said:

"My name is Houston—Temple Houston. Would you mind telling me your name."

"Ben Franklin."

"Ah! You have been called after a very worthy gentleman, although I never had the honor of his acquaintance. I hope you are as good a man as your namesake."

"I fear not," I said, "but I am doing the best I know how."

"Good! None of us can do better. Where are you from?"

"I am from Missouri."

"Missouri. Good old Missouri! Well, my friend, I guess you will have to be shown. Come along." He seized me by the arm....

"Where are we going, Mr. Houston?" I asked.

"Going! Thunder and lightning! Where do two gentlemen go when they meet?"

"Thank you, I don't drink."

By all the veracious legends of the West, this is where the badman jerks out his gun and makes the tenderfoot dance up to the bar and order a murderous dose of peace destroyer. But Houston was not that sort of badman.

"No?" he exclaimed in some surprise. "I commend your principles. Whiskey will ruin any man. Have a cigar?" And he pulled out a box of Havanas.

The Riggins case was not tried at that time, but it finally came on in the district court at Enid. Because of the local feeling against his client, Houston obtained a change of venue to Garfield County. In the meantime Franklin acquired an associate in the case—an attorney who was something of a fighter himself, Moman Pruiett.

Pruiett had run away from home at Leitchfield, Kentucky, at age thirteen. He landed at Rogers, Arkansas, on the Frisco, and shined shoes until the railroad built to Fayetteville, where he worked at night in a hotel selling papers and washing dishes for his supper. After the Frisco pushed on to Hackett City, he got a job in the railroad station. In 1888, at age sixteen, he was caught kiting freight bills and sentenced to two years in the Arkansas Penitentiary. He was pardoned a few months later because of his youth, good conduct, and a strong petition presented to the governor by his mother. She took him to Paris, Texas, where the family now ran a boardinghouse. In November, 1890, he was sentenced to five years in prison for stealing three thousand dollars sewed in the coat of a local tailor, James Riley. His mother went to work again, and Moman was out in a couple of years, back in Paris cleaning up the spittoons and offices of attorney Colonel Jake Hodges and dreaming of greatness through the lawbooks. He swore that he had been railroaded in both instances and vowed to devote the rest of his life to "emptying jails."

Well versed in law and full of hate, he migrated to the Smith Paul's Valley region of the Chickasaw Nation, Indian Territory, where Federal Judge David E. Bryant, struck by the keen knowledge of this cocky, unbroken, animal-handsome ruffian, admitted him to practice in his "sandyland court," established in 1895. Here Pruiett proved uncannily adept at getting before juries to acquit the guilty and soon had all the business he could handle.

In his sensational career by his own count he defended 343 accused murderers, 304 of whom escaped punishment. The remaining 38 were found guilty and given sentences ranging from four years to life. The only client of his ever sentenced to death was granted presidential clemency. In 1902, at age forty, he was a fancy dresser and high liver, with a mane of black hair, black eyes, beetling black brows, and a slink in his walk that probably came from aping cow-country heroes. He was also a straight-whiskey man and a dedicated poker player, and he always kept a six-shooter handy. His name had become sacred to the criminal element and illiterate victims of crimes of passion, and he was well into his reputation as the greatest master of backwoods psychology, actor, hypocrite, fakir, lawyer, and publicity expert that the courts of Oklahoma were likely to know.

Pruiett had watched Houston for years. Some said that he imitated Houston. Pruiett claimed that he had hoped that they would cross swords on his home grounds or at least on a neutral battleground but that Houston contained his activities south of Kansas across No Man's Land into the stretches of West Texas and was too wary to venture down the Washita. Against his better judgment, but at the request of an old friend, Bill Whittinghill, Pruiett consented to go to Enid to help prosecute Riggins. Of course, the Sears family had put up an attractive cash inducement, and the case was getting a lot of territorial publicity.

Houston was aware of all this, and, according to Ben Franklin,

> directed most all of his harsh talk toward Pruiett. Once or twice it looked like the two fire-eaters would have to settle the point of law with guns. When the eloquent lawyer for the defense had occasion to refer to me it was always "the gentleman from Missouri." I guess he saw that I wasn't a fighter, and he disdained to pick a quarrel with me. Houston did not examine the witnesses, but he sat at the elbow of Enid attorney W. S. Denton, who did. . . .

From the start to the wind-up he was intensely observant and watchful of every point.... had the details of the case in his head more thoroughly than any lawyer connected with it. He could repeat from memory disputed points, and in that particular seemed almost infallible. Again and again he was on his feet objecting to the territory's tender evidence, and at last the judge reprimanded him a trifle harshly, which Houston took in a very good part.

At this interval, according to Enid's populist newspaper *Coming Events*,

Mr. Pruiett made his closing argument, ... characterized by the fiery zeal for justice and law and order. He wove a web of circumstantial deduction which was convincing and conclusive.... His "fiery zeal" caused him to tread on the blunt toes of the figurative Houston boot. He told the jury, "the defendant's lawyer, who wore buckskins and twisted his hair up like a multitude of rats' tails, had but one virtue to his claim to fame, and that was the undying reputation of an illustrious father."

Pruiett believed that anything was fair in a murder trial—he had even been known to furnish his own witnesses. At one point, provoked by Houston's manner of utter contempt for him throughout the proceedings and relying on a false belief circulated about the territory that Temple was of Indian blood, he cried:

"Spawn of the teepee!"

Houston's swarthy complexion deepened, but he made no answer. He had only to fall back on the fact that Sears had brandished his pitchfork and that Riggins had reason to believe that his life was in danger.

Franklin continued:

Houston's great forte, as I learned, was in summing up at the close.... His speech was made late Christmas eve, and to a man of Houston's caliber as a rhetorician it was a point outweighing a gold mine. The courtroom was crowded with men and women anxious to hear him. The eloquent lawyer painted rainbows, prismatic waterfalls, sent shooting stars across the blue skies and tolled deep bells in old cathedral spires. He brought to the jury in coloring as vigorous as that sketched by any artist, the babe in the manger, the wise men who journeyed on camel back across the desert, the startled shepherds on Bethlehem hills and the angel chorus heralding the birth of peace on earth, good will to men.

I don't suppose many juries could have stood that. I know ours couldn't. Riggins was a free man within minutes after Houston sat down. I never begrudged him his victory. He earned it.

Afterward Judge Beauchamp made a noble gesture. He asked Pruiett to leave town or stay off the streets lest Houston kill him. Then he took Temple by the arm and under guise of court business led him from the building.

Pruiett went to his hotel room, debating whether to stay or leave. Houston had killed a man; for Pruiett that experience was yet to come. But violent physical encounters had been his lot since childhood; he had no intention of showing cowardice now. He took his blue-steel revolver from his old carpetbag, shoved it into the waistband of his trousers, and strode downstairs for a drink.

Soon Temple came in and joined three or four friends at the other end of the bar. The group ordered, laughed, and talked, but Houston was conscious of Pruiett's presence and finally edged toward him.

"The gentleman from the Chickasaw country is a pretty talker," he said sarcastically, holding his glass as if ready to toss it into Pruiett's face.

Pruiett said nothing but stood "looking unwaveringly" into Houston's eyes.

"The jury was not misled by it," Houston added.

Pruiett replied, "The jury is always right."

Houston emptied his glass, tilting it awkwardly. "Would the gentleman from the Chickasaw country condescend to drink with the son of the immortal emacipator of Texas—who wears his hair on his coat collar like a multitude of rat's tails?" Houston remained "menacingly sarcastic."

Pruiett explained that he confined his professional feelings to the courtroom, tried to give satisfaction to those who employed him, and was able to look any man in the face, even his adversary, without an apology. He concluded, "I would be glad to drink with Temple Houston, an able lawyer."

Temple weighed his remarks briefly. "You are indeed a pretty talker," he said. Drinks were poured and tossed off, then each man nodded, and they separated, Pruiett keeping up his eye-to-eye gaze until he made his exit.

In later years he loved to brag about facing down Houston, which was not quite true. The *Enid Eagle* said, "Pruiett left town on the midnight train."

20

The Tub Stands on Its Own Bottom

Houston was in Guthrie again in January, "greeting his many friends" but primarily "on business before the board of equalization," and "nothing political except that attaches" to a bill before the Seventh Legislature. The bill provided that the commissioners of any county, upon petition signed by "at least twenty-five homesteaders or freeholders, legal voters and residents," could divide such county into stock districts of "not less than 72 square miles nor more than 144," with due consideration to streams, timber, and prairies, "whether it be better adapted to agriculture or stock raising use." After a district was established, one-fourth of its voters and residents could petition a special election to decide "if and when domestic animals would be permitted to run at large, methods of distraint, and other such police regulations." Violators were subject to a fine or imprisonment in the county jail and in addition were liable in a civil action for recovery of damages and costs by the person whose lands were trespassed.

Despite the ill-feeling between cattlemen and settlers in western Oklahoma, there was an element of common interest between the groups. The farmer and small stock raisers joined in protesting fencing of large enclosures to be leased by non-resident capitalists. Surrounding large tracts of land subject to homestead entry and building drift fences not only impeded travel across the country but kept settlers and small stock raisers from water and intimidated prospective settlers from going inside the enclosures to take claims.

The big cattlemen maintained that the law should not be strictly enforced. The land was poorly suited to agriculture because of drought and was therefore better adapted to the

THE TUB STANDS ON ITS OWN BOTTOM

grazing business. Cattle raising, the principal industry, would be virtually destroyed if pasture fences were taken down. While the United States Department of the Interior was empowered to proceed against offenders in the courts and showed a willingness to be as lenient as possible so as not to hamper the growth of the industry, it was beyond the province of the government to turn over public domain to the adjustment of private parties. Every session of the territorial legislature since 1893 had passed some statute to alleviate the conflict and support and encourage the settler in his honest rights.

In 1903 in Woodward County alone over half of the quarter sections that remained had been filed on, and applications on thousands of acres more were pending. A great many settlers had come in 1901 after being unsuccessful in drawing for lands in the Kiowa-Comanche-Apache land opening. The population had trebled, and several new communities had sprung up, such as Yelton, Charleston, and Brule (present-day Buffalo). Old trails had been abandoned, and section lines had been opened for highways. There were seventy-two postoffices. Church buildings had been erected in every community; there was a schoolhouse within reach of every child—182 organized districts and 113 open for instruction with an enrollment of nearly 4,000 pupils; and thirteen county newspapers were published in Curtis, Mooreland, Mutual, Oleta, Quinlan, Shattuck, Supply, and Woodward. Six were published in Woodward. Alfalfa, milo maize, kaffir, and broomcorn were cash crops, wheat produced forty bushels an acre, and the splendid farm homes were surrounded by thrifty young orchards of peach, apple, grapes, and berries. While cattle still headed the livestock list, the territorial governor reported quite a number of swine, mules, and horses. Deposits in Woodward's two banks totaled over $150,000.

Houston and Marum consistently pushed Woodward's progress and the upbuilding of all the northwestern country. While in the legislature, Marum had introduced and secured passage of the bill establishing the normal school at Alva and had promoted irrigation projects in sections with little rainfall

301

Bird's-eye view of Woodward, ca. 1900.

and in No Man's Land along the Cimarron. Both men strongly supported the movement to create one state out of Oklahoma and Indian territories and were active members of every statehood organization and convention.

Asked by a *State Capital* reporter, "How about Northwestern Oklahoma and Woodward County?" Temple replied:

My boy, you ought to see that part of the Lord's vineyard. No words of mine can describe its beauty. It is a waving paradise, a symphony of rolling grasses and yellow grain. You have read in the sacred word of how the devil took our Savior up to the summit of a high mountain and offered him all within the range of his vision if he would fall down and worship the prince of darkness—well, I've sometimes thought that the barren hills and rocky deserts of that country presented but a poor recompense for so groveling an act as devil worship; but if his Satanic Majesty could have made his offer from the vantage ground of one of the beautiful elevations of Woodward county, with its rippling streams, its singing birds, its flowering prairies, shady woodlands, its waving fields of grain and its tens of thousands of cattle feeding in knee deep grasses, the fact that our Savior was of divine origin would alone have saved Him. Had He been of mortal flesh he would have yielded and the Bible would never have been written.

Temple called northwestern Oklahoma "the richest agricultural section in the Territory" and Woodward the "Belle of the Short Grass Region."

His legal work increased so greatly that he was away from his office much of the time and found need of a partner who could give more attention to the business than Marum did. They dissolved the partnership but continued as personal friends and supported each other's civic schemes and enterprises. In April, Temple formed a new partnership with T. M. Grant, which lasted a few months and then was dissolved when Houston formed a partnership with A. M. Appelget. The firm of Appelget & Houston thrived into the summer months of 1904.

Temple never seemed more happy during this period, and Colonel Forrest recalled that he became a teetotaler. He was engaged in many social turns, and you would scarcely meet him on attendance in court without finding him jollying with acquaintances. He would stand for hours and greet man after man, invariably full of irresistible and new anecdotes always applicable... and notwithstanding his reputation as a dangerous man to affront, nobody thought of being timid in his presence. He joked others and accepted jokes thrown at him in the heartiest spirit, and in distant departure from too frequent occurrence on such occasions, never applied epithets nor made unpleasant references to the personalities of those present.

Houston had emerged a giant behind the bar as well as before it. Political leaders acknowledged his quality and dauntless courage. Committeemen of several factions visited him to sound out his views on current issues. Other attorneys sought his advice on extension of Oklahoma laws and procedure over Indian Territory and uniting the bar associations of Oklahoma and Indian territories so that their members might get acquainted before the territories were merged and be in better temper to form a constitution for the new state. For it would be the lawyers who would write the constitution, and there would be many offices to fill. A place on the supreme court bench or a senatorial seat after statehood was in line with his thinking, though he would not decline to helm the ship of the new state.

He had sought to establish a personal individuality, to carve his own fortune, and the opportunity had arrived. Men listened to his sensible answers and went away nodding, with no mention that he was descended from a distinguished sire. At last his tub was going to stand on its own bottom.

Then Temple attended a term of district court at Taloga to participate in the defense of Ed McHaffie, slayer of W. G. McDonald. McDonald had been a well-known Dewey County Republican and a delegate to several territorial conventions. The trouble rose out of an old political disagreement. McDonald was driving into Taloga one day when McHaffie rode up behind him and asked if he was ready to fight it out. McDonald replied that he was, got out of his wagon, and reached for his Winchester. Before he could fire, McHaffie put two pistol balls in him, but neither took effect. McDonald raised his rifle, but it failed to fire. McHaffie emptied his pistol into McDonald, and the noted politician fell dead.

McHaffie surrendered to the sheriff. McDonald, better known as "Mc of D," had been a unique character but well liked. Feeling ran high. The killing occurred on August 31, 1898, but had remained untried because of legal delays.

Finally McHaffie was brought to trial. The prosecution presented its evidence and rested. Houston rose to address the jury. There was a sudden halting of a brilliant speech, a blind groping of feeble hands. He sank back in his chair, fumbling for papers that were not there.

Judge Pancoast, realizing that something was seriously wrong, declared a recess. Temple was assisted to his hotel, suffering severe nausea and feverish in the neck and head. His associates took over when court reconvened.

Temple was ill for several days. He said nothing about it and was soon back in his Woodward office. His many friends, though puzzled, were pleased that he had recovered.

Few outside his family and home physician knew that for some time he had suffered from a most uncomfortable disease—Saint Anthony's fire, or erysipelas. The treatment had been iron-and-quinine tonics, but he had found the best relief in alcohol. For the past months he had experienced a recurrence that manifested itself in attacks at irregular intervals. This had been his first attack in public, and a few uninformed wags attributed it to too much tabasco sauce and whiskey.

Within a week he drove to Roger Mills County in a buggy to defend some criminal cases and then started to Canadian, Texas, to defend a case there. On the prairie ten miles from the city he was "seized with the most violent convulsions and lay unconscious and practically dead for an hour" before he was discovered by a passing cowboy. "Notwithstanding the severe attack at that time and the feeble condition in which it left Mr. Houston," said Colonel Forrest, "he defended the case the next day, then boarded a train that night to Vernon, Texas, and participated next morning in the trial of a murder case in which his firm was employed."

On January 6, 1905, several northwestern Oklahoma weeklies carried this brief item: "Temple Houston, the noted criminal lawyer of Woodward, is reported to be ill in a hospital."

Shortly after returning from Texas, inflammation began on his face, his eyes were swollen, and a most intense pain spread throughout his body. Local physicians, after doing all they could to relieve him, took him to the hospital at Topeka. An abscess had formed, and prompt surgery was necessary. But the doctors shook their heads. Streptococcus had wandered into the bloodstream, and general pyemia was the result.

He was in and out of the hospital for the next six months, until he was finally brought home and confined to his bed, paralyzed and partly blind. It was an agonizing time for his friends, wife, and children. His torture was exhibited in writhing and spasmodic convulsions. The Woodward doctor could only administer a sedative.

The night of August 15, Temple Houston's star of destiny exploded in a blaze of excruciating pain. A blood vessel in his brain hemorrhaged. Within moments the West's most colorful lawyer lay dead in his palatial home of many gables on Texas Street.

Chief Justice Burford made the funeral arrangements. Members of the Woodward bar were pallbearers. During his illness Houston had asked to be buried in Oklahoma, and the family was compelled to refuse to have the body taken to Texas. On Sunday afternoon, August 20, he was laid to rest in the cemetery just west of the city. Personal friends and admirers from throughout the territory and the Texas Panhandle and the entire population of Woodward were present for the occasion.

The Reverend Father Kemp delivered the oration and said in part:

> I see people of every station and class in life gathered around the bier of our departed friend. The feelings of sympathy and interest

manifested by you are a tribute greater than which it is possible for me to give him. Your presence here speaks for him. . . .

Humanly speaking, he should or ought to have lived longer—a man of a mighty and powerful intellect; a man who was a promoter of this place, whose labor for the welfare of the community was unceasing.

I have loved wisdom and pursued it, and in it my heart has rejoiced.

To know things . . . was the aim of his life. To use the knowledge, acquired after hours of hard study, for the good of his fellow man, was his greatest pleasure. We all admire wisdom, we all admire intellect, we all admire brains, but when a man uses that wisdom and intellect for the welfare of the community at large, and of each of its members in particular, then we honor, revere, esteem, love such a man. Our departed friend was such a man. He was a genius "sui generis." Would to God that his mantle could be thrown on the shoulders of some of our citizens to make Woodward what he would have made of it if he had lived longer.

The *Oklahoma State Capital* evaluated Houston:

. . . by profession a lawyer, incidentally a scholar of aesthetics and classics, by accident a pioneer, and by nature a fighter. He scrapped because he thought he was right. True, he did not take the requisite amount of time to decide the question in all its moral ramifications. His heart led him and he followed its dictates. . . . He forged ahead in a new country into which he was thrown with the sort of indomitable energy which makes the present Oklahoma a possibility. . . . Oklahoma should inscribe in her book of records a paragraph to one of her most forceful, if not one of her most effective pioneers.

The *Dallas Times-Herald* expressed bitterness:

A chip off the old block, he had great gifts and strong passions. The gods were kind to him—he was not kind to himself. Eloquent as an orator, able as a lawyer, and frank and engaging as a comrade, he should have won renown in the law and politics in the state of his nativity, but . . . he cast his lot with Oklahoma. . . . now clamoring for statehood. . . . missed the mark and died far from the land of his birth.

At a special meeting of the territorial bar association President Jesse James Dunn delivered an appealing eulogy. Among

Richard Dix as Yancy Cravat in a scene from *Cimarron*, RKO Radio production, 1931. Temple Houston was the model for Edna Ferber's character in her magnificent twice-filmed novel.

other comments he said, "Temple Houston belongs to the ages."

Biographer Claude Weaver lamented: "I knew him in the glorious dawn, but the clouds came all too soon.... The overwhelming sense of loss appalls us in the contemplation of his God-given talents, noble impulses, exalted ideals, wasted and gone down to oblivion."

The most touching tribute was paid by Minnie Stacey, who credited the change in her life to Temple's plea. From Cana-

Richard Dix as Yancy Cravat, defending the "fallen woman" in *Cimarron*.

dian, Texas, she sent her condolences to the family and a garland of wild prairie flowers.

Temple Houston died young and might not be remembered today, except for two things: Thousands of people treasure his lectures and courtroom speeches, and twenty-five years after his death he became the model for Edna Ferber's character Yancey Cravat in her magnificent twice-filmed novel *Cimarron*.

Bibliography

Manuscripts and Documents

E. G. C. Austen, Channing, Texas, to J. Evetts Haley, August 4, 1925. Panhandle-Plains Historical Society, Canyon, Texas.

Biennial Report of the Attorney General to the Governor of Oklahoma Territory, 1899-1900. Guthrie, Okla., 1901.

Biographical Directory of the American Congress 1774-1949. Washington, D.C.: U.S. Government Printing Office, 1950.

Arthur Black, Arnett, Oklahoma, to Linnaeus B. Ranck, February 5, 1938. Indian-Pioneer History, Foreman Collection. Vol. 90, pp. 322-35. Oklahoma Historical Society, Oklahoma City.

E. E. Carhart to J. Evetts Haley, July 20, 1926. Panhandle-Plains Historical Society, Canyon, Texas.

Logan Coffee, Miami, Texas, to J. Evetts Haley, July 16, 1926. Panhandle-Plains Historical Society, Canyon, Texas.

S. B. Burck, Appt., v. Abner Taylor, 152 U.S. 634.

William W. Cullar, Woodward, Oklahoma, to Alson J. Chase, June 15, 1937. Indian-Pioneer History, Foreman Collection. Vol. 21, pp. 304-307. Oklahoma Historical Society, Oklahoma City.

Dictionary of American Biography. Vols. 2, 9, 11, 12, 15. New York: Scribner's, 1931-35.

Charley Ferchau, Gage, Oklahoma, to Linnaeus B. Ranck, August 27, 1937. Indian-Pioneer History, Foreman Collection. Vol. 24, pp. 171-74. Oklahoma Historical Society, Oklahoma City.

J. T. Godfrey, Sheriff, et al., v. *W. P. Wright* et al., 8 Okla. Rep. 151.

Governor's Message to the Seventh Legislative Assembly of the Territory of Oklahoma, January 13, 1903. Guthrie, Okla., 1903.

James A. Griggs, Gage, Oklahoma, to Linnaeus B. Ranck, April 8, 1938. Indian-Pioneer History, Foreman Collection. Vol. 80, pp. 206-15. Oklahoma Historical Society, Oklahoma City.

C. W. Herod to Linnaeus B. Ranck, April 28, 1938, "Some Side Lights on the Life and Professional Career of Temple Houston,

Early Day Lawyer of Woodward, Oklahoma." Indian-Pioneer History, Foreman Collection. Vol. 80, pp. 430-43. Oklahoma Historical Society, Oklahoma City.
House Journal (Texas State Legislature). Austin, 1887.
Dick (Richard) Houston, Woodward, Oklahoma, to Linnaeus B. Ranck, May 3, 1938. Indian-Pioneer History, Foreman Collection, Vol. 80, pp. 496-504. Oklahoma Historical Society, Oklahoma City.
Laura (Mrs. Temple) Houston to L. F. Sheffy, December 20, 1929. Panhandle-Plains Historical Society, Canyon, Texas.
Index-Digest and Notes of All Criminal Cases Decided in Texas to 1895. Compiled by A. B. Peticolas and J. V. Vanderberge of the Victoria Bar. Saint Louis: Gilbert Book Company, 1895.
Laws of Texas, 1823-1897. Compiled by H. P. N. Gammel. 10 vols. Austin, 1898.
Letters of Temple Houston, 1896, 1900. Houston Collection, Library, Oklahoma Historical Society, Oklahoma City.
Letters of Temple Houston to Claude Weaver, March 19, June 15, August 27, and October 23, 1885, May 25, 1891. Weaver Collection, Western History Collections, University of Oklahoma Library, Norman.
Letters of H. P. ("Tex") Willis to Claude Weaver about Temple Houston, April 16, May 10, and July 29, 1949. Weaver Collection, Western History Collections, University of Oklahoma Library, Norman.
Clyde Mattox v. United States, 13 S. Ct. 50-54; 146 U.S. 140; 156 U.S. 237.
Message of the Governor of Oklahoma to the Sixth Legislative Assembly, January 9, 1901. Guthrie, Okla., 1901.
L. E. Moyer, Gage, Oklahoma, to Linnaeus B. Ranck, October 2, 1937. Indian-Pioneer History, Foreman Collection. Vol. 108, pp. 475-88. Oklahoma Historical Society, Oklahoma City.
John H. Pitzer, Probate Judge v. The Territory of Oklahoma on relation of A. J. Jennings, County Attorney, 4 Okla. Rep. 86.
Percy Powers, Mangum, Oklahoma, to Ruth Kerbo, August 30, 1937. Indian-Pioneer History, Foreman Collection. Vol. 40, pp. 376-81. Oklahoma Historical Society, Oklahoma City.
Ranck, Linnaeus B. "Some History of Old Day County" (from interviews with O. E. Bull, O. A. Black, and O. E. Enfield of Arnett, Okla). Indian-Pioneer History, Foreman Collection. Vol. 102, pp. 472-76. Oklahoma Historical Society.

―――. "Temple Houston, Early Day Woodward Lawyer." Indian-Pioneer History, Foreman Collection. Vol. 113, pp. 161-164. Oklahoma Historical Society.

"Relics of Oklahoma. Colonel Houston Has an Extensive Collection of Curios." Fred Barde Collection. Book 8, p. 10, February-September 1902. Library, Oklahoma Historical Society, Oklahoma City.

William C. Renfrow, as Governor and Chairman, Thomas J. Lowe and E. D. Cameron, as Secretary, Composing the Board for Leasing School Lands in the Territory of Oklahoma v. B. R. Grimes, J. A. Murphy, A. T. Wilson, Young Short, J. E. Love, J. T. Word, I. T. Pryor, G. T. Hume and W. E. Herring, 6 Okla. Rep. 608.

Report of the Attorney General of the State of Texas, 1885-1886. Austin, 1886.

Report of the Attorney General of the Territory of Oklahoma, December 1, 1902. Guthrie, Okla., 1902.

Report of the Governor of Oklahoma to the Secretary of the Interior, 1899. Washington, D.C.; U.S. Government Printing Office, 1899.

Report of the Governor of Oklahoma to the Secretary of the Interior, 1901. Washington, D.C.: U.S. Government Printing Office, 1901.

Senate Journal (Texas State Legislature). Austin, 1887.

Session Laws of 1895, Third Legislative Assembly of the Territory of Oklahoma. Guthrie, Okla., 1895.

Session Laws of 1897, Fourth Regular Session of the Legislative Assembly of the Territory of Oklahoma. Guthrie, Okla., 1897.

Session Laws of 1899, Fifth Regular Session of the Legislative Assembly of the Territory of Oklahoma. Guthrie, Okla., 1899.

Session Laws of 1901, Sixth Regular Session of the Legislative Assembly of the Territory of Oklahoma. Guthrie, Okla., 1901.

Session Laws of 1903, Seventh Regular Session of the Legislative Assembly of the Territory of Oklahoma. Guthrie, Okla., 1903.

"Some Temple Houston Verses: An Early Morning Inspiration of the Late Oklahoma Man." Fred Barde Collection. Book 15, p. 43, July-November, 1905. Library, Oklahoma Historical Society, Oklahoma City.

Alfred Son v. Territory of Oklahoma. 5 Okla. Rep. 526.

"Temple Houston's Genius: A Missourian's Experience with the Late Cowboy-Lawyer." Fred Barde Collection. Book 15, p. 54, July-November, 1905. Library, Oklahoma Historical Society, Oklahoma City.

"A Tribute to Temple Houston, Funeral Oration Delivered by Rev. Father Kamp at Woodward, Oklahoma." Houston Collection, Library, Oklahoma Historical Society, Oklahoma City.

John W. White, Shattuck, Oklahoma, to Linnaeus B. Ranck, September 30, 1937. Indian-Pioneer History, Foreman Collection. Vol. 94, pp. 55-64. Oklahoma Historical Society, Oklahoma City.

James Ewing Williams, Pampa, Texas, to J. A. Meek, August 11, 1936. Panhandle-Plains Historical Society, Canyon, Texas.

Theses

Alsup, Frances McNeill. "A History of the Panhandle of Texas." Master's thesis, University of Southern California, Los Angeles, 1943.

Barton, Jerry Tyson. "The Economic Development of the Texas Panhandle." Master's thesis, North Texas State College, Denton, 1950.

Boswell, Grover Cleveland. "History of the Bar Lo Ranch of the Eastern Panhandle of Texas." Master's thesis, Hardin-Simmons University, Abilene, Texas, 1933.

Burton, Harley True. "A History of the J. A. Ranch." Master's thesis, University of Texas, Austin, 1927.

Ford, Dalton. "History of Donley County, Texas." Master's thesis, University of Colorado, Boulder, 1932.

Israel, T. C. "The History of Oldham County, Texas." Master's thesis, University of New Mexico, Albuquerque, 1932.

Jeter, W. D. "The Fort Worth and Denver South Plains Railway." Master's thesis, Texas Technological College, Lubbock, 1949.

Lowe, Ida Marie Williams. "The Role of the Railroads in the Settlement of the Texas Panhandle." Master's thesis, West Texas State College, Canyon, 1962.

McClure, Charles Boone. "A History of Randall County and the T Anchor Ranch." Master's thesis, University of Texas, Austin, 1930.

Randels, Ralph Emerson. "History of Grazing and Crop-Growing in Woodward County, 1893-1907." Master's thesis, University of Oklahoma, Norman, 1938.

Newspapers

Arapaho Bee, October 1895.

Ardmore State Herald, October 1895.
Austin Daily Statesman, March–April 1883, November 1884, January–March, July, December 1885, January–February, April 1896, January–March 1887, May 1888.
Beaver Herald, March 1895, July 1896, February 1898.
Beaver South and West, May, October 1896.
Cheyenne Sunbeam, November–December 1893, various items 1894, 1895, 1904–1905.
(Clarendon) Northwest Texan, January–February 1886.
Daily Oklahoman, June 1894, January, August, October, December 1895, May, September–December 1896, February, May, August, November–December 1897, March–April, December 1898, February, April, August–September, December 1899, January, April–November 1900, August 1905, July 1936.
Dallas News, January 1887.
Dallas Times-Herald, August 1905.
Day County Tribune, July, December 1893, May 1894, July 1896, January 1897.
Edmond Sun-Democrat, May 1897.
El Reno Democrat, August 1902.
El Reno Globe, November 1895.
El Reno News, December 1895, May 1898.
Fort Smith Elevator, August 10, 1888; November 1890; January 1891.
Fort Worth Gazette, July 1884, January, November–December 1885, January–February 1886, January–March 1887.
Galveston News, January 1886, January–March 1887.
(Grand) Canadian Valley Echo, July–August 1902.
Guthrie Daily Leader, April, August, November 1894, January–February 1895, November 1897.
Guymon Herald, September 1905.
Houston Post, May 1948.
Kingfisher Free Press, August 1904, April 1914.
Lenora Leader, January 1905.
Mangum Star, August 1905.
(Mobeetie) Texas Panhandle, various issues 1882–90.
Noble County Sentinel, July 1896.
Norman Transcript, July 1896.
Oklahoma Daily Press-Gazette, January, March–April 1894.
Oklahoma State Capital, June, November–December 1893; January, April, December 1894; January–February, April–June, August–

October 1895; July-August, October, December 1896; March, May, November-December 1897; January-February, July September 1898; February, April-June, August, October, December 1899; January, March-November 1900; May, November 1902; November 1903; May 1904; August-September 1905.

Oklahoma City Times-Journal, December 1893, February, May, June, October 1895, February, July-August 1896, May 1897, December 1907.

(Pauls Valley) Chickasaw Enterprise, October 1895.

(Stillwater) Eagle-Gazette, April 1894.

Taloga Occident, various issues 1892-93.

Tascosa Pioneer, July, September, November-December 1886; April, June, October 1887; January-February 1888.

(Vinita) Indian Chieftain, February 1897.

Vinita Leader, October 1895.

Wichita Eagle, January 1888, October 1895, December 1896.

Woodward Advocate, various issues 1893-95.

Woodward Bulletin September 1897, November 1900.

Woodward Jeffersonian, September-December 1893, July 1895.

(Woodward) Live Stock Inspector, various issues 1895.

(Woodward) News and Advocate, April 1900.

Woodward News, June 1894, February 1898, August-September 1905, special number, vol. 10, commemorating the tenth birthday of Woodward County, Woodward, Oklahoma Territory, 1903.

Books

Armstrong, J. B. *The Raw Edge.* Missoula: Montana State University, 1964.

Bancroft, Hubert Howe. *History of the North Mexican States and Texas.* Vol. 2, 1801-1889. San Francisco: History Company, 1889.

Carriker, Robert C. *Fort Supply, Indian Territory: Frontier Outpost On the Plains.* Norman: University of Oklahoma Press, 1970.

Casady, Klina E. *Once Every Five Years: A History of Cheyenne, Oklahoma, 1892-1972.* Oklahoma City: Metro Press, 1974.

Cotner, Robert C. *James Stephen Hogg: A Biography.* Austin: University of Texas Press, 1954.

Crouch, Carrie J. *A History of Young County, Texas.* Austin: Texas State Historical Association, 1956.

Friend, Llerena B. *Sam Houston: The Great Designer.* Austin: University of Texas Press, 1954.

Goodspeed, Weston Arthur. *The Province and the States.* Vol. 6 Madison, Wis.: Western Historical Association, 1904.
Haley, J. Evetts. *Charles Goodnight: Cowman and Plainsman.* Norman: University of Oklahoma Press, 1949.
———. *George W. Littlefield, Texan.* Norman: University of Oklahoma Press, 1943.
———. *Jim East: Trail Hand and Cowboy.* Canyon, Texas, 1931.
———. *The XIT Ranch of Texas and the Early Days of the Llano Estacado.* Norman: University of Oklahoma Press, 1953.
———, and William Curry Holden. *The Flamboyant Judge: James D. Hamlin.* Canyon, Texas: Palo Duro Press, 1972.
Hamner, Laura V. *Light 'n Hitch.* Dallas: American Guild Press, 1958.
———. *The No-Gun Man of Texas: A Century of Achievement, 1835-1929.* Amarillo, Texas: privately printed, August, 1935.
Handbook of Texas. 2 vols. Austin: Texas State Historical Association, 1952.
Harris, Sallie B. *Hide Town in the Texas Panhandle: 100 Years in Wheeler County and Panhandle of Texas.* Hereford, Texas: Pioneer Book Publishers, 1968.
Harrison, Walter M. *Me and My Big Mouth.* Oklahoma City: Britton Publishing Co., 1954.
Hoyt, Henry F. *A Frontier Doctor.* Boston: Houghton Mifflin Company, 1929.
Huckabay, Ida Lasater. *Ninety-four Years in Jack County, 1854-1948.* Austin, Texas: Steck Co., 1949.
James, Marquis. *The Cherokee Strip: A Tale of an Oklahoma Boyhood.* New York: Viking Press, 1945.
———. *The Raven: A Biography of Sam Houston.* Indianapolis: Bobbs-Merrill Co., 1929.
Jennings, Al. *Through the Shadows with O. Henry.* New York: H. K. Fly, Co., 1921.
———, and Will Irwin. *Beating Back.* New York: D. Appleton and Co., 1914.
Key, Della Tyler. *In the Cattle County: History of Potter County, 1887-1966.* Quanah-Wichita Falls, Texas: Nortex Offset Publications, 1972.
Laune, Seigniora Russell. *Sand in My Eyes.* Philadelphia: J. B. Lippincott Co., 1965.
Lewis, Willie Newberry. *Between Sun and Sod.* Clarendon, Texas: Clarendon Press, 1938.

McCarty, John L. *Maverick Town: The Story of Old Tascosa.* Norman: University of Oklahoma Press, 1946.
Memorial and Genealogical Record of Texas. Chicago: Goodspeed Brothers, 1894.
Miller, Thomas Lloyd. *The Public Lands of Texas, 1519-1970.* Norman: University of Oklahoma Press, 1972.
Morris, Lerona Rosamond, ed. *Oklahoma: Yesterday-Today-Tomorrow.* Guthrie, Okla.: Co-Operative Publishing Co., 1930.
Nix, Evett Dumas, as told to Gordon Hines. *Oklahombres: Particularly the Wilder Ones.* Saint Louis: Eden Publishing House, 1929.
Nordyke, Lewis T. *The Angels Sing.* Clarendon, Texas: Clarendon Press, 1964.
———. *Cattle Empire: The Fabulous Story of the 3,000,000 Acre XIT.* New York: William Morrow and Company, 1949.
Paddock, Capt. B. B. *A Twentieth Century History and Biographical Record of North and West Texas.* Vol. 1. Chicago: Lewis Publishing Co., 1906.
Parker, Watson. *Gold in the Black Hills.* Norman: University of Oklahoma Press, 1966.
Peattie, Roderick, *The Black Hills.* New York: Vanguard Press, 1952.
Perry, George Sessions. *The Story of Texas A&M.* New York: McGraw-Hill Book Co., 1951.
Porter, Millie Jones. *Memory Cups of Panhandle Pioneers.* Clarendon, Texas: Clarendon Press, 1945.
Pruiett, Moman. *Moman Pruiett, Criminal Lawyer.* Oklahoma City: Harlow Publishing Corp., 1944.
Raine, William MacLeod, and Will C. Barnes. *Cattle.* Garden City, N.Y.: Doubleday, Doran & Co., 1930.
Rainey, George, *The Cherokee Strip.* Guthrie, Okla.: Co-operative Publishing Co., 1933.
Rathjen, Frederick W. *The Texas Panhandle Frontier.* Austin: University of Texas Press, 1973.
Robertson, Pauline Durrett, and R. L. Robertson. *Panhandle Pilgrimage: Illustrated Tales Tracing History in the Texas Panhandle.* Canyon, Texas: Staked Plains Press, 1976.
Seale, William. *Sam Houston's Wife: A Biography of Margaret Lea Houston.* Norman: University of Oklahoma Press, 1970.
Sheffy, Lester Fields. *The Francklyn Land and Cattle Company: A Panhandle Enterprise, 1882-1957.* Austin: University of Texas Press, 1963.

Shirley, Glenn. *Toughest of Them All.* Albuquerque: University of New Mexico Press, 1953.

———. *West of Hell's Fringe: Crime, Criminals, and the Federal Peace Officer in Oklahoma Territory, 1889-1907.* Norman: University of Oklahoma Press, 1978.

Speer, William S., and John Henry Brown, ed. *The Encyclopedia of the New West.* Marshall, Texas: United States Biographical Publishing Co., 1881.

Stanley, F. *Rodeo Town* [Canadian, Texas]. Denver, Colo.: World Press, 1953.

———. *Story of the Texas Panhandle Railroads.* Borger, Texas: Hess Publishing Co., 1976.

Sullivan, Dulcie. *The LS Brand: The Story of a Texas Panhandle Ranch.* Austin: University of Texas Press, 1968.

Sullivan, Sgt. W. J. L. *Twelve Years in the Saddle for Law and Order on the Frontiers of Texas.* Austin: Von Boeckmann-Jones Co., 1909.

Texas: A Guide to the Lone Star State. New York: Hastings House, 1969.

Texas Almanac and State Industrial Guide. Austin, 1945-46, 1947-48, 1952-53.

Thoburn, Joseph B. *A Standard History of Oklahoma.* 5 vols. Chicago: American Historical Society, 1916.

———, and Muriel H. Wright. *Oklahoma: A History of the State and Its People.* 4 vols. New York: Lewis Historical Publishing Co., 1929.

Tolbert, Frank X. *An Informal History of Texas: From Cabeza de Vaca to Temple Houston.* New York: Harper and Brothers, 1961.

Webb, Walter Prescott. *The Texas Rangers: A Century of Frontier Defense.* Boston: Houghton Mifflin Company, 1935.

Wisehart, M. K. *Sam Houston: American Giant.* Washington, D.C.: Robert B. Luce, 1962.

Wortham, Louis J. *A History of Texas: From Wilderness to Commonwealth.* 5 vols. Fort Worth, Texas: Wortham-Molyneaux Company, 1924.

Articles

"A Panhandle Pioneer." *Frontier Times* 4, no. 2 (November 1926): 44-47.

"A Temple Houston Story." *Oklahoma State Capital,* undated clipping.

Allen, Ruth Alice. "The Capitol Boycott: A Study in Peaceful Labor Tactics." *Southwestern Historical Quarterly* 42, no. 4 (April 1939): 316-26.
Arnot, John. "LITs Make Ranch History." *Amarillo Sunday News and Globe*, Golden Anniversary Edition, August 14, 1938.
"Autobiographical Sketch of Ex-Governor A. J. Seay's Public Life." *Oklahoma State Capital*, April 11, 1909.
Barde, Fred. "Fred Barde's Impression." *Oklahoma State Capital*, August 24, 1905.
Bierer, A. G. C. "Early Day Courts and Lawyers." *Proceedings of the Twenty-Third Annual Meeting of the Oklahoma State Bar Association.* Oklahoma City, February 21-22, 1930, pp. 193-205.
Cotner, Robert C. "Attorney General Hogg and the Acceptance of the State Capitol: A Reappraisal." *West Texas Historical Association Year Book* 25 (1949): 50-73.
Crane, R. C. "Act of 1876 Created Panhandle Counties." *Amarillo Sunday News and Globe*, Golden Anniversary Edition, August 14, 1938.
———. "Temple Houston, Plains Statesman." *Amarillo Sunday News and Globe*, Golden Anniversary Edition, August 14, 1938.
Cross, Cora Melton. "Mose Hays Tells of Early Days." *Frontier Times* 5, no. 6 (March 1928): 228-31.
Dealey, Edward M. "The Story of Old Tascosa." *Frontier Times* 4, no. 1 (October 1926): 33-41.
"David P. Marum." *Chronicles of Oklahoma* 8, no. 3 (September 1930); 352-53.
Doyle, Thomas H. "The Supreme Court of the Territory of Oklahoma." *Chronicles of Oklahoma* 13, no. 2 (June 1935): 214-18.
"Early Day History in Oklahoma." *Oklahoma City Weekly Times-Journal*, December 27, 1907.
"El Reno Democratic Convention." *McMasters' Magazine* 13, no. 7 (July 1900): 30-38.
Finch, O. H. "Judge O. H. Nelson." *Panhandle-Plains Historical Review* 19 (1946): 18-23.
Forrest, Col. R. B. "Corrects the Many Errors." *Oklahoma State Capital*, September 12, 1905.
Fraker, Elmer L. "The Election of J. Y. Callahan." *Chronicles of Oklahoma* 33, no. 3 (Autumn 1955): 354-59.
Gracy, David B. "George Washington Littlefield, Portrait of a Cattleman." *Southwestern Historical Quarterly* 68, no. 2 (October 1964): 237-58.

Haley, J. Evetts. "The Grass Lease Fight and Attempted Impeachment of the First Panhandle Judge." *Southwestern Historical Quarterly* 38, no. 1 (July 1934): 1–27.
Harper, Roscoe E. "Homesteading in Northwestern Oklahoma Territory." *Chronicles of Oklahoma* 16, no. 3 (September 1938) 326–36.
Higgins, Thomas A. "Stories Relating to Oklahoma Territorial Courts and Law." *Chronicles of Oklahoma* 38, no. 1 (Spring 1960): 101–106.
Hobart, T. D. "Some of the Characters and Customs of Old Mobeetie." *Panhandle-Plains Historical Review* 2 (1929); 123–29.
Holden, W. C. "Law and Lawlessness on the Texas Frontier, 1875–1890." *Southwestern Historical Quarterly* 44, no. 2 (October 1940): 188–203.
Horton, L. W. "General Sam Bell Maxey: His Defense of North Texas and the Indian Territory." *Southwestern Historical Quarterly* 74, no. 4 (April 1971): 507–24.
"Incidents in the Life of Col. Temple Houston." *Daily Oklahoman*, August 20, 1905.
Isaacs, Mrs. Sam. "Captain and Mrs. G. W. Arrington." *Frontier Times*, 17, no. 8 (May 1940): 365–66.
"John E. (Jack) Love, 1857–1918." *Chronicles of Oklahoma* 10, no. 4 (December 1932): 604–606.
Johnson, Vance. "Great XIT Ranch Required Vast Outlay of Men, Money and Cattle." *Amarillo Sunday News and Globe*, Golden Anniversary Edition, August 14, 1938.
"Judge Jerry Rowland Dean, 1841–1917." *Chronicles of Oklahoma* 20, no. 2 (June 1942): 205.
Kahlbau, Edna. "Old Tascosa, Once Gay Capital of the Open Range, Silent Now." *Amarillo Sunday News and Globe*, Golden Anniversary Edition, August 14, 1938.
Kountz, Nina. "The First Judge in the Panhandle." *Frontier Times* 4, no. 7 (April 1927): 5–8.
Laune, Paul. "The Story of the Woodward Murals." *Oklahoma Today* 21, no. 3 (Summer 1971): 3–6.
———. "Temple Houston." *Oklahoma Today* 14, no. 4 (Autumn 1964): 14–16.
Laune, Seigniora Russell. "The Brilliant, Eccentric Temple Houston." *Sturm's Oklahoma Magazine* 12, no. 2 (April 1911): 20–23.
McMillin, Bob. "Temple Houston—Spellbinder." *Oklahoma's Orbit*, December 19, 1965.

Mitchell, Billy. "Judge A. J. Fires, Childress Pioneer." *Panhandle-Plains Historical Review* 19 (1946): 24-28.
"More About Houston in Oklahoma." *Historia* 8, no. 4 (October 1, 1919): 6-8.
Nelson, Bonnie Stahlmen. "Temple Houston, Son of General Sam." *Tulsa Sunday World,* February 23, 1964.
Nelson, O. H. "First Panhandle Stockmen's Association." *Frontier Times* 4, no. 4 (January 1927): 25-28.
"Not Guilty: A Speech by Temple Houston." *Daily Oklahoman,* July 5, 1936.
Officer, Mrs. Helen Bugbee. "A Sketch of the Life of Thomas Sherman Bugbee, 1841-1925." *Panhandle-Plains Historical Review* 5 (1932): 8-22.
Ogletree, D. W. "Establishing the Texas Court of Appeals, 1875-1876." *Southwestern Historical Quarterly* 47, no. 1 (July 1943): 5-18.
"Old Day County, Oklahoma Territory." *Chronicles of Oklahoma* 12, no. 2 (June 1935): 219-22.
Oringderff, Nora Belle. "Temple Houston Lives in Family's Memory." *Daily Oklahoman,* October 20, 1957.
Oswald, James M. "History of Fort Elliott." *Panhandle-Plains Historical Review* 33 (1959): 1-58.
Peery, Dan W. "The Indians' Friend, John H. Seger, His Stories of Myths, Legends, and Religions of the Cheyenne and Arapaho Tribes." *Chronicles of Oklahoma* 10, no. 3 (September 1932): 348-52.
Ranck, M. A. "Some Remnants of Frontier Journalism: A Record of Pioneer Life and Spirit." *Chronicles of Oklahoma* (part 1) 8, no. 4 (December 1930): 378-88; (part 2) 9, no. 5 (March 1931): 63-70.
Randels, Ralph E. "The Homesteader and the Development of Woodward County." *Chronicles of Oklahoma* 17, no. 3 (September 1939): 286-95.
Rathjen, Frederick W. "The Texas State House: A Study of the Building of the Texas Capitol Based on the Reports of the Capitol Building Commissioners." *Southwestern Historical Quarterly* 60, no. 4 (April 1957): 433-62.
Richardson, David. "Glimpse of Life in Brazoria County in Ante-Bellum Period." *Galveston Daily News,* April 11, 1942.
Riddle, Roy. "Casimero Romero Reigned as Benevolent Don in Brief Pastoral Era." *Amarillo Sunday News and Globe,* Golden Anniversary Edition, August 14, 1938.

Rippy, J. Fred. "British Investments in Texas Lands and Livestock." *Southwestern Historical Quarterly* 58, no. 3 (January 1955): 331–33.

"Robert J. Ray, 1864–1931." *Chronicles of Oklahoma* 9, no. 4 (December 1931): 484–86.

Roberts, Mrs. Lige. "True Son of the Raven Handled Gun at Tascosa Like Plainsman." *Amarillo Sunday News and Globe*, Golden Anniversary Edition, August 14, 1938.

Romero, J. I. (as told to Ernest R. Archambeau). "Spanish Sheepmen on the Canadian." *Panhandle-Plains Historical Review* 19 (1946): 45–72.

"Sam Houston in Indian Territory." *Historia* 8, no. 3 (July 1, 1919): 1–4.

Sheffy, L. F. "Old Mobeetie—The Capital of the Panhandle." *West Texas Historical Year Book* 6 (1930): 3–16.

Shirk, George. "The Start of the Law." *Daily Oklahoman Sunday Magazine*, April 29, 1951.

Shirley, Glenn. "Temple Houston, Lawyer with a Gun," *Western Tales* 1, no. 1 (April 1960): 12–15, 44–45.

———. "Temple Houston, the Man with the Silver Tongue." *Real West* 13, no. 85 (September 1970): 14–20, 48.

Sinise, Jerry. "Tascosa—Portrait of a Cowtown." *Southwest Heritage* 1, no. 3 (Summer 1967): 4–8.

Timmons, Herbert, and Carolyn Timmons. "These Are Our Boys on Boot Hill." *Amarillo Sunday News and Globe*, Golden Anniversary Edition, August 14, 1938.

Tinkler, Estelle D. "Nobility's Ranche: A History of the Rocking Chair Ranch." *Panhandle-Plains Historical Review* 15 (1942): 1–88.

Weaver, Claude. "Personal Recollections of Temple Houston." *Sturm's Oklahoma Magazine* 12, no. 3 (May 1911): 22–23.

Webb, Walter Prescott. "George W. Arrington: The Iron-Handed Man of the Panhandle." *Panhandle-Plains Historical Review* 8 (1935): 7–20.

Williams, Judge R. L. "The Judicial History of Oklahoma." *Proceedings of the Fifth Annual Meeting of the Oklahoma State Bar Association, Oklahoma City, December 21–22, 1911,* 107–62.

Wolfskill, George. "William Carey Crane and the University of Texas." *Southwestern Historical Quarterly,* 54, no. 2 (October 1950): 190–203.

Index

Adair, John: 31
Adobe Walls: 29, 33, 36, 41, 104
Agricultural and Mechanical College (Bryan, Texas): 17
Alamo: 99
Alamo, Ind.: 51
Alamo Museum: 101
Albany, Ky.: 143
Albany, Texas: 26
Alexander, Charles: 208
Alfred Son v. Territory of Oklahoma: 259
Alien Contract Labor Law: 150
Allen, Eliza: 9
Allen, "Old Rise-Up Bill": 174
Alva, O.T.: 199, 301
Amarillo, Texas ("Ragtown"): 33, 48, 162
American Pastoral Company: 102, 128
Amherst County, Va.: 194
Anadarko, O.T.: 291
Anderson, A. W.: 183
Anderson, Bill: 112
Ann Arbor, Mich.: 183
Apperson, L. P.: 281
Appleget, A. M.: 183
Appleton City, Mo.: 212
Arapaho, O.T.: 190, 224–25
Ardmore, I.T.: 226
Armstrong, Marion: 64, 67
Armstrong County, Texas: 33, 162
Arnett, Harmon: 225
Arrington, George W.: 58, 93, 96–97, 101, 105, 138, 132–33
Asa Whitney Trail: 16
Asp, Henry E.: 220
Atchison, Topeka and Santa Fe Railroad: 29
Austen, E. C. G.: 119–21
Austin, Stephen F.: 20

Austin, Texas: 8, 126, 139–40, 143, 149, 151
Austin Statesman: 139–40, 152, 159

Babcock, Amos: 149, 156
Baby Doll Ranch: 78
Baca County, Colo.: 213
Bailey County, Texas: 103
Baker, Wharton: 283
Baltimore, Md.: 12
Bankhead, H. C.: 38
Banks, William: 189–90, 256
Bar CC Ranch: 36, 48, 93, 102
Barde, Fred: 206, 248
Barnes, Cassius M.: 242, 291
Bar Ninety-Six Ranch: 133
Barnum, Will: 264–65
Bar O Ranch: 78
Bar WA (connected) Ranch: 109
Bates, W. H. ("Deacon"): 33, 95–97, 102
Baton Rouge, La.: 67
Baylor Female College: 19
Baylor University: 14, 19, 164
Bayou La Fourche: 21
Beach, Miss: 93
Beale, A. J.: 232, 234, 237
Beals, David T.: 33, 95, 102
Beard, Jim: 54
Beating Back: 213
Beauchamp, J. K.: 292–93, 298
Beaver County, O.T. (No Man's Land, or Neutral Strip): 3, 36, 41, 95, 167, 192, 208, 242, 292, 303
Bedford County, Tenn.: 174
Beef Bonanza, The (book): 102
Belle of Mobeetie: 57
Belle of the Short Grass Region: *see* Woodward, O.T.
Bell Ranch: 112

325

INDEX

Ben Hur (book): 53
Bennett, E. L.: 45
Betsy Nan: 57
Bierer, Andrew G. Curtin: 192, 264, 285
Big Black Campaign: 144
Bismarck, Dakota Territory: 16–17
Bixler, Mort L.: 232, 234, 236–37, 239
Black Hills Expedition: 16
Black Kettle (Cheyenne Chief): 30
Black Republican: *see* Abraham Lincoln
Blaine County, O.T.: 167, 192, 199, 292
Bland, Richard P. ("Silver Dick"): 231–32
Boies, Horace: 231
Boles, Eva: *see* Willis, Eva
Boles, Newton: 45, 53
Bolton, Will E.: 202
Bonaparte, Napoleon: 17, 19, 197, 220, 252
Bond Switch, I.T.: 223
Bonney, William (Billy the Kid): 33, 35, 53, 67–68, 76, 104, 108, 112
Bosque County, Texas: 261–62
Boston, Mass.: 96
Bousman, Louis: 72, 116–19, 122–24
Boynton, Fannie: 93
Boynton, G. W.: 43, 93
Brackenridge, George W.: 132
Bracketville, Texas: 30
Brady, Jim: 57–58
Bray, R. E.: 284
Brazoria, Texas: 20
Brazoria County, Texas: 21, 90, 92, 99, 206
Breeding, William: 188–91
Brereton, John J.: 93
Briggs, Theodore: 114, 120
Briggs, William A.: 183
Brisbin, James S.: 102
Brophy, John: 111
Brown, Ella ("Diamond Girl," alias Ella Holmes): 57
Brown, G. A. ("Gyp"): 80, 82, 272

Brown, Henry Newton: 68, 71–72
Brown, I. M.: 45
Brown, John: 53
Brown, Thomas Jefferson: 129–31
Brown County, Texas: 123, 261
Browning, James Nathan ("Honest Jim"): 26, 48, 53, 77, 80, 82–83, 85–86, 101, 129–33, 135, 139, 148
Browning, Joe: 83
"Browning's Cow": 139
Brule, O.T.: 301
Brunt, W. C.: 232, 234, 237
Bryan, William Jennings: 231, 237, 239, 276, 283, 288
Bryant, David E.: 295
Buckner, Simon B.: 237
Buell, George P.: 30
Buffalo, Okla.: *see* Brule
Buffalo, Texas: 147
Buffalo Bayou, Brazos and Colorado Railroad: 21
Buford, Sam: 108
Bugbee, Thomas S.: 33
Burford, Elijah Hastings: 194
Burford, James: 194
Burford, John H.: 3, 7, 192, 194, 196–97, 200–201, 241, 264, 266, 268, 271, 291–92, 306
Burnet County, Texas: 150
Burns, D. V.: 194
Burwell, B. F.: 265–66
Bussy, Hess: 225
Buster, Sterling: 82
Butler, Benjamin: 96–97
Butts, Ed: 57
Byers, A. A.: 239

Cabinet Saloon: 216–17
Caddo County, O.T.: 291–92
Cage, Duncan S. ("Dunk"): 108, 116, 120–21
Cage, Hays: 116, 120–21
Caldwell, Kan.: 96, 247
Callahan, James Yancey: 237, 239, 274, 284, 287
Campbell & Goodwin-Austen: 68, 108

INDEX

Camp Douglas: 13
Camp Supply: *see* Fort Supply
Canadian, Texas: 163-64, 186, 222, 256, 305, 308-309
Canadian County, O.T.: 3, 167, 188, 192, 213, 292
Cantonment Gibson: 11
Capitol Building Commission: 153
Capitol Freehold Land and Investment Co., Ltd.: 103, 150, 156
Capitol Syndicate: *see* Capitol Freehold Land and Investment Co., Ltd.
Carhart, Lewis Henry: 41, 77-79
Carson County, Texas: 103, 162
Castro County, Texas: 60, 103
Cattle Exchange Saloon: 43, 48
Cattle King Hotel: 217, 222-23, 240
Cedar Point: 11
Cedar Valley Land and Cattle Co.: 102, 128
Central Hotel: 223, 241
Chambers, Lon: 112, 121-22
Chandler, O.T.: 232, 283-84
Chapman, Amos: 187-88, 256
Charleston, O.T.: 301
Checotah, I.T.: 225
Cherokee Outlet: 3, 96, 162, 167-68, 199, 215
Cherokee Outlet Colony (homeseekers): 183
Cheyenne, O.T.: 181, 186-88, 207, 294
Cheyenne-Arapaho Reservation: 3-4, 163, 167-68, 173, 181
Cheyenne Sunbeam: 186-87
Chicago, Ill.: 231, 233, 237
Chickasaw Nation: 224, 295
Childress, Texas: 162, 165
Childress County, Texas: 165
Chilton, Fred: 115-19, 122-23
Churubusco, Mexico: 143, 145
Cimarron (book): 309
Cincinnati, Ohio: 247, 276
Clampitt, Bert: 45
Clampitt, Frank: 43, 84
Clarendon, Texas ("Saints' Roost"): 41, 55, 77-81, 87, 94, 102, 123,
125, 128-29, 131, 134-36, 138-39, 163
Clarendon Land Investment and Agency Co.: 79, 128
Clarendon Northwest Texan: 130, 141
Clark, Edward: 286
Clark, George: 140-41
Clark, John: 285
Clark, R. B.: 218
Clark County, Ark.: 83
Clarke, S. R.: 285
Clarksville, Texas: 148
Clay County, Texas: 25, 103-104
Cleveland, Grover: 170, 174, 192, 213, 228-29, 231-34, 241, 264, 283
Cleveland County, O.T.: 167, 192, 280, 283-84, 292
Clifton, "Dynamite Dick": 223, 225
Clinton County, Ky.: 143
Cochran County, Texas: 149
Coffee, Logan: 267, 271
Coke, Richard: 140, 152, 160-61
Coldwater, Kans.: 213
Cole, Liddie: 57
Collin County, Texas: 129
Collins, Bert: *see* Red Buck Waightman
Collins, Lieut.: 93
Collins, Mrs. L. B.: 242
Collingsworth County, Texas: 36, 58, 94
Co-lo-neh ("Raven"): *see* Houston, Sam
Colony, O.T.: 198
Colorado City, Texas: 131
Columbia, Texas: 20-21, 90
Columbus, Ohio: 226
Comanche, Texas: 123, 261-62
Comanche County, Kans.: 213
Comanche County, O.T.: 291-92
Coming Events (newspaper): 297
Cone, John: 62, 118
Confederate Brigadiers: 144
Connet, Alfred: 174
Contreras, Mexico: 143, 145
Cook, John: 53
Cook, T. M.: 256, 258

327

INDEX

Cooke County, Texas: 83
Corsair, The (poem): 23
Cotter, T. S.: 188-90
Cottle County, Texas: 102, 165
Covington, Ind.: 53
"Cowboy Capital of the Plains": *see* Tascosa, Texas
Cowboy Strike of 1883: 105
Crane, William Carey: 19
Crawford (merchant): 252
Crawford (rancher): 207
Crawfordsville, Ind.: 51, 53, 194
Creede, Colo.: 35, 76
Creek Nation: 168, 211, 225
Crescent G (cattle brand): 34
Creswell, Henry Whiteside: 36, 48, 58, 102
Cromwell, W. O.: 284
Cross, Laura: *see* Houston, Laura
Cross, William: 283, 287
Crozier & Nutter: 225
Cullar, William W.: 205
Cummings, Charley: 62
Cunningham, A. G.: 183
Curtis, O.T.: 301
Cushing, O.T.: 225
Custer, George A.: 16, 30
Custer County, O.T.: 3, 167, 188-89, 192, 258, 292

Daily Oklahoman: 286
Dale, Frank: 192, 212, 241, 262, 264
Dallas, Texas: 78-79, 98, 129, 147, 181
Dallas County, Texas: 60, 103, 149, 162
Dallas Times-Herald: 307
Darlington (Indian agency): 190
Daughters of the Republic of Texas: 247
Davidson, John W. ("Black Jack"): 30
Davis, Edmund J.: 25, 143, 160
Davis, Jefferson: 12, 147
Day, Lieut.: 93
Day County, O.T.: 3-4, 167, 192, 202, 220, 284, 292
Deaf Smith County, Texas: 60, 103, 183

Dean, Jerry Rowland: 183, 185, 241-42
Decker, John: 48
DeKalb, Ill.: 36
Denton, W. S.: 232, 234, 239, 280, 284-85, 296
Denver, Colo.: 74, 76, 183, 213
Denver, Texas and Gulf Railroad: 162
Dewey County, O.T.: 3, 167, 192, 200, 255, 257, 292, 304
Diamond F Ranch: 78
"Diamond Girl": *see* Brown, Ella
Diamond Tail Ranch: 78, 241
Dickens County, Texas: 102
Dickerson, John: 43
Dickerson, Wiley: 43
Diggs, James: 280, 284
Dills, Lucius: 51, 101-102, 138
Dobbs, Kid: 108, 111-12, 121-22
Dodge, Grenville M.: 162
Dodge City, Kans.: 29-30, 36, 39, 41, 62, 64, 67, 78, 108-109, 173
Donley County, Texas: 36, 42, 87, 94-95, 123, 125, 135-36, 162
Doolin-Dalton outlaws: 223
Dreiling, Sol: 289-91
Driskill Hotel: 137, 160
Duke, F. B.: 164
Dull Knife (Cheyenne chief): 247
Dunn, Jesse James: 199, 307
Duran, Dolores: 35, 64, 118
Dyer, Grainger: 48, 50
Dyer, Leigh: 34, 81
Dyer, Mary Ann: *see* Goodnight, Mary Ann
Dyer, Walter: 34

East, James H.: 33, 67, 104-105, 112-13, 119, 120-21
Edmond, O.T.: 223
El Dorado, Kans.: 263
Elgin, Ill.: 265
Elizabethtown, N.Mex.: 62
Elliott, Joel H.: 30
El Paso, Texas: 162
El Paso County, Texas: 142
El Reno, O.T.: 186, 188, 196, 198, 213, 225, 232-33, 239, 247, 258, 260, 292

INDEX

El Reno Democrat: 293
El Reno Globe: 246
Emory, Charlie: 116-19, 123-24
Emory, Sally: 66, 110, 115-17, 123
Emory and Henry College: 212
Enid, O.T.: 3, 202, 232, 274, 276, 284, 292, 295-97
Enid Daily Eagle: 228-29, 299
Equity Bar: 66, 116-17, 119
Emerson, Henry F.: 170
Eureka Springs, Ark.: 147
Evans, J. F.: 26, 94, 128

Fair God, The (book): 53
Fannin, James W.: 20
Fargo, Dakota Territory: 17
Farwell, Charles: 149, 152, 156
Farwell, John V.: 149-50, 152, 156
Fayetteville, Ark.: 295
Feather Hill: 43, 50
Ferber, Edna: 309
Ferguson, Thompson B.: 199, 274, 292-93
Fires, Amos J.: 165
Flatcreek, Tenn.: 174
Fleming, Henry: 50-51, 58, 60, 92
Floyd County, Texas: 97, 102
Flynn, Dennis T.: 228, 233, 239, 274, 286-87
Folsom, N.Mex.: 162
Forrest, R. B.: 208, 223-24, 260, 283, 285, 293, 303, 305
Fort Abraham Lincoln: 16
Fort Bend County, Texas: 21
Fort Bliss: 30
Fort Clark: 30
Fort Concho: 30, 39
Fort Davis: 30
Fort Dodge: 30, 41
Fort Duncan: 30
Fort Elliott: 30, 35, 38, 41, 45, 58, 67, 78, 87, 92, 163
Fort Garland: 30
Fort Griffin: 30, 39, 58
Fort Lyon: 30
Fort McKavett: 30
Fort Richardson: 30
Fort Sill: 30, 39, 247
Fort Stanton: 30
Fort Stockton: 30

Fort Sumner: 35
Fort Supply, O.T.: 30, 35, 39, 167, 172-73, 187, 205, 242, 301
Fort Territt: 30
Fort Union: 30
Fort Worth, Texas: 26, 41, 144, 162
Fort Worth and Denver City Railroad (Texas Panhandle route): 26, 91, 125, 162-63, 165
Fossett, William D.: 224-25
Four Sections Act: 142
Francklyn Land and Cattle Company: 102-103
Franklin, Ben: 294-97
French, W. H.: 284, 286
Fritchie, Gus: 122
Frog-mouth Annie: 57
Frying Pan Ranch: 36, 112

Gaady, L. J.: 183
Gainesville, Texas: 98, 152
Galbraith (fugitive): 261-62
Galbraith, C. A.: 212, 220, 235
Galveston, Texas: 21, 26, 248, 252
Galveston News: 134, 136, 139
Garfield County, O.T.: 3, 168, 192, 280, 284, 292, 295
Garrett, Patrick F.: 35, 67, 104, 112-15
Garst, Frank: 213
Garvey, Jack: 216-17
Gass, W. T.: 129, 133
Gatlin, Bill: 110, 113
Geary, O.T.: 224
Gentry, Al: 138
Georgetown, Texas: 15, 17
Get Even Cattle Company: 109, 114
Giaour, The (poem): 23
Gibbs, Barnett: 98
Gibson, Bill: 73
Giddings, D. C.: 98
Gillette, Frank E.: 292
Gilmer, Texas: 24
Glidden, J. F.: 36, 128
GMS (cattle brand): 34
Godfrey, Lula: 93
Godfrey, Maj.: 93
Goodnight, Charles: 31, 33, 55, 61,

INDEX

79–81, 93–95, 105–106, 126–34, 138, 140–41
Goodnight, Mary Ann (Mrs. Charles): 31
Goodnight-Loving Trail: 31
Goodwin, F. M.: 43
Gough, John B. ("Catfish Kid"): 116–17, 119–20, 123–24
Granada, Colo.: 29, 31
Grand, O.T.: 3
Grand Central Hotel: 43
Granite Cutters Strike: 150
Grant, T. M.: 183
Grant, Ulysses S.: 160
Grant, Whit M.: 234
Grant County, O.T.: 168, 192, 280, 292
Gray County, Texas: 103, 162
Grayson County, Texas: 96, 129
Greer County, Texas: 25, 36, 91, 164, 167; included in Oklahoma Territory, 272–73, 292
Griffin, Roy: 106
Griffith, T. J.: 286
Griggs, James: 222
Grigsby, William H.: 45, 82–83, 89, 101, 129–30, 132
Grimes and Murphy (cattlemen): 215
Groesbeck, Texas: 64
Groom, B. B.: 137
Gunter, Jot: 34
Gunter, Jule: 34, 102, 107
Guthrey, E. Bee: 264–65
Guthrie, O.T.: 181, 210, 235, 241, 261, 264, 276, 300
Guthrie Daily Leader: 209

Hackamore (cattle brand): 110
Hackett City, Ark.: 295
Hainer, Bayard: 264
Hale County, Texas: 97
Hall and McDonald (saloonkeepers): 172
Hall County, Texas: 33, 162
Hamburg, Henry: 43
Hamilton, Harry: 284
Hamilton, Robert: 48

Hammock, Wilson M.: 170, 181
Hammon (Indian agency): 186–88
Hammon (Indian farmer): 189
Hansford Land and Cattle Company: 33, 104, 128
Harbold, Jim: 256
Hardeman County, Texas: 256
Hardin, John Wesley: 123
Hare, Silas: 129, 133
Harp, Mose: 36
Harper's Ferry: 53
Harris, Tom: 106–109, 111, 114–15
Harrison, Pres. Benjamin: 196
Hartley, Texas: 120
Hartley County, Texas: 30, 103, 162
Harvard University: 78
Harvey, W. H. ("Coin"): 229
Hatch, Sadie W.: 263–64
Haybaugh, James: 218
Hays, Mose: 86
Hazelwood & Moody (store): 186
Hedrick, Joe: 218
Hemphill County, Texas: 36, 41, 86, 162–63, 256
Hennessey, Pat: 247
Henrietta, Texas: 26, 48, 103
Herod, C. W.: 208, 215–17
Herring, P. L.: 215
Hickman, Ky.: 31
Higgins, Texas: 162, 183
Hill, Chief (Cheyenne): 188–90
Hill, David B.: 231
Hobart, Garrett A.: 230, 239
Hobart, O.T.: 89, 291
Hockley County, Texas: 103, 149
Hodges, Jake: 295
Hoffer, Fannie: 93
Hoffman, Fred: 255, 257–59
Hoffman, Roy V.: 235, 239, 280, 284
Hogg, James Stephen: 132, 134, 152
Hogtown: 64, 76, 94, 109, 114–16, 121, 134
Hollicott, John: 95
Holmes, Ella: *see* Brown, Ella
Home Rangers: 112, 114
Hondo (cattle brand): 110

330

INDEX

Hopkins, Bee: 93
Horseshoe Bend: 9
Houston, Andrew Jackson: 8
Houston, Antoinette: 8
Houston, Elizabeth Paxton: 8
Houston, Laura (Mrs. Temple): 21, 45, 90-92, 101, 167, 199, 207, 223, 242, 247
Houston, Louise: 101
Houston, Margaret: see Williams, Margaret
Houston, Margaret Moffette (Mrs. Sam): 8, 11, 13-15, 19
Houston, Mary Lea: 206
Houston, Mary Willie: 8
Houston, Nancy Elizabeth: see Morrow, Nancy Elizabeth
Houston, Richard: 206
Houston, Sam: 8-13, 24, 144, 146-47, 210
Houston, Sam, Jr.: 8, 13-14, 206, 240
Houston, Temple, Jr.: 101, 206
Houston, Temple Lea: defends friendless cowboy, 3-7; birth of, 8, 12; early life and education of, 14-20; law practice of, at Brazoria, Texas, 20-21; San Jacinto speech by, 22-25; appointed district attorney of the Thirty-fifth Judicial District of Texas, 25-26; arrival of, at Mobeetie, 42-43, 45, 48, 51, 53; early cases of, at Mobeetie, 55-58; "west-side" cases of, at Tascosa, 60, 71-73, 76-77; cases of, at Clarendon, 77, 81-83; influence of fellow lawyers of, 84-87; and court week at Mobeetie, 88-89; marriage of, to Laura Cross, 90-92; prosecutes cattle thieves, 93, 96-97; in Texas Senate and private practice, 97-102, 104, 110, 114, 124-26; and "grass lease" fight, 127, 133, 137-42; endorses Samuel Bell Maxey, 143-45; rejects candidacy for U.S. Congress, 148-49; dedicatory oration of, at Texas state capitol, 151-59; loses taste for politics, 160-61; law practice of, at Canadian, Texas, 163-66; moves family to Woodward, O.T., 167; as companion of John E. Love, 172; law partnership of, with Robert J. Ray, 174, 181; and *Advocate* comments on legal ability, 183; defends Tom O'Hara, 185, 188, 190-91; and travels with Burford court, 194, 196-201; feared by Judge McAtee, 202; law partnership of, with David P. Marum, 205; as "Lone Wolf of the Canadian," 205; eating habits of, 205-206; family life of, 206-207; and travels with Swindall and Laune, 207-208; described by other western Oklahoma lawyers, 208-209; suggests changes in legislative act governing Oklahoma attorneys, 210; clashes with Jennings brothers, 215-19; charged with manslaughter, acquitted, 219-20; and Jennings gang, 222-26; poetry of, 227; and politics of 1896, 227-28, 232-37, 239; altercation of, with J. B. Jenkins, 240-41; described by Seigniora Laune, 242; lectures of, on astronomy, 242; address of, at Northwestern Normal School, Alva, 244-46; lectures on "Antiquities of America," 246; collects relics, 246-49, 252-53; described by Woodward County rancher, 253-54; defends Alfred Son, 257-61; defends M. R. Lee, 261-62; defends Clyde Mattox, 262, 264-66; defends Minnie Stacey, 266-71; and politics of 1900, 273-76, 280-84 287-88; defends Sol Dreiling, 289-91; defends Robert Riggins and clashes with Moman Pruiett, 293-99; supports stock-district legislation for western counties and growth of northwestern Oklahoma,

331

300–302; law partnership of, with T. M. Grant and A. M. Appleget, 303; defends Ed McHaffie, 304–305; illness of, 305–306; death of, 306–309
Houston, William Rogers: 8
Houston, Texas: 21
Houston & Texas Central Railway: 33
Houston Post: 152
Houston Tap and Brazoria Railroad: 21
Howard, G. L.: 62, 67, 70
Hunter, Capt.: 190
Hunter, Prucilla: 57
Huntsville, Texas: 8, 11, 13, 124, 256
Huselby, Mark: 45
Huselby House: 43
Huston, A. C.: 286–87
Hutchinson County, Texas: 33, 41, 103

Independence, Texas: 11, 19
Iowa, Reservation: 167
Ireland, John: 97, 112, 128, 150
Irwin, Clinton F.: 265, 284
Isaacs, George: 256
Isaacs, Mrs. Will: 93

Jack County, Texas: 25, 103
Jacksboro, Texas: 30, 103
Jackson, Andrew: 8–9, 11
Jacobs, James R.: 280, 284–85
James, Frank: 66, 74
James, John Garland: 19
JA Ranch: 31, 62, 78–79, 93–94, 107, 131–32
Jefferson, Pres. Thomas: 174
Jenkins, Charles: 123
Jenkins, J. B.: 240–41
Jenkins, Jess: 109–10, 114–17, 123, 134
Jenkins, William M.: 291–92
Jennings, Alphonso J. (Al): 212–13, 216, 220, 222–26, 242
Jennings, Edward: 212–13, 215–18, 220, 242

Jennings, Frank E.: 212, 220, 222–23, 225–26
Jennings, J. D. F.: 170, 212, 215–18, 222–23
Jennings, John: 212–13, 215, 217–20, 222
Jinks, Capt.: 73, 115
Johnson, Andrew: 97
Johnson, Corinda: 57
Johnson, J. W.: 276, 280, 285
Johnson, "Skillety Bill": 186–87, 191
Johnston, Gen. Albert Sidney: 144
Jones, Frank: *see* Mattox, Clyde
Jones, George: 112
Jones, James Kimbrough: 232–34
Jones, John B.: 25
Jones, R. P.: 252
Jones-Plummer Trail: 39
Judkins, W. D.: 170
Jumbo District (Texas Eleventh Congressional District): 148

Kansas City Star: 268
Kansas City Times: 253, 275
Kaufman, Texas: 98
Kaw Reservation: 192
Kay County, O.T.: 168, 192, 262, 264, 281, 284, 286, 292
Kearse, Thomas: 286
Keaton, James R.: 241, 265
Kemp (priest): 306
Keyes (buffalo hunter): 72–73
Kickapoo Reservation: 228
Kimball, Henry: 61–62, 71, 117
Kimball, W. D.: 80
Kincaid, A. O.: 170
King, Ed: 108, 112, 115–20, 122–24
King, J. H.: 234
King County, Texas: 165
Kingfisher, O.T.: 213, 237
Kingfisher County, O.T.: 3, 167, 192, 292
Kiowa, Kans.: 162
Kiowa-Camanche-Apache Reservation: 173, 211, 234, 256, 291, 301
Kiowa County, O.T.: 291–92
Koogle, "Old Bill": 139

INDEX

La Junta, Colo.: 64
Lamar County, Texas: 143
Lamb County, Texas: 103
Lang, Johnny: 112, 115–18, 129, 123–24
Lanham, Willis Tucker: 148
Lansing Penitentiary: 265–66, 284, 291
Larque, "Mexican Frank": 71–72
Las Vegas, N.Mex.: 41, 64, 109, 112
Laune, Paul: 290
Laune, Seigniora: 241–42
Laune, Sidney Benton: 183, 185, 241–42, 289–91
Laurel Leaf (cattle brand): 93
Lawson, George: 225
Lawton, O.T.: 291
Lea, Margaret Moffette: see Houston, Margaret Moffette
Lea, Nancy: 8
Leahy, David D.: 247
Leavenworth, Kans.: 36, 108, 226, 264
Lebanon, Tenn.: 174
Ledbetter, James F. ("Bud"): 225
Lee, M. R.: 261–62
Lee, W. M. D.: 35, 108–10, 128
Leigh, Fred: 69–70
Leitchfield, Ky.: 295
LE Ranch: 35, 62, 64, 106–107, 112
Lerch, Frank: 152
Lewis, H. A.: 67
LFD Ranch: 34
Liberty, N.Mex.: 109, 111
Life and Adventures of Ben Thompson, the Famous Texan (book): 129
Lightning Express (mail line): 41, 64, 68, 108
Limestone County, Texas: 64
Lincoln, Pres. Abraham: 12
Lincoln County, N.Mex.: 35, 112
Lincoln County, O.T.: 192, 281, 283, 285–86, 292
Lincoln County War: 68
Lipscomb, Texas: 41
Lipscomb County, Texas: 36, 162
LIT Ranch: 34, 62, 102, 106–107, 112

Littlefield, George W.: 34, 68, 102
Live Stock Inspector (newspaper): 202, 210
Logan County, O.T.: 167, 192, 286, 292
Lone Wolf of Yellow House Canyon: see Woodman, W. H.
Long, Johnny J.: 43
Long, Mrs. Johnny: 101
Long's General Store: 43
Long S Ranch: 48
Longview, Texas: 132
Los Angeles, Calif.: 264
Love, John E.: 170, 172, 213, 215, 217–20
Loving, Oliver: 31
Lowell, Mass.: 96
LS Ranch: 35–36, 62, 69, 106–13, 115, 121–22, 124
Lubbock, F. R.: 129, 132
LX Ranch: 33–34, 62, 64, 95–96, 102, 104, 106–107, 112, 115

McAllister, J. E.: 107–108, 111, 113, 115, 121–22
McAllister, Mrs. J. E.: 121–22
McAnulty & Pope Cattle Co.: 91
McAtee, John L.: 3, 6–7, 192, 194, 202, 241, 292
McCarney (gambler): 79–80
McClelland, Bruce: 134
McClelland, J. W.: 280–81
McCloud, Paul: 218
McCormick, Frenchy: 66–67
McCormick, Mickey: 67, 116–17
McCray, Shannon: 220
McCullar, Henry: 71–72
McCurry, W. W.: 115–16, 120
McDonald, W. G. ("Mc of D"): 304–305
McKennon Opera House: 246
McGee, Tom: 256
McHaffie, Ed: 304–305
McKenzie, Jake: 256
McKinley, William: 230, 239, 241, 264, 274–75, 283, 288, 291–92
McKinney, Texas: 98, 129
McKinney & Huffman's Hardware (store): 43

333

INDEX

McMasters, James E.: 62, 67, 69–71, 122
McNelley, L. H.: 25
McPherson, Kans.: 183
Mackenzie, Ranald S.: 30
Macon County, Mo.: 293–94
Madsen, Chris: 199, 256–57
Maley, John: 73
Malone, Sheriff: 190
Manchester, Ohio: 212
Mangum: in Texas, 164; in O.T., 272–73, 292
Marion, Ill.: 212
Martin, Jack: 71
Martinez, Felix: 115–16, 120
Martinez, Jermo: 110–11
Marum, David P.: 183, 205, 215, 220, 227, 239, 273, 284, 301, 303
Maryville, Tenn.: 9
Mason, Barney: 112
Mason, Fred: 241
Mason, Joe: 43
Masterson, Bat: 76
Masterson, Ben: 48
Matador Land and Cattle Co., Ltd.: 102
Matador V (cattle brand): 102
Matlock, Avery L.: 53, 98, 26
Mattox, Clyde: 262–66
Maxey, Samuel Bell: 98, 143–47, 160
Maxwell, Pete: 35
Mays, Jim: 108
Medicine Lodge Treaty: 29
Meridian, Texas: 261–62
Miami, Texas: 267
Middleton, John: 68
Midland Hotel: 236, 253
Mike Buffalo Thigh (Cheyenne): 190
Miles, Nelson A.: 30
Miller, George Lynn: 199
Miller, John: 43
Miller, L.D.: 51, 77, 82, 84, 101, 110, 124
Mill Iron Ranch: 78
Minco, I.T.: 224, 226
Mint Saloon: 43
Missouri Reservation: 192

Mitchell, E. F.: 232–33
Mobeetie, Texas: 25–26, 28–29, 39, 41–43, 50, 53, 55, 60, 64, 67, 71, 74, 78, 83, 86–87, 91–93, 101–102, 104–105, 123, 125, 131, 137–39, 161, 163
Mobeetie Panhandle: 60, 101, 141
Monroe, James: 9
Montague, Texas: 83, 89, 98
Montague County, Texas: 53, 101, 125
Montgomery, George A.: 45
Montgomery County, Ind.: 51
Montoya, Mariano: 61
Moody, Dan: 165
Moore, Lee: 256
Moore, W. C. ("Outlaw Bill"): 33–34, 95, 109
Moore County, Texas: 41, 60
Mooreland, O.T.: 301
Morgan, Josiah: 36
Morrison, Tom: 78, 80–81
Morrow, Joseph Clay Stiles: 15
Morrow, Nancy Elizabeth: 8, 15, 17
Motley County, Texas: 98, 102
Moyer, L. E.: 183, 208
Mullen, John: 263
Munson, W. B.: 34, 132
Murdock, J. G.: 136
Muskogee, I.T.: 223, 226
Mustang Mae: 66
Mutual, O.T.: 301
Myers, Elijah: 150

Nall, S. B.: 81
Nashville, Tenn.: 9
Nations, Hannah: 93
Neal, A. L.: 51, 101
Neff, Robert: 284, 286–87
Nelson, O. H.: 33, 134, 137
New Goodnight Trail: 31
Newkirk, O.T.: 262, 264–65
New Orleans, La.: 17, 20, 248–49
Nix, E. D.: 222
Noble County, O.T.: 168, 192, 280, 281, 292
Noble County Sentinel: 237
Nolan County, Texas: 25, 39
Norman, O.T.: 232
Norman Transcript: 237

INDEX

Northern Pacific Railroad: 16
North Fork Cantonment: 30
Northwestern Normal School: 244, 275
Norton, Charlie: 48
Norwood, Ed: 73

O'Brien, Thomas L.: 170
Ochiltree County, Texas: 36, 41, 253
O'Hara, Tom ("Red Tom"): 185–88, 190–91
Oklahoma City, O.T.: 170, 232, 234, 241, 263, 265, 280, 283–84, 293
Oklahoma County, O.T.: 167, 192, 285, 292
Oklahoma Daily Press-Gazette: 190
Oklahoma Livestock Association: 202
Oklahoma State Capital: 190, 210, 226, 246, 303, 307
Oklahoma Times-Journal: 210, 266
Oklahombres (book): 222
"Old Betsy" (Houston's revolver): 5, 77, 81, 89, 202, 222, 227, 236, 240
Oldham County, Texas: 33–35, 41, 60, 67, 80, 87, 103–104, 110, 112–13, 123, 162
Ole Buck: 66
Oleta, O.T.: 301
O'Loughlin, Ellen: 43, 48
O'Loughlin, Thomas: 43, 48, 50
Omaha World Herald: 231
O'Malley, Morris: 223, 225–26
O'Malley, Pat: 223, 225–26
Oo-loo-te-ka (Cherokee chief): 9
Organic Act (May 2, 1890): 181, 193
Osage Nation: 168, 192, 211, 264–65, 281
Otey, James T.: 80
Oto Reservation: 192
Owen, Robert L.: 235–36

Paducah, Texas: 165
Palace Saloon: 45
Palestine, Texas: 147
Palmer, J. F.: 281

Palmer, John E.: 237
Palo Pinto County, Texas: 31
Pancoast, J. L.: 292, 305
Panhandle Stock Association: 26, 33, 93, 105, 135, 137–38
Paris, Texas: 98, 143–44, 147, 295
Parke County, Ind.: 194
Parker, Dangerfield: 172, 187
Parker, Quanah: 33
Parks, J. H.: 80
Parmer County, Texas: 60, 103
Pattison, Robert E.: 231
Patton, F. M.: 48, 83, 139
Pawhuska, I.T.: 292
Pawnee County, O.T.: 168, 192, 280, 286, 292
Payne County, O.T.: 167, 192, 225, 285, 292
Peacock, J. W. ("Waddy"): 106
Pearson, Deputy Sheriff: 262
Pecos County, Texas: 142
Peery, Dan W.: 239, 280
Pell, Albert: 102
Pendleton, C. L.: 43
Pendleton's Wholesale & Retail Whiskey Store: 43
Perry, Albert: 112
Perry, O.T.: 234, 292
Petrie, John: 94–95
Philadelphia, Pa.: 274
Pierce, Frank: 264
Pierce, L. C.: 119–21
Pitzer, John: 260
Poe, John W.: 112
Ponca City, O.T.: 264
Ponca Reservation: 192
Pottawatomie County, O.T.: 192, 222, 228, 292
Pottawatomie-Shawnee Reservation: 167
Potter County, Texas: 33–34, 36, 60, 162
PPP Ranch: 112
Prairie Land and Cattle Co.: 34, 102, 128
Prentiss, Seargent Smith: 23, 53
Presidio County, Texas: 142
Price, R. C. ("Daddy"): 174
Price, William R.: 30
Princeton University: 78

INDEX

Pruiett, Moman: 295-99
Pryor & Hume (cattlemen): 215
Pueblo, Colo.: 162
Purlington, George: 190

Quanah, Texas: 186, 272
Quantrill, William Clarke: 48
Quapaw Agency: 167
Quarter Circle Heart Ranch: 79
Quarter Circle T Ranch: 33
Quigsby, Maj.: 260
Quillin, Mollie: 89
Quillin, Tom: 89
Quillin, William W.: 89
Quinlan, O.T.: 301
Quitman, Texas: 132

"Ragtown": see Amarillo
Ranche and Cattle Co., Ltd.: 102
Randall County, Texas: 36, 60
Rath, Charlie: 43
Rath & Hamburg Mercantile: 43
Ray, Robert J.: 170, 174, 181, 210, 215, 220, 227, 233, 284-85
Read, Clare S.: 102
Reagon, John Henniger: 147
Reams, Callie: 283
Reasor, Charley: 112
Redwine, W. H.: 286
Renfrow, William C.: 170, 211, 232-33, 235, 280
Reynolds, A. E.: 35
Reynolds, C. F.: 35
Rice, Jo: 66
Riggins, Robert: 293-94, 296-97
Riggs, Willie ("Wild Bill"): 57
Riley, James: 295
Riley, Tom: 45, 86
Rinehart, Frank: 225
Rinehart, Ira: 62
Roach, I. N.: 26
Robert (interpreter): 187
Roberts, Oran M.: 24-26, 97, 149
Roberts County, Texas: 36, 103, 162
Robinson, Tobe: 108, 120
Rockbridge County, Va.: 8
Rocking Chair Emma: 66, 115, 128
Rock Island, Ill.: 149
Rock Island Railroad: 224, 226

Roger Mills County, O.T.: 3, 167, 181, 186, 192, 285, 292-93, 305
Rogers, Ark.: 295
Romero, Don Casimero: 61-62
Roosevelt, Pres. Theodore: 283, 288, 291-93
RO Ranch: 36, 78, 94
Rosenfield, Rosie: 81-82
Ross, Lawrence Sullivan ("Sul"): 132, 152-53, 161
Ross, Leslie P.: 280-81, 283-84, 287
Rowe, Alfred: 36
Rowe, Bernard: 36
Rowe, Vincent: 36
Rowe Brothers: 128
Rudabaugh, Dave: 67
Rudolph, Charles Francis: 124-26
Russell, Bob: 67
Russell, H. A.: 64
Russell, Seigniora: see Laune, Seigniora
Ryan, Jack: 64, 70-71, 74, 76

Sac and Fox Reservation: 167
Saint Anthony's fire: 305
St. James Hotel: 64
Saint Jo, Texas: 125
Saint Louis, Mo.: 67, 96, 230, 237, 276
Saint Paul, Minn.: 16-17
Saints' Roost: see Clarendon, Texas
Sales Act Amendment of 1887: 142
Sam Houston Normal School: 170
San Antonio, Texas: 83, 99
San Augustine, Texas: 24, 170
Sanborne, Henry W.: 36, 128
San Jacinto, Battle of: 8, 11-12, 89
Sand in My Eyes (book): 241
Sandoval, Agapito: 61
Sanger Brothers (company): 78
Santa Anna, Antonio López de: 11, 19, 242
Santa Fe Railroad: 149, 161-62, 173, 220, 224
Santa Fe Trail: 162
Satanta: 33
Schnell, Mattheas: 149
Scott, Gen. Winfield: 145
Scott, Henry W.: 192, 240

336

INDEX

Scott, Lucien B.: 35-36, 109-10, 128
Sears, Frank: 293-94, 296-97
Seay, Abraham J.: 196
Sedgwick County, Kans.: 192
Seger, John H.: 198
Seiling, O.T.: 258
Seminole Indian Nation: 211
Seven Cities of Cíbola: 252-53
Sewall, Arthur: 232, 237, 239
Shackelford County, Texas: 26, 83
Shanholster, Minnie: 257
Shattuck, O.T.: 301
Shawnee, O.T.: 222, 280
Sheets, Jesse: 117-18, 121-23
Shelton, J. M.: 119-20
Sheridan, Philip: 30
Sherman, Texas: 41, 60, 78, 133
Shiloh, Tenn.: 13
Shoe Bar Ranch: 78, 94
Seige of Corinth, The (book): 23
Sierra Blanca, Texas: 162
Silverites: 231, 234
Sioux Falls, S.D.: 276
Sipes, Jasper: 280-81, 285
Siringo, Charles A.: 33, 67
Slater, Mo.: 222
Smith, B. B.: 172, 215, 220
Smith, Hoke: 234
Smith, Sherman: 183
Smith, Soapy: 109
Smith, Thomas: 256, 258
Son, Alfred: 255-61
Soule, J. S.: 286
Spade Ranch: 78, 94
Spike S. Ranch: 225
Spiller, E. B.: 101, 103
Spotted Horse (Cheyenne): 188
Spotted Jack: 57
Springer, A. J.: 50
Springer, N.M.: 62
Spur Ranch: 93
S. R. E. Land and Cattle Co.: 128
Stacey, Minnie: 266-67, 271, 308
Stanton County, Kans.: 237
Star Cross (cattle brand): 110
Starr, Patsy: 57
Steele, George W.: 196
Steeple Bar (cattle brand): 110
Stephens, C. M.: 51

Stevens County War: 199
Stevenson, Adlai E.: 283
Stockham (hotel manager): 236
Street, John. O. B.: 101, 103
Stroker, Johnny: 45, 84
Stucker, Zack: 89
Sugarland, Texas: 21
Summerfield, John: 34
Swindall, Charles: 183, 207
Swinney, Lincoln: 264-66
Swisher County, Texas: 60

T Anchor Ranch: 34, 62, 102, 106-107, 112, 132
Tabletop (cattle brand): 110, 113
T-48 (cattle brand): 110
Taloga, O.T.: 200, 205, 255-57, 304
Tarsney, John C.: 241, 258, 265
Tascosa, Texas ("Cowboy Capital of the Plains"): 41, 55, 58, 60-62, 64, 66-69, 74, 76-78, 80, 87, 94, 102, 104-106, 109, 113, 116, 120, 125-26, 131, 134, 163
Tascosa Pioneer: 124, 141, 148-49
Taylor, Abner: 149-50, 152
Taylor, Babcock & Company: 149
Taylor, Capt.: 285
Tazewell County, Va.: 212
Tecumseh, O.T.: 222, 261-62
Teller, Henry M.: 230
Templeton, John D.: 112, 128-32, 139
Terrell Election Law: 143
Territory of Oklahoma v. Temple Houston and Jack Love: 220
Terry, Charles: 64
Texas and Pacific Railroad: 162
Texas Military Institute: 19
Texas Panhandle Route: see Fort Worth and Denver City Railroad
Texas Rangers (Frontier Battalion and Special Force): 25
Texline, Texas: 162
Thompson, H. C.: 218
Thompson, Maurice: 194
Throckmorton, James W.: 98, 129, 147
Through the Shadows with O. Henry (book): 213

337

INDEX

Thurman, Allen G.: 174
Todd, J. F.: 286
Thombstone, Ariz.: 74
Tom Green County, Texas: 152
Tony Ridge: 50, 92
Topeka, Kans.: 306
Torrey, Ellsworth: 34–35
Travers, O. H.: 281, 285
Trinidad, Colo.: 31, 76
Trujillo, N.M.: 108–109
Turkey Track Ranch: 36, 48, 104, 112
Turner, Bud: 115–16, 120
Tyler, Texas: 24

U Bar U Ranch: 48
University of Indiana: 194
University of Pennsylvania: 15
University of Texas: 103
University of Virginia: 78
Urréa, Gen. José: 20

Valley, Frank: 115–19, 122–23
Van Buren, Pres. Martin: 23
Vance, Constable: 189
Van Horn, Maj.: 78
Varden, Dolly: 57
Velasco, Battle of: 20
Velasco, Texas: 20–21
Vernon, Texas: 186, 306
Vinita, I.T.: 41
Vivian, C. B.: 67, 72, 123
Voorhees, Daniel W.: 53

Waco, Texas: 140–41, 152
Waightman, Red Buck: 256–58
Waite, Fred: 68
Waldeck Plantation: 90
Walker, Delos: 284
Walker, Kirby: 187–88
Wallace, H. H.: 113–14, 119, 121–22, 133
Wallace, Lew: 53, 194
Walton, William M. ("Buck"): 129, 132–35, 140
Ward, Deputy Sheriff: 266
Ward, Tom: 202
Washburn, Texas: 162
Washington, Cindy: 43

Washington County, Texas: 15, 165
Washington-on-the-Brazos: 8
Washita County, O.T.: 167, 189, 192, 198, 285, 292
Watkins, Gene: 110–11
Watonga Republican: 199
Watson, Thomas E.: 237
Weatherford, Texas: 26, 140
Weaver, Claude: 99, 308
Webb, Charley, 123
West, Little Dick: 223, 225
West Virginia State University and Military Academy: 213
Wharton, Lon: 235–36, 281
Wharton, William Harris: 20
Wheeler County, Texas: 25, 30, 39, 48, 51, 53–55, 60, 80, 93, 97, 101, 103, 110, 123
White, Benjamin Horton: 79–81
White Deer Pastures: 102
White House Club Saloon: 264–65
White Oaks, N.M.: 108
Whitney, William C.: 232
Whittinghill, Bill: 296
Wichita-Caddo Reservation: 173, 211, 224, 291
Wichita, Kans.: 247, 263
Witchita Eagle: 247, 273
Wichita Falls, Texas: 91, 162, 165
Wiley, Moses: 51, 80, 84
Williams, Deacon and Co.: 102
Williams, Justice of the Peace: 215
Williamson County, Ill.: 212
Willingham, Cape B.: 64, 67–69, 72, 104, 108, 116, 133
Willis, Benjamin Franklin: 51
Willis, Eva: 53
Willis, Frank: 51, 53–55, 58, 60, 72–73, 81–83, 85–86, 89, 94, 97, 124, 126, 128–30, 132–36, 138–39, 143, 194
Willis, Sir John: 51
Willis, W. T.: 283
Willis, William H.: 152
Wilson, J. D.: 81
Wilson, Scotty, 113
Wilson & Short (cattlemen): 215
Williams, Margaret: 8, 15, 19, 165

338

INDEX

Williams, Weston Lafayette ("West"): 15, 165
Wisby, Joe: 276, 280, 285
Wood, Samuel N.: 199
Wood County, Texas: 132
Woodman, W. H. ("Lone Wolf of Yellow House Canyon"): 45, 67, 72, 77, 80, 82, 84–88, 102, 114, 124, 128, 130, 133, 135, 138, 205
Woodruff, Lem ("Pretty Ed"): 115-20, 123-24, 126
Woods County, O.T.: 168, 192, 199, 228, 292
Woodson, A. A.: 190
Woodward, O.T.: 167, 172-74, 181, 183, 185, 200, 202, 205, 207, 210, 212-13, 215, 220, 222-24, 226-27, 233, 236, 240-42, 248, 262, 266-67, 273, 275, 288, 293, 301, 305-307

Woodward Advocate: 174, 183, 185
Woodward County, O.T.: 3, 168, 192, 210, 253, 280, 289, 292, 301, 303
Woodward Jeffersonian: 174
Workman, J. M.: 218
Wright and Fransworth (store): 122
Wrightsman, C. J.: 280
Wyand, Clyde H.: 183
Wybrant, O. C.: 183

XIT Ranch: 103, 110, 149

Yale University: 78
Yandell, Bill: 72-73
Yates Center, Kans.: 263
Yelton, O.T.: 301
Young, Josh: 165, 252
Yuma, Ariz.: 144